Protest and Response in Mexico

The MIT Press
Cambridge, Massachusetts,
and London, England

Protest and Response in Mexico

Evelyn P. Stevens

This book was set in CRT Vega,
printed on Finch Title 93,
and bound in Columbia Millbank Linen MBL-4019
by The Colonial Press Inc.
in the United States of America.

Library of Congress Cataloging in Publication Data

Stevens, Evelyn P
Protest and response in Mexico.

Bibliography: p.
1. Strikes and lockouts—Mexico. 2. Communication and traffic—Mexico. 3. Violence—Mexico. I. Title.
HD5331.A6S75 301.6'3'0972 74-2232
ISBN 0-262-19128-8

Contents

Acknowledgments

Some books can be written in the monastic isolation of the author's study, with only his private muse for assistance. A book like this, however, is the result of so much help from so many individuals that to thank each by name would fill a chapter in itself. Nevertheless, a beginning must be made, even at the risk of almost unforgivable omissions due to faulty memory rather than to lack of gratitude.

The initial phase of the research was made possible by a Fulbright fellowship. At a very early stage of the work, Sidney Verba was generous with his advice and clarification of theoretical problems, as well as suggestions about research design. Chalmers Johnson offered helpful criticism of the first draft of the manuscript and continued to be an unfailing source of encouragement. George Foster and May Nordquist Díaz drew on their anthropological experience to enrich my understanding of Mexican culture, while Rogelio Díaz Guerrero frequently took time from his teaching and his psychiatric practice to deepen my insights into Mexican attitudes and behavior.

My intellectual debts continued to accumulate as the work progressed. Enrique González Pedrero at the National Autonomous University of Mexico and Mario Ojeda of the Colegio de México made it possible for me to use the documentary resources of their institutions, as did Hector Fix Zamudio, director of the Instituto de Investigaciones Jurídicas at the National University. Iván Illich and Tarsicio Ocampo at the Centro Interamericano de Documentación in Cuernavaca allowed me to check my documentation against theirs, to assure maximum coverage and accuracy.

People whose work is devoted to library resources are invaluable allies of researchers. I was particularly fortunate in being able to appeal for help not once but innumerable times to Elena McLin de Rodríguez, director of the Mexican

Academic Clearing; Georgette Dorn, the reference librarian at the Latin American, Portuguese, and Spanish Division of the Library of Congress in Washington; and Armando González of the Hispanic Law Division, also of the Library of Congress.

As the work neared completion, colleagues took time to read and criticize the manuscript, helping me to avoid the consequences of my worst follies. Foremost in this group were Wayne Cornelius, Rafael Segovia, and Lorenzo Meyer. The follies that remain are entirely my responsibility.

I shall keep my promise to preserve the anonymity of the railroad men, doctors, students, and those in other walks of life who provided me with material for the case studies in this book. They know who they are, and they know that I am grateful.

When I became ill with hepatitis at an important stage of my field work, it was the humane care of Señorita Vina and her staff at Number 24 Tequilas Street that hastened my recovery and enabled me to complete the project.

By this time Agnes Conley has been thanked so often by authors for her expert typing and proofreading that I can only add a fervent amen. Inés Stevens graciously allowed herself to be pressed into service for making last-minute changes.

Many authors conclude their acknowledgments by thanking their spouses for their forbearance during the painful process of creation. My husband, George Sayers, did much more than put up with my foibles; he not only encouraged me but lovingly egged me on, and by his fierce devotion to his own work he has shown me the real meaning of professionalism. This book is a halting first attempt to show him that I understand.

E.P.S.

Introduction

1

Why would anyone want to write a book about protest and response in Mexico? And why should anyone want to read such a book? Aside from a precious coterie of Latin Americanists, who could possibly be interested in the aspirations, frustrations, and occasional achievements of strikers, reformers, and agitators in Mexico? Do we not have enough troubles of our own? Do we have any *right* to inquire into the troubles of our neighbors?

These and other related questions are all ways of asking what is the relevance of a study of this kind, at this particular juncture of human events. The easy answer, of course, is that protest movements were a very prominent feature of the world's political landscape during the 1960s and have shown a tendency to persist during the early part of the present decade. In this sense, they are a timely topic, one that preoccupies alert citizens in many different countries.

In a broader sense, protest is an aspect of a political problem which has troubled and fascinated both the theorists and practitioners of politics for at least 2500 years. Aristotle examined the extreme limits of the problem in Book V of his *Politics*, under the heading "Causes of Revolution and Constitutional Change"; twentieth-century political scientists have continued the inquiry, with only a slight variation of nomenclature, referring now to "systemic change."

During the 1950s and at least part of the 1960s, many American scholars fell into the habit of discussing the topic of change in a context loaded with inarticulate ethnocentric assumptions. They talked about legitimacy and stability as though these attributes were the exclusive properties of politics in industrialized, urbanized Western nations, which were brandished as yardsticks of performance for the rest of the world. The terms "development" and "underdevelopment," or "modern" and "traditional" were euphemisms for saying that we had found the secret for institutionalizing nonviolent rapid change, while "those other" countries were sill oscillating between immobility and violence.

The late 1960s, with their widespread outbursts of violent protests in the nations which heretofore had called themselves developed, put an end to smugness. When one of the leading exponents of interest group theory almost literally had his book thrown at him during the riots at Columbia University, pluralism no longer seemed a magic formula for the achievement of domestic peace and prosperity. The new-found humility of political inquiry in this country may yet have the effect of refocusing interest on questions of fundamental and general importance.

In its historical development since the Middle Ages, the nation-state has been shaped largely by the necessity of maintaining enough order within the boundaries of the political system so that the sovereign could mobilize enough resources to preserve the system from annihilation by outside enemies. In addition to these historic tasks, the sovereign (the government) of the modern nation-state has added another: that of choosing the goals of national growth and development and of choosing the ways and means by which these goals will be achieved.

If government is to perform this new task with any degree of success, it will find it necessary to mobilize the resources of the nation-state to a much greater extent than that required for minimal maintenance of order. Priorities must be established, according to which some programs will be emphasized while others will be neglected for either a short or a seemingly endless period of time. The goals *could* be economic, aesthetic, or spiritual, but as a matter of fact, the sovereigns of most nation-states in the twentieth century have chosen to emphasize the economic aspects of growth and development. These goals are not immutable, of course; they may undergo change as government receives and evaluates information about the feasibility of their achievement in terms of the human and material costs involved.

Goal choices and their corollaries, the establishment of priorities, involve what Easton has called an "overarching" set of values whose supremacy may be challenged by groups within the polity that cherish a different set of values. In attempting to influence the decision-making process, these groups may make known their needs, demands, or aspirations through protest activities, which can be seen as a special form of information transmittal, directed toward the government.[1]

When we use the term "protest," we are referring to something more than an expression of nonconformity with the status quo; we bind ourselves to consider the effectiveness of a particular type of activity to bring about change. A quick glance at history shows that groups and individuals have experimented with a variety of other techniques to accomplish the same objectives, among which have been reform movements, *jacqueries,* revolutions, assassinations, and palace coups.

The choice of method is far from haphazard. To draw a parallel, it may help to recall that although accidental death is statistically frequent, an individual who plans to commit suicide actually has a limited repertoire of possibilities for doing the job with neatness and dispatch. Among the limiting factors in such cases are the availability of efficient agents and freedom from interference by those who might wish to frustrate the attempt. These limitations also narrow the range of possibilities for political activists; the highly successful techniques of one era may lead to complete failure in another. What we call protest today can take place only against a background of belief in the respectability of something called participatory democracy, which in turn has been stimulated by a decline of belief in the effectiveness of interest group politics. In an ironic twist, one generation's poison is another generation's innocuous potion.

The term interest group calls to mind an image of a number of individuals associated in a comparatively peaceful effort to achieve a limited objective. Many protest groups may also have limited objectives, but their efforts are characterized by a refusal to accept some or all of the previously sacred definitions of the "rules of the game." The interaction of these two elements can cause problems for an observer who is trying to analyze the objectives and probabilities of success of a group. Many violent outbursts may be aimed at the achievement of very parochial ends, while a few may have far-reaching implications. In addition, the observer who is apprehensive about radical (deep-rooted) change may be concerned about the cumulative result of the many separate protests. By its very nature, the formal apparatus of government—any long-established government—has a built-in bias against radical change. Sophisticated leaders of protest groups are therefore aware that they will have to overcome some degree—minimal in some contexts, enormous in others—of formal opposition to their activities. They do not expect that all or even any of their demands will be granted as soon as they are presented. They must be prepared either to violate *some* rules of the game or at least to rationalize their way around the rules so as to eliminate the objections of some of their followers and most of their opponents.

To try to analyze the motives of a protest leader is to embark on an extremely risky venture. Is he trying to achieve some small gain for his group, or is he manipulating the group by convincing its members that his objective is a limited one, while in reality he has grandiose visions of radical change? While this is a central concern of the intelligence operations of any government, it often becomes peripheral in broader studies of political change, because results may vary with the conscious aims of individuals or groups.

Why "Response"?

One way to appreciate the impact of protest is to recall that the expression of wishes, needs, or demands for change must be directed at someone or something. When American protesters marched on Washington, or when Mexicans massed in front of the presidential palace in Mexico City, it was because the members of these groups thought that either in a real or a symbolic sense they would find, at the seat of national government, the groups or individuals who could bring about the changes they wanted. In the popular terminology of the day, they were trying to reach the power structure, and they expected the decision makers to respond to their message by gratifying their demands. According to the democratic theory which has grown by accretion around the notion of the social contract, governments are praised or condemned in direct proportion to their degree of responsiveness to the demands of their citizens. By the same token, lack of responsiveness is often adduced as justification for revolution.

Revolutionary governments always justify their creation by the claim that they will be more responsive than the governments they have supplanted. In a very real sense, this is the basis of the modern claim to legitimacy. Once this legitimacy is established, however, the simplistic view of government as a mechanism for receiving demand inputs and producing satisfaction outputs begins to be eroded. The argument is advanced that gratification of some demands would threaten the general good (or prejudice the achievement of the national goals), which is, after all, more important than the wishes of individuals or groups.

Constitutions proclaim the rights of citizens; penal codes and administrative regulations, following close on the heels of the constitutions, begin to qualify the new freedoms in order to protect the new system. When not checked, the tendency toward self-perpetuation inherent in all systems may result in a hardening resistance to change of any kind.

Responsiveness may be diminished not only by the natural history of the revolution but by the conservativeness of the masses, who are quick to fear that gratification of demands formulated by protest groups will somehow impinge on their own welfare. Large sectors of the population regard all innovators with suspicion and cling to established ways because they are familiar and comfortable. Elites become conservative also, especially when the security of many officials is contingent on the continuance of particular procedures. Fears of functional superfluity, fears of the high costs of a new revolution, and awareness of the interdependence of parts of the prevalent system, all tend to make them reluctant to upset the applecart.

Under the circumstances, response by decision makers may take the form of negation of demands. In the face of these naturally conservative tendencies, it is a wonder that *any* political system should be able to continue for any length of time to gratify the demands of any considerable sector of its citizenry. An interest in the question of protest and response thus becomes an inquiry into the arrangements for institutionalizing change.

Why Mexico?

Every political system has some mice in it. If somebody has invented a better mousetrap, we want to know about it so that we can acquire one, and if some political system has a more effective way of accommodating to change, we may want to consider adopting some of its features or adapting them to our own system. On the other hand, we may save ourselves much time, effort, and heartbreak if we can learn from the experiences of our neighbors to avoid repetition of costly mistakes. These motives are valid justification for studying comparative politics.

For nearly two hundred years, many scholars have regarded the American political system as a model mousetrap, to be imitated all over the world. Under these circumstances, the comparative study of politics in this country was often little more than an exercise in self-congratulation and a search for the elements in other systems which prevented them from becoming as good as ours. There are salutary aspects of the current ego deflation in America, not the least of which is the rejection of ethnocentrism as a basis for political science research.

However, the new mood of penitence has already produced a hair shirt literature of its own that is equally biased in the other direction. The current crop of American books and articles about protest and response in this country is more concerned with our fall from grace than with a search for alternatives. To achieve some perspective, it may be helpful to look outside our own system to see how others approach similar problems. We must be prepared to face the possibility that the methods employed by others are either morally unacceptable to us or practically unworkable in our cultural context. In either of these eventualities, our comparative study may sometimes lead to the conclusion that the all-purpose foolproof mousetrap has yet to be invented.

During the twentieth century, the appeal of the pluralistic democratic model has been challenged by totalitarianism, much of whose attractiveness stems from the rapidity with which it promises to achieve radical changes in economic and social structures. Proponents of both models are concerned with the problem of change, but in very different ways. To the totalitarian, some kinds of change are desirable, while others are not. The easily defined goal of economic growth and the more elusive ones of political, economic, and social development usually figure at the top of his list of priorities; either those changes that do not contribute to the achievement of these goals or those that are seen as detouring the polity away from the straight and narrow path leading to these goals are regarded as threats which must be eliminated. The notion of change qua change is therefore rejected; the millenarian vision of a changeless utopian plateau requires prompt and stern repression of distracting tendencies.

From the totalitarian perspective, the absence of a centralizing force and purpose makes democracy seem like the punch line of a bad political joke. Pluralism is oriented to the near future, not to the distant future; it therefore has no reliable standard by which to judge the demands for change which arise in the present. Pluralism wanders down the disorderly, unselective, incremental primrose path of trying to keep everybody happy all of the time or, failing that—which it inevitably must do—at least to keep most of the people reasonably content most of the time. The only value sacred to a democrat is his institutions, and those institutions retard *all* changes, without succeeding in permanently blocking any of them.

These were the two choices offered to the thoughtful citizen. Or, at least, so it seemed for a long time. The human mind delights in dichotomies; elaborate systems of thought and action have been built on either-or choices. Caught in his own semantic trap, the political analyst constructed a totalitarian-democratic continuum and tried to locate all modern political systems somewhere along the line between the two ideal types. Thus, if a particular system was perceived as being or becoming less democratic, it was thought that it must by definition be more totalitarian or be moving toward totalitarianism. That a number of known systems had developed peculiar characteristics which defied classification under either of the major rubrics constituted a disquieting reality which first one, then another, political scientist was forced to face. Finally, in the classic fashion of scientific revolutions, the neat theoretical edifice crumbled under the burden of accumulated facts, and the profession was forced to seek alternative explanations.

Some elements of a more satisfactory approach had been cropping up from time to time. In 1964 they were fitted into a coherent framework which has already proved useful to students of comparative politics. An essay by Juan Linz rejected the democracy-totalitarianism dichotomy and examined instead the distinctive nature of authoritarian regimes, focusing on Spain to illustrate the unique characteristics of this kind of political system.[2]

According to this description, the authoritarian regime is characterized by limited pluralism, lack of a well-defined ideology, depolitization (absence of mobilization, except at certain stages in their development), and the exercise of power by a leader or small group (for example, junta) "within formally ill-defined limits but actually quite predictable ones." [3] By limited pluralism it is meant that while some political groups may be allowed to exist and some may actually be called into being by express action of the regime, they lack autonomy and exist only at the pleasure of the leader or elite coalition. Other incipient groups, whose leaders naïvely assume a right to organize, are suppressed by legal or illegal means, or a combination of both.

Linz points out that although such regimes lack a guiding ideology, they are characterized by a distinctive mentality which permits the elite to share a clearly formulated program allowing very little deviation. Those who disagree with these policy preferences are prevented from pressing for alternatives, sometimes through the use of violent repression. Except under circumstances when activated groups can be controlled and made to serve limited short-term objectives of the regime, authoritarian leaders avoid confrontation by encouraging political apathy and discouraging mobilization. In this sense, depolitization of the masses promotes political stability by funneling demands for change through the narrow neck of selective repression.

There are other points to Linz's argument, some of which will be examined later, but we shall pause for a moment to try to establish a connection between the foregoing discussion and the present study. Why subject the Mexican political system in particular to scrutiny? In spite of the fact that there is more literature in English on Mexico than on any other Latin-American nation, only a small portion of this impressive output helps the student to understand the actual operation of its political system. Too much effort has been expended in trying to force the square peg of political reality into the round hole of previously formulated theory. If Linz's descriptive and classificatory excursion can throw new light on the problem, it might render a wide range of questions about Latin-American politics more understandable.

A laudable step in this direction has already been taken by one of Linz's students, who takes some structurally derived generalizations about decision making in an authoritarian regime and applies them to an analysis of a decision made by President Adolfo López Mateos in 1961, which was successively implemented during the subsequent decade.[4]

Among the implications of Linz's original statement which are spelled out by the 1971 paper is one connected with the notion of limited pluralism. If, as it is argued, the only interest groups allowed to exist are those which are mobilized by the authoritarian leadership for the purpose of validating the decisions of that leadership, then there should be a high correlation between the groups' "demands" and the leaders' decisions. Such an arrangement would allow much more autonomy to the elite than that available to the elite of a totalitarian regime, bound as it is by a rigid ideology, or the elite of a pluralistic democratic regime, which is restricted by the conflicting demands placed upon it. A review of the circumstances surrounding the 1961 decision seems to bear this out.

Another feature of authoritarian regimes postulated by Linz is the low degree of subject mobilization, accomplished by a gradual depolitization of the masses after they are no longer needed to achieve a particular objective (for example, revolution). The resulting apathy of the silent majority becomes the keystone of the regime's stability. The author of the Mexican study cites indigenous sources to show that between 50 and 70 percent of the population is inactive, or marginal to the political process, but does not try to explain how this apathy can be transformed, as it was during the Mexican Revolution, into violent mobilization.

It is this explosive potential and the reaction to it, rather than the decision-making process itself, which is the central theme of the present study. While some authoritarian regimes have shown a remarkable stability and resistance to unplanned change, it would be unwise to preclude the possibility of future change. Once we accept that possibility, our interest in detecting early signs of it is awakened. Efforts to voice protests against the existing policy preferences would probably constitute the major category of such signs. These would be expressions of nonconformity arising from sources other than the officially created or officially tolerated interest groups described above, and their activities could be expected to elicit a characteristic pattern of reaction by the elite. We shall look at this pattern of protest and response in Mexico in order to examine the actual behavior of the participants and to formulate a series of propositions about the Mexican political system in particular and authoritarian systems in general.

One of the theses advanced in this book is that Mexican decision makers have evolved a mix of control and permissiveness, with respect to the flow of information, which has enabled them to pursue a relatively steady course toward the achievement of economic goals. Some groups have been permitted to express dissent from the choices of national goals, but this dissent is quarantined so that the disagreement is prevented from spreading. This behavior provides the elite with information concerning the effect of its policies while at the same time it places that kind of information beyond the reach of the bulk of the citizenry, assuring that the natural inclination toward apathy will not be disturbed by uncomfortable facts.

Depolitization in this sense succeeded for many years in reducing the use of violence for controlling dissidents. Violence is a costly tool, and for more than thirty years the Mexican government had been economical in its use of it, preferring to rely as long as possible on the effectiveness of depolitization. Violence was never abandoned; most of it, however, was clandestine and kept from public view by control of information. An example of this is the killing of the peasant leader Rubén Jaramillo in 1962.

Because of another aspect of the Mexican control-permissiveness mix, the actual recourse to killing has been much less frequent than might otherwise have been expected. This aspect could be called the legality-illegality mix. By preference the regime has often used illegal or dubious means to isolate or eliminate protest leaders instead of using the legal tools at its disposal. This preference can be partly explained by a desire to avoid the publicity of trial procedures, even though the outcome of a trial could be practically assured.

The significance of these observations can be appreciated in the chapters that follow. We shall see a number of reasons for agreeing with the contention that the authoritarian model is qualitatively different from both democracy and totalitarianism. The changes that can be observed in the regime's response to protest are changes of degree, not of kind. In trying to deal with the new kinds of protest which arose in the 1960s, the regime did not become either more democratic or more totalitarian; it became more authoritarian.

The Revolution (and Mexicans still spell the word with a capital letter), which erupted in 1910, revealed an accumulated momentum for social change, manifested as a search for new dignity for the masses, as well as acceptance of the reality of ethnic diversity. In the economic sphere, the impulse toward an accelerated growth rate had emerged even before the outbreak of the Revolution, but during the presidential term of Lázaro Cárdenas (1934–1940), a real effort was made to reconcile equitable distribution of the new wealth with continuation of the trend toward sustained growth. In the area of political activity, a change gradually took place in the social basis of the decision makers and resulted in an expanded elite whose power was derived from new ways of organizing and manipulating the electoral support of the masses.

To return to our metaphorical mousetrap: the mice were there from the beginning, but for a long time the squeaks were hardly audible. By the 1940s some of Mexico's intellectuals whose ears were particularly sensitive to that sort of noise began to suggest the need for modifications in the mousetrap's design. But who listens to intellectuals? By the 1950s some numerically important groups of agricultural and industrial workers began to challenge the post-Revolutionary rules of the game for channeling and containing economic demands.

By the late 1960s the squeaks had grown to a nearly continuous roar. The student revolt of July–October 1968 was the first indication to the rest of the world that Mexico's methods for institutionalizing change might not be adequate to handle the new developments.

This is a book about the student revolt, but to understand that revolt and the government's response to it, we must first examine in detail two of the major movements of the decade which preceded it. To grasp the nature of the change from earlier presentation of demands (or rather, "petitions," as the Mexicans preferred to call them) to the subsequent outbreak of protest, it is necessary to devise a framework within which events can be studied and the basis laid for predictions about future events.

How This Study Was Conducted

That fortuitous circumstances often exert a decisive effect on the direction of research is an abundantly documented fact of which the present study offers additional proof. A long-standing interest in the interrelationship between information and decision making led to the initial study of communication processes in Mexico, the results of which can be found in Chapters 2 and 3 of this book.

This is not, however, a book about communications, in the sense that is usually implied by that word. The complex network of information transmittal which crosses and recrosses the boundaries of formal-legal institutions is embedded in a cultural context which must be appreciated if we are to understand how some of the components from other political systems function differently in Mexico.

To obtain the data for the communications study, it was necessary to undertake field work, involving a period of residence in Mexico, during 1965–1966. Previous visits, as well as reports from other scholars, indicated that one of the main difficulties would be the suspicion and reserve manifested toward foreigners in general, but especially toward American researchers. This attitude escalated dramatically as a result of the widespread publicity given in Latin America to the Camelot affair. Camelot was the multimillion dollar research project sponsored by the U. S. army to identify and describe incipient revolutionary movements in Latin America. When the project was exposed and denounced in 1965, it was discovered that several American social scientists, seduced by almost unlimited research grants, had been persuaded to participate in the project. The affair became an international scandal and for some time made it extremely difficult for Americans to conduct any research abroad. Another set of circumstances, however, counteracted the disadvantage, and it was here that fortuitous circumstances came into operation.

During the last weeks of 1964, it became apparent that a protest movement which had taken place among resident physicians and interns in some government hospitals, mainly in Mexico City, was gathering momentum and might affect a wide area of the government's health services. That is exactly what happened; the doctors' strikes began on 26 November 1964 and continued intermittently until September 1965. The most important effect of the situation on the conduct of research was that some of the participants in the events became so aroused and so frustrated that they lost some of their habitual reserve and spoke with unusual frankness to the interviewer. Complete fluency in Spanish enabled me to talk directly and at length with the participants and to follow up on leads furnished by verbal innuendos, which are often lost when filtered through an interpreter. These interviews provided much of the material for the case study found in Chapter 5.

Several of the most articulate informants, while discussing the impact of their activities, referred repeatedly to the railroad strikes of 1958–1959, which they described as the first widespread protest movement of Mexico's post-Revolutionary period. Indeed, the occurrence of the railroad strikes and their eventual outcome was seen by these informants as a conclusive answer to the often-posed question: "Is the Mexican Revolution dead?" [5] These references prompted the researcher to ask whether there were any similarities between the two strike movements, that is, whether any regularities might be observed in the way that the protesters conducted their activities and the methods employed by the government in responding to them. If such regularities did exist, the possibility was envisioned of abstracting a pattern of protest and response to reveal some distinguishing characteristics of the Mexican political system. It was therefore decided that another case study in Mexico would have to be undertaken as soon as possible. The opportunity did not present itself until the summer of 1968.

When that case study was initiated in 1968, involving, in part, interviews with some of the veterans of the 1958–1959 railroad strikes, these individuals seemed as communicative as the doctors, in spite of the fact that they had had ample time to adjust to their frustrations. It was almost as though they had been waiting for someone to listen to their experiences, and the fact that the listener was a foreign scholar had become insignificant in the face of other developments.

While research was being conducted on the railroad strikes, a series of events occurred which soon proved to be related to the main concern of the present inquiry. For the first time in my experience, access to the government archives was barred; traffic in the downtown section of Mexico City was detoured away from the main squares, while beyond the helmeted and bayonet-carrying soldiers I could see the smoke of burning buses. These were the opening incidents of the student strike, whose repercussions were far more widespread than either of the previous protest movements. As events unfolded, it became obvious that a study of this strike would also have to be undertaken, to complete the trilogy that is the core of this book.

The research for all three studies focused on behavior, not attitudes. Changing circumstances, as well as refinements of methods, resulted in an emphasis on different research techniques for each of the studies. For the doctors' strikes, it was both necessary and practicable to conduct a large number of open-ended in-depth interviews with participants. In the interview schedule, opening questions began with "When did you first become aware of a problem? With whom did you talk? What did you say? What did they say? What did you do next?" Some interviews extended through several sessions and aggregated as much as ten hours; the average, however, was about two hours. Interviews were also conducted with other Mexicans whose professions or interests were directly related to topics discussed in this study, such as psychiatrists, sociologists, anthropologists, economists, journalists, bureaucrats, and political party officials.

For a thorough understanding of information acquired through interviews, it was soon found necessary to directly observe the behavior of political participants. Literally hundreds of hours were spent in the national and district headquarters of the Partido Revolucionario Institucional (PRI) and Partido de Acción Nacional (PAN) and in other locations, attending meetings and rallies of political parties and protest groups, listening to business being transacted, and absorbing the oratorical style of speakers.

Scores of hours were also spent at meetings of the Alianza de Médicos Mexicanos. Although at one point an informant remarked, "You have almost lived the doctors' strikes with me and my colleagues," it should be stressed that no special privileges were accorded to the researcher at such meetings; all of them were public and open to all interested persons.

The third and last of the main tools employed in gathering information was the assembling of primary documentation from a number of sources, among them, the files of the Hemeroteca Nacional, Biblioteca del Congreso, Museo Nacional de Antropología, and field notes on peasant political organization and communication made available through the courtesy of Mexican anthropologists. The main written sources concerning the strikes were: (a) news stories, articles, cartoons, editorials, and advertisements appearing in newspapers and magazines of general circulation; (b) official government bulletins; (c) stories and articles appearing in the bulletins and broadsides published and distributed by groups of striking railroad workers, physicians, and students; (d) minutes of meetings and committee reports of the Alianza de Médicos Mexicanos (usually in mimeograph form); and (e) eyewitness accounts and memoirs published by participants in the movements. Observations for which no source is cited come from my field notes.

The research techniques developed during the 1965 field work were modified and utilized to good advantage during the return visit to Mexico in 1968. Most of the data on the railroad strikes which form the core of the second case study were gathered at that time. Although those strikes took place several years before the doctors' strikes, their outcome has had a continuing impact on the responses of the Mexican elite to protest activities.

In the case of the student strikes, research has been facilitated by the published accounts of many Mexican participant-observers and foreign journalists who were present to cover the Olympic games which took place in the autumn of 1968. This material, together with the documents presented by the government during the subsequent trial of student leaders, augmented the information obtained through many of the methods used for the previous studies.

In the following chapters it will often be necessary to refer to organizations and government agencies whose full titles in Spanish are somewhat cumbersome. To avoid confusion and to save space, it was decided to use the full title in Spanish, accompanied by its acronym, only on first mention. Thereafter, only the acronym is used. A glossary at the end of the study gives full titles in Spanish, the English translations, and the acronyms.

Some explanation is necessary regarding the use of information obtained through interviews. In Mexico, the fear of sanctions is prevalent among members of protest groups. At the beginning of each interview, I found that informants who had been most actively involved in the protest movements were being evasive and uncommunicative. After they were assured that their anonymity would be protected, they were much more cooperative. For that reason, *all* interviews were coded by number on the field notes, and a separate record was kept of the key to the names of the informants. Throughout this study, only the code number has been cited, and descriptions of informants have been eliminated or reduced to a minimum. This position makes it impossible to thank by name the many individuals in this category whose cooperation made these studies possible.

2 Communication, Mexican Style

Although this is not a book about communications, a description of the way Mexicans communicate may yet offer us some important insights into the operation of their political system. For example, we may wish to learn why the Mexican government finds it unnecessary to impose the kind of censorship of mass media that the Spanish and Greek regimes have instituted. Exposure to samples of Mexican journalistic techniques may illustrate the relationship between skepticism and irresolution which immobilizes a large part of even those sectors which might otherwise support protest movements. When we try to penetrate the core of interpersonal communication processes—only to find ourselves misled and burned in the bargain—we can sympathize with the ordinary Mexican who distrusts everyone, yet half believes every rumor he hears, and delays any positive action often until the action itself has lost significance. Almond and Verba observed the gap between professed belief in political efficacy and the actual performance of Mexicans, but they had no satisfactory explanation.[1]

Communication style is an important clue to the cultural matrix of any political system. While it is not the independent variable (cause) that accounts for the form of the system, it influences the way the system operates. If, as Kalman Silvert suggests, the comparative study of politics should better equip us to grasp the *differences* between superficially similar systems, then our excursion into the subject covered by this chapter will be worthwhile.[2]

The importance of communication style as an indicator of a society's value preferences is only beginning to be appreciated, but it is already obvious that further research along these lines will throw new light on political behavior. This is so, suggests an anthropologist, because the elements of communication style show the same congruence with a society's world view as do certain structural characteristics which were identified and described by earlier investigators.[3]

Consider, for example, the implications of a story which was given front page prominence by a major Mexican newspaper in 1966. A visiting Englishman who was totally blind lost his Seeing Eye dog on arrival at the Mexico City airport. Upon being released from its crate by a curious baggage handler, the dog became confused and ran out of the terminal. Some hours later he was found by a sixteen-year-old boy in a shantytown area near the airport, but the boy made no effort to locate the owner of the obviously valuable animal.

Meanwhile, the Englishman, reduced almost to immobility, sent out frantic appeals through the mass media for the return of his dog. Although he eventually learned of these appeals, the finder did not at first contact the dog's owner. After a week, a neighbor informed him that the Englishman had offered a generous reward. "Remembering that the money would enable his father to have a much-needed operation," related the newspaper story, "the dutiful son returned the dog to its owner and collected the reward."

The story is rich in clues to many of the value preferences of Mexicans. We can see lack of concern for physical handicaps, indifference to strangers, affection for animals, disregard for the personal property of others, and—above all—stress on the obligations of filial piety. That the incident occurred is not in itself significant; the same essential elements have undoubtedly cropped up in many places in the world: a blind man, a lost dog, a finder, and a happy ending when owner and dog are reunited. What is important is that the newspaper editor emphasized the overriding claims of kinship ties, taking precedence over other claims such as honesty, charity toward the physically disabled, and courtesy toward strangers. The editor's decision to publish this story and his choices of narrative elements accurately reflect aspects of Mexican attitudes and enable one to predict with some assurance how many Mexicans will behave in other situations involving some of the same kinds of values.

A number of sociologists and social anthropologists have found this notion so interesting that a whole new field of study, called sociolinguistics, has developed, principally during the past decade. Specialists in the field continue to offer fresh evidence of something that observers had long sensed intuitively: style influences the quantity of information transmitted as well as the content of the messages themselves. These characteristics are observable in both formal and informal communication, in both interpersonal and mass media processes.

Mexicans communicate at the oral level in ways which are quite different from those of other Spanish-speaking countries. The most striking difference, often remarked by Mexicans who have visited Spain, is in the pitch and volume of the voice. Whereas Spaniards converse in tones resembling shouts, adult Mexicans of both sexes speak very softly, often seeming to be transmitting confidential information, even when the subject of their conversation is in no way secret.

To speak loudly is interpreted as aggression, as gratuitous offense, as "looking for trouble," and a man who is thus addressed is expected to retaliate with immediate physical violence, if he is able to do so. If this is impossible, he will harbor a grudge and try to avenge himself on another occasion.

The low key of normal speech makes a drunkard's shouts even more startling than they might be in another cultural context. Mexicans get drunk, asserts Octavio Paz, when they can no longer tolerate the crushing burden of civility, when the pressures of violence must find an outlet.[4] When they shout, they have thrown off all restraints and are ready to couple their verbal aggression with physical assault. "We are," observes one writer, "individuals of oscillations; although we usually maintain our refined manners and conduct, we are also given to passing over to the opposite pole. In Mexico, extreme courtesy is as natural as extreme violence." [5]

This always imminent possibility of transition to violence is what gives to customary Mexican verbal communication its quality of hesitancy and trepidation. While some cultures require their members to maintain physical distance from each other and to avoid touching each other in normal social situations, Mexican culture requires that individuals keep their verbal distance.

In addition to softness of vocal tone, Mexicans employ circumlocution in what appears to be an attempt to put a cushion of words between themselves and their listeners. A bald statement, a direct question or answer, is interpreted as rude and vulagr, as an invitation to quarrel, probably involving a covert threat of violence. For this reason, speculates the writer already cited,

> on our lips the Spanish language becomes an instrument of roundabout indirect allusion, of definition by approximation. . . . The being designated by the indirect words is right there, but the speaker does not approach it straightforwardly but rather caresses it and wraps it in his tissue of approximate concepts.[6]

Redundancy pervades the most routine business communications, as in this sample:

Telephone caller: "Good morning, Miss. Would you have the kindness of telling me whether Mr. Pérez is in his office?" (Instead of "Is Mr. Pérez there?")
Secretary: "Just imagine, sir, right now he isn't here." (Instead of "No, sir.")[7]
This habit of talking excessively and saying very little has been hilariously exploited by the popular Mexican comedian Cantinflas (Mario Moreno). In Mexico, and also in other parts of Latin America, redundancy coupled with vagueness is called a *cantinflismo*.[8]

The repugnance to calling a spade a spade is not confined to Mexico. While peninsular Spanish is rich in obscene or profane words, as well as in euphemisms, all Latin-American countries have extensive vocabularies of double entendre words, which fill even ordinary conversation with verbal land mines for the unwary.[9] Mexican Spanish is extraordinarily well endowed with this kind of circumlocution, often making it necessary for refined persons to engage in agonizing verbal gymnastics to avoid offense. Some students of this phenomenon interpret it as additional evidence of the poorly controlled tendency to aggressiveness which they see in the Mexican modal personality.[10]

Another manifestation of this propensity for circumlocution is the custom of referring to certain individuals by code names. This is especially prevalent in government circles; it protects the speaker by throwing a screen of apparent ambiguity around his utterance and at the same time excludes all but initiates from the import of his message. In this context, the code has a function similar to the specialized vocabularies developed by such groups as the hippies in the United States: it provides a bond of solidarity among the initiates.[11] If outsiders show signs of adopting the vocabulary, it is quickly discarded and a new one is developed.

Mexicans in all levels of politics must master the specialized vocabulary appropriate to their particular area of activity. Not to understand a coded reference is to lack the information necessary to orient one's actions. To reveal this ignorance exposes a man to loss of face, to being "burned" (*quemado*), that is, too naïve to be trustworthy. Once burned, a man is barred from further participation in meaningful political activity,[12] unless he is fortuitously resurrected by a more powerful political figure.

No student of politics is unaware of the importance of rumors and rumormongers in almost all societies of any degree of complexity. Riesman and associates have noted an American variant in their description of the "inside dopester." [13] In Mexico, the style of interpersonal communication lends added importance to such a figure. It is also possible that in systems where the factual content of mass media is low, rumor nets expand to cover the gap, and the role of rumormonger is of proportionately increased importance, compared with societies having a more open style of communication. Economically, the scarcer a commodity (in this case, news), the greater the number of middlemen (rumormongers) handling that commodity. A later section in this chapter will deal with the scarcity of news in the mass media.

Many government agencies and sections of the PRI employ individuals whose chief value appears to be associated with their access to a wide range of rumor sources. All politically active people must spend a relatively large proportion of their time receiving and transmitting rumors, but the monger is distinguished by the fact that he derives his status solely from his role as information broker.

Political survival and advancement are conditioned by an individual's ability to accurately appraise the reliability of his informants and by his capacity for reacting appropriately to information which he judges to be correct, that is, factual. The broker's continued survival depends largely upon his batting average of proved factual information. Thoroughly unreliable transmitters are eliminated early, but there are gradations of excellence among the survivors.

Information brokers specialize in different areas of competence, both horizontally and vertically. A man may be able to assemble a composite picture of the positions of several different agency heads with regard to a proposed economic measure, or, on the other hand, he may know the personnel of one agency so well that he will be able to say which individual at what level of the agency's hierarchy will try to implement or obstruct a decision made at the top.

One of the elements which gives the broker his special importance is the generalized attitude toward information as a potentially dangerous weapon. Mexicans act as if they believe that to surrender a datum to another person is to place a loaded gun in his hands. It may be for this reason that when an individual is forced to supply information, even of an apparently routine factual nature, he surrenders a gun loaded with blanks (falsified data).

Whatever the basis for this attitude, there can be no question about its effect on the style and quantity of communication. Data are both scarce and unreliable. Much writing about Latin America laments that the situation can be easily remedied by introducing adequate data-gathering techniques.[14] Whether such a solution is feasible for other areas of Latin America is not of direct concern at this moment; however, the existence in Mexico of behavior patterns inimical to the compilation of quantifiable data suggests that the problem may be more complex than has heretofore been intimated.

One kind of behavior encountered by survey research teams is illustrated by the experience of a group of psychology students from the National Autonomous University of Mexico who conducted interviews in different sections of Mexico City. It was reported that "there were about 20% refusals to answer the questionnaire mainly because of fear of getting involved in something that might bring a variety of reprisals." [15] The reluctance to supply even the most innocuous information is so generalized a characteristic of Mexican style that it becomes a central consideration in the design of any research project there.

Another reaction reported by teams working in a different cultural context may also exist in Mexico. Investigators found that their population sample rapidly became contaminated, that is, individuals interviewed during the first few days talked with individuals who had not yet been interviewed. When the latter were interviewed, they tended to answer in such a way as to conform with the community's understanding of what the survey team "wanted" to hear or, conversely, what the community had decided to let the team know about. It should be noted that this was not a problem of proper design of the questionnaire but rather of inability to isolate the sample from the effects of gossip. The investigators concluded that some of the survey research techniques which have yielded much valuable information for social scientists in the United States may not produce good results in other cultures.[16]

The example also illustrates the efficiency with which the informal network of communications can protect the community from an invasion—the invaders, in this case, being the research team. While the present study was being conducted, a few informants admitted that this type of protective technique is widely employed in dealing with foreign social science researchers. "We derive considerable amusement," commented one such source, "in seeing these false representations quoted seriously in articles in foreign professional journals."

This is not intended as a claim that reliable data are completely lacking.[17] Rather, it is a reminder of some of the special conditions which characterize the transmission and reception of information in the Mexican political system.

To sum up, it may be said that interpersonal communication by Mexico's Spanish-speaking population is characterized by a high degree of indirectness, evasiveness, cryptic remarks, and deliberate falsification.[18]

A trait shared by Spanish-speaking and Indian-speaking Mexicans is a strong reluctance to complain to or present demands to persons of superior authority. To express nonconformity is interpreted as a manifestation of hostility which can only be countered by an even more hostile reaction.[19] Perhaps because of this, Mexicans tend to bottle up their grievances until they release them in startling violent manifestations, either during bouts of drunkenness or in mass movements. An early example of rioting in Mexico City by the ordinarily docile common people is recorded for 1692. A behavioral profile of Mexican history since independence would show plateaus of apparent quiescence broken by jagged peaks of violence. The period 1934–1958 seems to represent a plateau, perhaps superficially similar to the thirty-four-year period, known as the "Porfiriato," immediately prior to the 1910 Revolution.

Mass Media: The Press

The quality of journalism presents a sharp contrast to the

softness, delicacy, and reticence of interpersonal oral communication. To read a Mexican newspaper is to venture onto a factual desert in the midst of an ideological hailstorm. Headlines scream, news stories bellow, and columnists and cartoonists belabor "enemies of the Revolution" with sledgehammer sarcasm.[20] During a fourteen-month period (January 1965–March 1966) a survey of major daily newspapers in the Federal District reveals that the bulk of material consisted principally of several types of stories.

First, there were the enthusiastic descriptions of the country's material and cultural progress. Emphasis was on benefits to be realized at some distant date. Present and future were confused, and vague plans appeared as faits accomplis. An example of this type of story, chosen at random, displays the headline "Irrigation, electricity and a port for the valley of the Balsas." [21] The lead paragraph of this front-page story states:

> The valley of the Balsas River, with an area of one hundred twelve thousand square kilometers and four and a half million inhabitants, will be supplied with irrigation, electricity and a port, thanks to the coordinated program of the ministries of Public Works, Water Resources and Navy, as well as the Federal Commission of Electricity.

The rest of the story, which occupies a total of thirty column-inches, consists of mutually congratulatory statements by the heads of the ministries and above named agencies. There is no mention of an expected commencement date for any phase of the work.

A variant of the optimistic headline technique was noted in a series of front-page stories, spanning a period of several weeks, on the granting of a loan to Mexico by the International Development Bank. The news was milked by publishing separate stories on different days about the probability of the granting of the loan, the uses to which it would be put if granted, comments by Mexican government officials about the anticipated effect on economic programs, actual granting of the loan, signing of the loan documents, and other aspects of the negotiation, until a total of ten such stories had appeared. The headlines and stories required very careful analysis to reveal the fact that all of them referred to the same loan. The casual or unsuspecting reader might easily get the impression that ten different loans had been granted.

Occasionally a courageous crusader took arms against the sea of verbosity, as witnessed by this example:

> The man in the street in Mexico lives in an atmosphere of fiction which is dangerous because it gives him the impression that what has been constructed and inaugurated is just a sample of the general progress achieved at all levels all over the nation. . . . We are getting used to thinking that only the visible side of the moon exists. Our country will not escape the influence of this publicity activity which aims at making Mexicans believe that many of their fundamental problems have been solved or are on the way toward . . . a solution.[22]

Stories of the type referred to by this critic produce a "Potemkin village" impression of generalized well-being and prosperity throughout the national territory. Even such serious problem areas as Yucatán, Baja California, and Laguna were depicted as future sites of vague but impressive rehabilitation projects.

Information on changes involving abandonment of plans or failure to begin work on a much-publicized project is usually impossible to obtain even by diligent research; the press is discreetly silent. This characteristic is not confined to Mexican journalism; it is encountered throughout Latin America. In the opinion of one observer, the disparity between planning goals and real achievements is a reflection of persistent faith in the magic power of words.[23]

In Mexico, the faith in words often appeared to coexist with extreme cynicism in many individuals interviewed. At one time or another, almost every one of the informants in this study made statements to the effect that the Mexican press was completely unreliable. "Let me put it this way," stated one person. "If I read something in the paper I must think to myself, 'Why am I being told this particular lie today?' " This same informant, a member of a liberal profession, later proffered as an incontestable fact the statement that Mexico's municipal governments have complete autonomy "because this is written in the Constitution." [24] Another informant stated very earnestly, "In Mexico we have the best Constitution in the world, and some day it will become a reality."

There seems to be an oscillation between optimism and despair, between an impulse to act energetically and a restraint of that impulse. It is possible to speculate that if fed such conflicting messages, most communication systems would develop serious operational difficulties.

The second category of published material was centered on the cult of glorification of the president of the nation. Even his most inconsequential remarks were quoted, repeated, and glossed by newspaper editors and columnists and television and radio commentators until they acquired the inviolability of sacred texts. Until 1968, it could be asserted that the chief executive was above public criticism; what he did and said was always right and just. The student strikes of that year, however, showed a trend away from such unquestioning acquiescence.

When some governmental activity went wrong and the effects of the mistake were too obvious to ignore, scapegoats must be found to deflect criticism from the president. Departmental secretaries of cabinet rank were the officials most frequently criticized in cases of this nature. It is part of their job, asserts one observer, "to suffer with stoicism all the criticisms . . . because in this respect it should be noted that political criticism is permitted with complete liberality, even to the extent of insults, but the top limit for these activities is the level of the secretaries; above that, only whispered criticism is allowed." [25]

At the mass media level, the president is immune even from good-natured joking. If the word caricature is understood as "grotesque or ludicrous exaggeration," there is no such thing as a published caricature of the president.

On the other hand, at the informal interpersonal level, sly references to public figures are exchanged with relish. During the 1970 presidential campaign, for instance, the PRI candidate was referred to as "the helicopter" or "Mr. Brassiere" because of his campaign motto, "Upward and Forward." The press confers humorous epithets on many public figures; the success of Mexico's most popular comic strip, *Los Supermachos* (the Super He-Men) was due largely to this kind of sardonic name-calling.[26]

The conduct of Mexico's foreign policy is reserved exclusively to the president, but his activities are narrowly limited by the nation's relative lack of military and economic power. Whether Mexico would—if it could—assume a more aggressive role vis-à-vis the affairs of other Latin-American nations cannot be predicted; the fact that historically its participation in international affairs has been minimal is elevated to the category of a transcendent moral principle. At intervals the president or his secretary of foreign relations restates the principle of nonintervention, and although the customary wording of this statement is familiar, it is treated each time by the mass media as a glorious new advance in foreign policy.

The last note in the triad of preferred subjects noted in the period under study concerned national history. Biographies of national heroes and villains were printed and reprinted at great length, followed by lively controversies concerning the details of the stories. Letters to the editor advanced such claims as that Pancho Villa could not possibly have led a charge against a particular town on a certain date during the Revolution because on that very date the writer of the letter was at Villa's side in a battle six hundred miles north of the alleged action. "La Hora Nacional," the national government's Sunday evening radio broadcast which was carried simultaneously by all stations in the country, fashioned many hour-long programs around the lives of national or regional heroes.[27] In the major newspapers, datelines on stories about foreign affairs usually carry the names of the principal United States news agencies. Because of this, the views of many Mexican readers about world events are greatly influenced by the same biases held by most American readers.[28]

Like most large-circulation newspapers in the United States, Mexican dailies are top-heavy with what professional journalists call "soft" news. In spite of their impressive bulk, experienced readers know that they can lay aside all but a few pages without missing a single "hard" story, that is, one based on actual events of some political, social, or cultural relevance. One newspaper has attempted to capitalize on this generally recognized characteristic by advertising that it is "more newspaper, not just more paper." But it does not live up to its promise.[29] Any student of contemporary American journalism would be quite correct in pointing out that most United States newspapers are guilty of the same sin. However, there are a few prestigious dailies, primarily in cities of the eastern seaboard but distributed nationally, to which educated and relatively affluent Americans can subscribe in order to be well-informed. Mexican readers are not so lucky in this respect.

Politically significant items are often published on the Mexican crime pages. Sandwiched between sensational stories about "passion murders" and bloody feuds may be found less lurid paragraphs that report the quelling of some peasant or labor uprising far from the capital. Some of these disturbances involve hundreds of people and may result in a number of casualties, but their importance is minimized, and the casual reader takes little notice of them.

An exception is the newspaper *El Día* whose few pages contain a much higher proportion of hard news, often including verbatim excerpts from important foreign speeches or government communiqués. Its small circulation is confined mainly to university students, members of liberal professions, and others who regard themselves as intellectuals. Since 1968, *Excelsior*, a large-circulation Mexican daily with a previous reputation of conservatism, has undergone the most remarkable transformation in recent Mexican journalistic history. Under new editorial direction, its orientation has moved to center left, and many of its writers are frankly critical of the regime.

In addition to the three types of stories described above, much space in newspapers and magazines is filled with classified and display advertising, social news (weddings, showers, christenings, obituaries, receptions, and parties), comic strips and other "boiler-plate" material purchased principally from United States syndicates, sports and entertainment pages, and paid publicity disguised as news. Some of this publicity is commercial, promoting products or services of certain firms. The bulk, however, consists of direct or indirect government publicity.

Direct publicity is that which is prepared in the offices of federal, state, or municipal governments as official information. This includes texts of the speeches of government functionaries (for example, the president, cabinet ministers, agency heads), official notices, and reports. The press and propaganda sections of federal, state, and municipal entities employ personnel to clip this kind of material and supervise its publication. Arrangements are usually handled openly and matter-of-factly between government agencies and newspaper or magazine business offices. It is estimated that from 20 to 30 percent of the newspapers' advertising income is derived from this source.[30]

Indirect publicity is designed to advance specific individuals within the party or government ranks, by presenting flattering accounts of their activities or planting favorable references in gossip columns. Payment for this kind of material is usually covert and handled on the basis of personal contact between the official concerned, or one of his trusted aides, and the newspaperman responsible for the item's appearance.

Display advertising in newspapers exhibits some distinctive characteristics, as to both style and quantity, a grasp of which is important for understanding Mexican communication processes. Most obvious of these characteristics is the large relative and absolute amount of linage devoted to political propaganda, which is a very important source of revenue.

It is a rare newspaper edition that does not contain several advertisements of this type. Most common are those which seem directed at influencing presidential action on some current issue. As an example, a businessmen's group may buy space to explain why the president should promulgate a decree granting them subsidies or exempting them from the application of certain regulatory measures. These advertisements are often worded like telegrams sent to the chief executive. After a lapse of a few days or weeks, they are frequently followed by other telegramlike advertisements thanking the president for actions taken, which are described, not as favoring their interests, but as necessary for the strength of the nation's economy.

There is reason to believe that much of this advertising is mere window dressing. The unsuspecting newspaper reader is asked to believe that the groups paying for the advertisements have no more direct way of approaching the president, but there is evidence to the contrary.[31] Representatives of the more important commercial and industrial interests often pay discreet visits, not usually at the highly visible national palace on the Zócalo in downtown Mexico City, but at the president's secluded official residence, Los Piños, near Chapultepec Park.[32] Such visits are not recorded on the president's official calendar, which is made available to news reporters.

On a less formal but extremely important plane, many businessmen have easy access to high-level government decision makers through the network of extended family or ritual coparenthood relationships.[33] Publishing newspaper advertisements may therefore be seen as reassertion of the revolutionary myth that there is absolute separation, even some degree of hostility, between government and business.

Another kind of advertisement also occupies a large amount of space in the daily newspapers. This category is devoted to statements of support for particular governmental actions or praise of the president for some policy promulgated by him. Many of the groups sponsoring these advertisements are directly supported or indirectly subsidized by the government, so that the texts in effect constitute public self-congratulation. The names of unions are often used as sponsors for this kind of advertisement.

Apocryphal groups are a third important category of advertisers. Their messages often appear over the signatures of fictitious persons or entities with such titles as "Ad Hoc Committee for the Defense of. . . ." A distinguishing characteristic of these messages is that they contain no clues as to the date of the group's organization, the location of its headquarters, if any, or the other interests or loyalties of the signatories. Sometimes the names of well-known persons are inserted, without their consent, among the list of fictitious names, thus lending an air of authenticity to the whole list. This type of advertisement has been frequently employed in other countries, but seldom to the extent to which it is seen in Mexico. As a matter of fact, most if not all of the devices employed in Mexico are prevalent over large areas of the world; none of the remarks in the descriptive sections of this book should be construed to indicate that a particular practice is peculiar to Mexico alone. What is distinctive, however, is the particular *style* imparted to a practice. In the apocryphal advertisements, for example, the Mexican penchant for hyperbole is seen in its most flagrant form; verbosity and poetic flights become ludicrous, while viciously slanderous attacks on opposition groups offend with their crudity. Many politically aware people feel that the signatory groups or individuals are simply fronts for government propaganda. They assume that their purpose is to advertise the government's intention to crack down on a protest group so that persons who wish to protect their political futures may disassociate themselves from the protesters in time to avoid reprisals.[34]

A typical apocryphal advertisement, underwritten by a group of irate citizens, may announce that decent people are disgusted with antirevolutionary communist plotting, and may plead that the government take "energetic action . . . even to the extent of using sufficient force" to eliminate the threat to peace and stability. Examples of this kind of broadside will be found in the case studies contained in the following chapters. The message, plain to the adept, is that the government is now ready to crack down on dissenters and *"sálvese quien pueda"* (that he who can should save himself). Failure to heed such a message can ruin a man's chances of advancement, make him a *quemado,* or even more seriously affect his life and liberty.

Individuals with particular axes to grind or grievances to air may also pay for advertisements. A widow dissatisfied with a judge's disposition of her late husband's estate may, after an unsuccessful judicial appeal, resort to this method of placing her case before a wider public. An individual whose name was included, without his authorization, in a list of signatories to an apocryphal advertisement, may try to set the record straight in a separate advertisement; another individual who may have unwisely lent his name to such an advertisement may later try desperately to salvage his personal fortunes by publicly proclaiming that his signature was forged.

The net effect of this use of advertising is to increase the publishers' revenues while substantiating their boast that they present both sides of controversial questions. The claim is deceptive on two grounds. The presentation is based on the unequal economic power of the government vis-à-vis genuine protest groups, resulting in the government's version of events constantly being presented while the protesters' version is presented only when they can scrape together the price of an advertisement. That the inequality runs even deeper than the availability of ready cash is evident when it is recalled that the government has other resources at its disposal, including the ever present possibility of applying sanctions by withdrawing the substantial subsidies provided by Productora e Importadora de Papel, Sociedad Anónima (PIPSA).[35]

Unlimited financial resources would still not guarantee continued publication of protesters' views. In the course of at least one of the cases studied, a point was reached where newspapers were unwilling to print such advertisements. Members of the doctors' committee who handled publicity for their organization allege that they delivered the text of an advertisement to one of Mexico City's largest daily newspapers, together with a check for publication charges. When the text failed to appear, they called on a representative of the paper, who returned their check and explained that an official from the president's office had requested them to cease publishing "calumnies about the government." [36] From that moment the newspaper published only the official version of events, and accepted only advertisements condemning the doctors' movement.

Even columns which carry the by-lines of well-known political commentators, when subjected to careful scrutiny, often prove to consist of publicity releases. Many reporters and columnists are employed only part-time in their editorial capacity; the rest of the time they either direct or are employed by the very firms which prepare and disseminate the publicity releases. The informants canvassed in this study who did both kinds of work seemed to see no conflict of interest in this duality of employment. An informant pointed out that his position as a journalist gave him added stature as director of a public relations firm, as it assured his clients of a publicity outlet through a major publication.

Only a few large newspapers employ a full complement of editors, reporters, and columnists; the "rewrite man" seems not to exist.[37] The smaller papers employ only skeleton staffs who do not go out of the editorial offices to cover beats. The news columns of these papers principally contain copies of government publicity releases, known to the trade as handouts. Limited staff and lack of interest prevent verification of the material received.

Most weekly magazines also have small staffs, the bulk of their published material consisting of a mix of paid publicity stories and articles by free-lance writers. The average pay for a two- or three-page article in one of the better-known magazines seems to be around 36 dollars. In 1964 one investigator reported that salaries paid to newspaper reporters ranged from a low of 800 pesos (64 dollars) to a high of 5,000 pesos (400 dollars) a month, but he observed that many of these journalists were enjoying a standard of living commensurate with a monthly income of 15,000–20,000 pesos (1,200–1,600 dollars) a month.[38]

A full-time general news reporter for a major daily newspaper usually covers about five beats, that is, sources of information roughly corresponding to important sectors of governmental and commercial or industrial activities. These sources are concentrated in the public relations offices of government departments and their subdivisions, similar offices of large companies or the offices of public relations firms. It is a commonly accepted practice for reporters to collect a monthly gratuity from each of their beats. In the trade this is called *trabajar el gancho* (to work the hook) because government publicity offices hang copies of current releases on hooks on a wall in the reception room. The more indolent reporters can simply step into the room, remove their copies from the hook, and proceed to the next station on their beat, without even greeting the publicity officers. It cannot be said that Mexican journalists are unaware of alternative methods of obtaining information. As early as 1934 a detailed and authoritative manual of good journalistic practices was published.[39] The author of the manual took special pains to caution reporters against relying on government publicity releases. Although the amount of payment for working the hook varies with the financial resources of the organization, it is said to average about 1,000 pesos (80 dollars) per beat per month.

If this estimate is correct, the combined income from salaries and routine gratuities would amount at most to approximately 10,000 pesos—a far cry from the 15,000–20,000 mentioned by several apparently reliable informants. When questioned on this point, these informants indicated a variety of possible additional sources of income, including clandestine payments of substantial bonuses over and above the monthly "little white envelope," salaries derived from positions as officers of the newspapermen's union, gifts, tax exemptions, and other fringe benefits.

One of these fringe benefits is access to the Journalists' Club, housed in a large building at the corner of Filomeno Mata street and Cinco de Mayo avenue in Mexico City, constructed and fully equipped by the national government during the administration of President Adolfo López Mateos (1958–1964). The building houses the offices of the government-approved unions of reporters and editors, as well as meeting halls, conference rooms, library, ballroom, restaurant, lodgings, baths, barber shop, and theater.[40]

A few informants indicated that some of the more obviously

affluent journalists were probably on the payroll of the Secretaría de Gobernación, the government ministry whose duties include responsibility for intelligence operations. As expected, this suggestion could not be confirmed.

It can be concluded from the foregoing that although the incomes of journalists can be only roughly calculated on the basis of available data, there can be no doubt as to their status as a privileged class of workers. They know that they owe the continued enjoyment of their privileges to the leniency of decision makers who prefer to feed them carrots but who are ready to apply the stick to them if they report unfavorably on government activities.

The Press and PIPSA

Poor timber resources force Mexico to purchase about 90 percent of its newsprint and other printing paper abroad. In 1964, these imports totaled 100,000 tons of paper, at an estimated value of 200 million pesos (16 million dollars).[41] Productora e Importadora de Papel, Sociedad Anónima (customarily referred to as PIPSA) was established in 1935 as a government financed and controlled corporation to handle the importation and distribution of this paper. It is possible, but not economically advantageous, for an individual or firm to bypass PIPSA and buy paper directly from a foreign supplier. In this case, an import license would have to be granted by the government and the private purchaser would have to pay an 80 percent ad valorem tax on the paper (PIPSA-purchased paper is tax exempt). Very few cases of such economic foolhardiness exist; a notable one was the magazine *Política*, the most strident critic of the PRI.[42] This magazine ceased publication in 1968 because of financial difficulties.

PIPSA engages in other related activities, such as provision of warehousing facilities, allocation of paper consumption quotas, and extension of credits to buyers. Newspapers and magazines of small circulations and precarious finances are spared the expense of providing storage space for newsprint as they are able to draw small quantities at regular intervals directly from the PIPSA stockpile. PIPSA can and does supply paper on credit and at its discretion may extend very favorable terms of payment to users, even to the point of carrying a debtor indefinitely. By the same token, the corporation can withdraw these privileges from any user at any time.

Many publications which are able to obtain consumption quotas from PIPSA derive an additional financial benefit, according to one informant, a publicist whose view was corroborated by other individuals.[43] This source states that consumption quotas are far in excess of amounts needed for actual press runs. The excess paper is sold at a profit to other enterprises which have been unable to obtain a quota assignment from PIPSA. This black-market profit is an important source of income, amounting in some cases to as much as 40 percent of the gross receipts of a publication.

The economic benefits derived by publications sheltered under PIPSA's umbrella are undoubtedly great. PIPSA's impact results in a press which is subsidized to a very large degree and which is greatly freed from being forced to suspend publication due to insolvency. It would be an exceptionally courageous publisher—or a very foolish one, depending on the point of view—who would bite the hand which feeds him. This may have something to do with the fact that journalistic criticism of the government is confined to sporadic barking, rather than sustained attempts to bite. One observer has commented:

The uniformity of this behavior is so impressive at first sight as to make us think that we are in the presence of a completely controlled press. . . . There is no necessity of police censorship because there is individual auto-censorship on the part of each journalist and collective self-restraint by the publishers of each newspaper.[44]

The point under consideration is not that of direct censorship, or even the much broader more nebulous issue of freedom of the press. The first of these two problems is extremely difficult to document, and the second is best left to such interested organizations as the Inter-American Press Association. What concerns us is the quality of communication.

In spite of these limitations, alert Mexican bureaucrats read their daily newspapers very attentively. They have trained themselves to interpret the language of official communiqués so that they yield a wealth of information not apparent to the ordinary reader. The general public is not equipped to understand the impact of government policies that are reported in this way; ordinary people are not usually able to formulate and express opinions about government policies.

The absence of feedback from the public, instead of benefiting government officials, "has hurt them, because it has left them with all the weight of responsibility . . . for making decisions without the possibility of sounding out large sectors of public opinion." As a result, the big daily newspapers limit themselves to "commenting with prudence and euphemisms, on events without offending powerful people, although occasionally for variety they will venture to kick a dead dog. . . ."[45]

When government is unable to provide the press with guidelines for reporting specific events, journalists' fear of making a wrong guess sometimes leads them to write stories so full of contradictory statements and tortuous syntax that they become completely unintelligible. Spanish-speaking foreigners often conclude after reading such stories that they have not yet mastered the subtleties of the Mexican variant of the standard Castilian language. Confidence in their linguistic competence is not restored until they learn that Mexicans are also unable to decipher the stories.

In the fall of 1965, a newspaper reader might have naïvely concluded that PIPSA's participation in the conduct of Mexican journalism was about to disappear. On Saturday, 2 October, most newspapers published a story concerning the fact that the corporation's thirty-year franchise, authorized by presidential decree, was about to expire and that a committee had been appointed to supervise the liquidation.[46] However, on Friday, 5 November, it was reported that the corporation's directors had met with President Díaz Ordaz on 21 October (a full fifteen days before it was mentioned in the press) to request an extension of the franchise.[47] On 11 December, to no one's surprise, it was announced that the president, "respecting the wishes of the newspaper and magazine editors," had extended the franchise for another thirty years.[48]

Magazines and Books

Spanish-language editions of foreign slick magazines are prominent on Mexican newsstands. In 1967, the latest year for which data were available, the highest circulation of any magazine in the nation was *Selecciones del Readers' Digest*, with an estimated 406,692 purchasers. *Life en Español* was third highest, with sales of approximately 186,000.[49] When *Life en Español* ceased publication, it was supplanted by a conservative news magazine, *Visión*. The chief need of Mexican readers, however, is not so much information about the outside world as more reliable indicators of events in their own country. Although the mass media practice self-censorship, diligent Mexicans can obtain some supplementary information about protest movements from sources which are not accessible to the general public. One such source is the collection of student licentiate theses at the Universidad Nacional Autónoma de México.

When a protest movement of considerable magnitude occurs, one or more concerned students often choose some aspect of the movement for study and discussion. The number of such theses is a rough index of the impact made by the event on public opinion. By far the largest number of these are by candidates for licentiate in law, but an increasing number can also be found among the political science students. The monographs show a concern for the legal and political problems raised by such movements. Thus, a few years after the railroad strikes, a number of studies appeared on subversion and the constitutionality of the Law of Social Dissolution, as well as the problem of legal existence or nonexistence of strikes. During and after the doctors' strikes, some theses were presented in the medical school concerning the distribution of medical services and related problems.

The studies vary widely, from those which merely cite a few classic works and repeat several safe platitudes to those which make a conscientious and thorough use of available secondary sources. The quality of the political science theses has risen steadily during the last decade, rewarding readers with valuable analyses of important aspects of Mexican political life. Most of the authors confine themselves to theoretical aspects of the problem, but they occasionally refer to the situation which originally roused their interest, and critical remarks of government procedure are aired. More rarely still, some reference is made to the actual behavior of individuals or groups involved in the events. The ministry of Gobernación quite justifiedly pays little attention to these studies, as their audience seldom extends beyond the narrow circle of the thesis committee, intimate friends, admiring relatives, and curious researchers. Predictably enough, authors critical of government procedures rarely obtain posts in the bureaucracy unless, like some Russian writers, they carefully point out that the abuses they describe belong to a historical epoch now fortunately superseded.

Watchful Mexicans with quick reflexes and a small supply of discretionary pesos have usually been able to buy books containing detailed accounts of protest movements, written by participants in the movements. The style of these works is sometimes disjointed, wildly polemical, and profuse with ideological cant, but they frequently fill in lacunae of data left by more socially acceptable media. Most of these books are produced by little-known publishing companies and have sometimes been withdrawn from sale shortly after their appearance, although some copies would continue to circulate clandestinely. Since 1968, the production of this kind of literature has increased enormously, with some titles running into four or five printings—a rare occurrence in Mexico's previous publishing history.

There is one matter on which Mexican students of mass communications express a unanimous opinion: reliable figures are almost nonexistent for circulation of newspapers and magazines. Public recognition of this fact is sometimes found in newspaper articles like the one which was headed by this paragraph: "Publicity in Mexico *ought* to be based on seriousness and truthfulness; therefore it is indispensable that there be an organization responsible for certifying . . . press runs of . . . newspapers and magazines." [50]

The reason for the absence of solid data on this subject, according to some informants, is that the figures supplied to the government are inflated in order that the publishing concerns may receive as high a quota as possible of PIPSA paper, so that resale of the surplus will net a profit.[51] As inflation rates are not uniform, it is impossible to adjust all estimates downward to arrive at more credible figures. It is said that advertisers and advertising agencies now commonly discount unverified circulation claims by anywhere from 35 to 50 percent, and the skepticism spreads even to those few publications which do offer verification.

Although four newspapers in the capital and five newspapers in other cities subscribe to the services of the Audit Bureau of Circulation, the circulation figures in their mastheads are not the ABC certified figures.[52]

Some publishers have tried to narrow the credibility gap by offering a variety of forms of certification of circulation, ranging from a notarized statement to the simple offer of proof on request.[53] For 1971 circulation figures for the principal newspapers published in the Federal District were:[54]

Esto (sports pictorial)	145,000
El Universal (daily)	165,000
El Universal (Sunday)	175,000
Ovaciones (daily)	220,000
Ovaciones (Sunday)	150,000
Excelsior (daily)	175,000
Excelsior (Sunday)	180,000
Novedades (daily)	140,000
El Diario de México	47,000

(Knowledgeable Mexican observers agree that most of these figures are grossly exaggerated.)

A complete list of newspapers for the Federal District would contain at least twenty more titles but, according to an observer, "other than differences of format and a few minor details, they [the newspapers] echo one another." [55]

An analyst of Latin-American mass communication feels that, even after discounting exaggerations, it is possible to state that "of all the countries of the *tiers monde,* Mexico is probably the one [which is] most penetrated by mass culture. . . . The network exists: it can be a powerful means of education and modernization." [56] However, these facilities are not available to the majority of the population. Some qualifying comments will illustrate the point.

Readership tends to cluster around the major urban centers. The Federal District (including Mexico City), Guadalajara, Monterrey, Torreón, Chihuahua, Vera Cruz, Mérida, and Puebla have flourishing local newspapers. Many of these are published by the García Valseca chain.

The Federal District is the undisputed publishing center of the nation, with twenty-six newspapers totaling a claimed daily press run well over a million copies. A few of the large Mexico City dailies circulate through the republic: *Excelsior,* with one-third of its circulation going outside the metropolitan area; *Novedades* (two-fifths); *El Universal* (one-fifth). However, at least 25 percent of this circulation is confined to a radius of 150 kilometers of the capital, and most of the remainder goes to the other major urban centers mentioned above.

While the number of newspapers published is impressive, it should be noted that 74 percent of this total consists of papers which at best are issued weekly or biweekly and which at worst appear only sporadically. There is no published periodical index for the nation, but the main card catalog of the Hemeroteca Nacional contains entries for literally thousands of small news sheets which have appeared for a few issues and then lapsed into oblivion. In addition, a rash of such publications breaks out in advance of the PRI's nominating procedures, in obvious attempts to promote the nomination of particular aspirants to office.[57]

The penetration of the press is further reduced by a high rate of illiteracy in rural areas. The overall percentage of nonreaders aged ten years or older was 23.81 in 1970.[58] Literacy rates were skewed in favor of urban areas; during the period covered, a large proportion of the rural population was unable to read, and only a small number of the literate rural people lived in the areas reached regularly by daily newspapers. The remainder of the literate rural population could obtain a newspaper only occasionally.

The year 1965 marked another of the Mexican government's periodic attacks on illiteracy. Much publicity was given to the campaign, with PRI workers enlisted at the local level to carry on the battle, whose rallying cry was "Teach a Mexican to read." For several weeks, major newspapers published daily installments of the government's officially approved primer, as well as reports from field workers on the numbers of new converts to literacy. But during the later stages of the campaign, a few articles also appeared warning against overoptimism and citing the experiences of previous efforts which had revealed that, unless the newly literate person has the opportunity to read, that is, unless there is an abundant supply of easy reading material readily available to him, he is likely to lapse again into illiteracy. This type of person is called a "functional illiterate" by educators.

Educators classify as "functionally literate" those individuals having a minimum reading vocabulary of approximately one thousand words. Acquisition and retention of such a vocabulary seems to depend largely on the individual's having at least three or four years of primary education.[59]

Another author has calculated that the aggregate number of absolute illiterates, functional illiterates, and literates who do not regularly read any daily newspapers, magazines, or books totals approximately 86 percent of the population, leaving only about 14 percent of Mexicans who are literate and who take the trouble to keep informed about current events.[60] It is this reduced group which can be described as the concerned public, with respect to the operation of the political system.

In 1970 there were still more than 1,100,000 persons five years of age or older, amounting to approximately 2.2 percent of the nation's total population, who not only were unable to read but could not speak or understand Spanish. These were Mexico's "monolingual" speakers of some of the more than 200 Indian dialects. However, the figure for 1960–1970 did show an improvement over the previous decade, as there was actually "a moderate absolute and relative decrease of [Indian-speaking] monolinguals . . . and both an absolute and relative increase of Spanish speakers." [61]

Of course, the monolingual Indians cannot be easily reached by other types of media, such as radio or television, which have been successfully used in the Spanish language in some areas to bypass the illiteracy problem.[62]

Beginning in 1959, the National Indigenous Institute initiated an experimental program for teaching Spanish to monolingual Indians in the Mixteca Alta region. It utilized its own low-frequency radio station to broadcast a series of recorded language lessons to isolated schoolhouses where qualified teachers were unavailable. The broadcasts were received on single-station radio sets in the schoolhouses and operated by native Indian educational promoters (trained to fill the lack of teachers) who only had to click the on-off switch. The results of this pilot project encouraged Institute officials to plan for extension of the program to other isolated regions, but lack of funds prevented this.[63]

Radio and Television

In 1969, there were 562 radio stations and 64 television transmitters operating in the republic. An estimated 13 million radio sets were in operation, in addition to which there were 2.5 million television receivers.[64] These figures do not include an estimate of pocket-sized transistor radios used in Mexico, and it is probable that the number is large, as can be testified by anyone who has ridden in a second-class bus anywhere in the country. The lack of data on this aspect of communications is particularly regrettable in view of the indications from other areas of the world that a "transistor revolution" is effecting radical changes in long-standing concepts of mass communications problems. The most authoritative source available estimates the number of radio receivers at 261 per 1,000 inhabitants, but the figure apparently refers only to standard-size sets.[65]

With the exception of the southwestern region of Mexico, radio transmitters provide near saturation of potential Spanish-speaking audiences, both rural and urban. Mexico's radio broadcasting is financed on a completely commercial basis, with little or no apparent subsidization from government funds. The two major staples of the broadcasting day are soap operas and record request programs, with sporting events occupying third place. In the Federal District, this order is reversed at certain times of the year when the Sunday afternoon radio coverage of the bullfights in Mexico City is preferred by the majority of listeners.

During the 1964 campaign, an attempt was made by a candidate of PAN, the principal opposition party, to broadcast a speech from a station in Mérida, in the state of Yucatán. (The voters of this city subsequently elected a PAN mayor.) It is alleged that moments before the broadcast was to begin, a Gobernación official called the station manager from Mexico City and ordered him to cancel the broadcast, under penalty of losing his operating license if he disobeyed.[66]

Under the new Federal Electoral Law, promulgated in January 1973, this kind of muzzling is no longer attempted. Chapter V, Section 2 of that law provides that all officially registered parties must be given ten minutes of television time and an even larger amount of radio broadcast time during each 15-day period in which to present their campaign publicity. Production and time costs are underwritten by the national government. The 1973 campaign for election of federal deputies saw the candidates of all registered parties (PRI, PAN, PPS, and PARM) taking advantage of this new provision.

During the period covered by this study, Mexican law required all radio stations to carry programs produced by the secretariat of Gobernación.[67] Chief beneficiary of this was *"La Hora Nacional,"* which since 1937 had been broadcast every Sunday between ten and eleven P.M. Every Mexican radio station technically capable of carrying the program was required to do so; the only alternative to station managers was to go off the air during that hour.[68]

This program was designed to sandwich small quantities of official propaganda between large slices of entertainment. Complaints about the quality of the program were widespread. One critic called it the worst program on the airwaves and stated that the public was being forced to turn off their radios every Sunday at that time.[69] For this reason, the program earned the nickname "The Hour of Silence" in the radio industry and its "continuous failure" caused some observers to question the wisdom of proposals that bad radio and television programming could be corrected by instituting increased government control of the medium.[70]

No survey has ever determined how many people listen to the program. When asked for an estimate of the total weekly audience the president's press secretary stated, "Everybody in Mexico listens to it. They have to. There is nothing else to listen to." When it was suggested that radio owners might choose to turn off their sets, he retorted, "Nonsense. No Mexican *ever* turns off his radio." [71] Personal experience indicates that there may be some merit in this observation, but at this juncture it can be stated only that the national government had no way of knowing how many of its citizens listened when it talked directly to them.

Nor can it be said that the government would learn much about the preoccupations of its citizens by attending to the information broadcast over the nation's stations. In a speech to the Cámara Nacional de la Industria de la Radiodifusión, the president of the republic, Gustavo Díaz Ordaz, outlined the government's standard of acceptability for program content in these terms:

> Before broadcasting a news item, before emitting a comment, before transmitting a program, think first and always whether it . . . helps to promote harmony amongst Mexicans or to exacerbate their differences and resentments.[72]

He went on to say that while the state (the national government) is not the owner of radio broadcasting facilities, it is their sole regulator whose principal interest is to maintain vigilance over the content of transmissions.

This reference to the national government's regulatory power was based on a series of statutes which established the limits of content of radio broadcasts and set up the machinery through which these limits were enforced. As to content, the code specified:

> It is forbidden to transmit news or messages whose text is contrary to the security of the State, or to international concord, to peace or public order, to the laws of the country and to the decency of the language or that prejudices the collective economic interests, causes scandal or in any form attacks the constituted government or the private life, honor, or interest of persons or which manifestly has for its purpose the commission of some crime, or which obstructs the operation of justice.
>
> It is also forbidden to transmit:
>
> I.—Matters of either frankly or disguised political or religious nature; II.—Matters of a personal nature which the Ministry [of Communications and Public Works] judges to constitute competition with the National Network; III.—Advertisements or publicity for cabarets, bars, and centers of prostitution or vice.[73]

The code provided for the appointment of interventors who were agents of the Ministry of Communications and Public Works. They were instructed to "examine *previously* and to authorize, when appropriate, all programs prepared for broadcasting by the stations under their jurisdiction, including programs authorized by the Ministry of Communications and Public Works, so that the content of these latter may not be altered." [74]

To enforce these provisions, broadcasters must furnish copies of all their scripts to the Office of Inspection and Intervention of the Ministry. Interventors, stationed in monitoring posts, compare actual broadcasts with the approved scripts and report any discrepancies, which may subject broadcasters to governmental sanction, including cancellation of their operator's license.[75] Under these circumstances, it is not strange that Mexican radio and television programs are produced in a wasteland even more barren than that north of the Rio Grande. All modern nations have instituted some degree of regulation of radio and television; Mexico's strictures on these media, as illustrated by the pertinent statutory sections, are somewhat more inclusive than most.

The exercise of this regulatory power, broadly interpreted, could effectively prevent the transmission of almost any kind of information. Radio program managers apparently play it safe by composing their news broadcasts from government information releases and refraining from broadening their format to include other types of educational or public service programs. This makes the work of the interventors much easier, but also much more boring.

A personal survey of program content, conducted by random monitoring of both AM and FM stations in the Federal District for ten hours each day during a two-week period in January 1966, failed to uncover a single item of new information which could alert government watchdogs. In fact, the only signal to emerge loud and clear from the welter of soap operas, *mariachi* music, and sentimental ballads could be summed up in one word: "BUY!" Article 67 of the Radio and Television Law prescribes a "prudent balance" between the amount of time given to advertising and the time dedicated to programming. This vagueness has allowed advertisers to use as much as twenty minutes per hour for commercial announcements, putting Mexico ahead (or behind) all other nations in this respect.[76] A market research firm reported that during a selected period of time, eight of the ten top-rated radio programs were soap operas, while the remaining two were comedy skits. Television fare was more varied, but the top ten programs did not include a single news telecast or any other type of educational program.[77]

A Mexican citizen who had been a member of the Ministry of Education's investigative commission commented on the quality of radio and television programs and concluded that both of these mass media are characterized by utter mediocrity. Moreover, he points out that because the program content is totally devoid of social or political significance, the audience cannot be considered part of the concerned public.[78]

Although not affecting the events chronicled in the forthcoming chapters, subsequent developments should be noted. The 1973 revision of the Radio and Television law reflects a complete victory of the private sector over the public sector for the control of these media. This will probably result in the same kind of voluntary self-censorship that is practiced by newspapers and magazines. In addition, growth of the television industry in Mexico during the past five years has clearly made it the most important communication medium throughout the urbanized areas of the nation.

Telephone and Postal Communication

As of 31 July 1967, there were 522,270 telephones in the Federal District, representing 55.23 percent of all the instruments in the republic.[79] How many of those instruments were in usable condition at a given time is not known. The caveat is not a gratuitous slur; the mechanical imperfections of Mexican telephone service are common knowledge. Complaints about the scarcity of telephones have been chronic for some years; the telephone company estimated that in order to catch up with the backlog of demand it would be necessary to install 732,000 instruments throughout the nation by 1970.[80] This goal was part of an ambitious plan announced in 1966 by the secretary of communications for the expansion of telephone, television, and telegraph facilities for which a total of 7 billion pesos (560 million dollars) was sought from foreign private investors. The announcement of this plan followed the established style of government news releases by promising a rosy future for the nation while admitting, almost as an insignificant detail, that the present situation was far from satisfactory.

By 1973 the telephone service had been nationalized and the number of telephones in the entire republic had risen to nearly 2 million, with about half of the total in the Federal District. The national telephone service was actually seeking new subscribers. A series of frustrating experiences in 1973 involving out-of-order telephone lines, convinced the author that telephone communication is still a somewhat hazardous venture.

During the period covered by this study, the telephone shortage affected middle-class Mexicans residing in the Federal District proportionately more than any other group. What this meant in terms of everyday living ranged from enduring constant petty inconveniences to trying to survive in spite of real hardship. Many of the young physicians who served as informants for the study of the doctors' strikes had no telephone in their homes. A prospective patient wishing to contact one of these doctors would have to send him a telegram or go to his house or office. Under these conditions, building a private practice would be almost impossible, even if other circumstances were propitious. The headquarters of the Alianza de Médicos Mexicanos did not have a telephone; communication was only possible by letter, telegram, or personal visit.

A common topic of conversation was the available strategies for obtaining a telephone. Family or friendship connections were the preferred channels; lacking such ties, some were hopeful that if they could scrape together the equivalent of 240 dollars, the purchase of a share of telephone company stock would get an instrument installed or at least put them higher on the waiting list. Apartments with functioning telephones rented at premium rates.

An incidental effect of these strategies was to make the telephone directory listings a very unreliable guide. Occupants of apartments and houses might change many times while the telephone numbers continued to be listed under the names of the original subscribers who had died, emigrated, or simply moved to other apartments or houses whose telephones, in turn, were listed under still other names.

In one such case, of personal knowledge to the author, a family had lived for over ten years in a house whose phone continued to be listed as belonging to the former occupant. When asked why he did not request a correct new listing, the head of the household replied that if the telephone company became aware of the change of occupants, it might cut off the services and assign the connection to someone else. To get another connection might mean waiting another ten years.

Occasionally the telephone company undertook a campaign to persuade subscribers to help update the directory listings, but many of those questioned were unconvinced that the promised advantages outweighed the dangers of losing their telephones. Others seemed to feel that the masquerade was a rather amusing game.

To complicate the picture still further, a large but undetermined number of middle-class Mexicans believed that having an unlisted number indicates prestige. It was reasoned that important government officials, rich people, and persons prominent in the sports and entertainment world could not be located in the directory; therefore, to be listed was a confession of social failure. Whatever the reasons for nonappearance of names in the directory, Mexicans seemed in this respect to be more advanced than their northern neighbors; Editorial Reports Service has recently recorded a similar trend in major United States cities.

There is a tentative quality about the telephone service which makes an adventure of each attempt to complete a call. Will one's own phone be in operating condition? Will the other telephone function properly? If, as is often the case, one of the two instruments is out of order, how many days—or weeks—will it take for service to be restored? Two of the physicians interviewed for this study assured the author repeatedly that their phone wires had been tapped during the strike period. They were undoubtedly sincere in their belief, but when questioned closely they admitted that line noises were such a common occurrence that they could not rule out the possibility that what they interpreted as telltale clicks were simply a new set of noises.

Much of the same uncertainty attaches to postal communications. During more than a year's residence in Mexico City, the author was aware of the loss of only one piece of mail. However, popular belief holds that the postal service is thoroughly unreliable, that inefficiency is rife, and that nothing of value should be confided to the mails.[81] Bills for goods and services are paid in person or, if this is not possible, checks are sent by trusted messenger rather than mailed. When, as a last resort, the postal service must be utilized for carrying a check, the sender usually writes a separate letter or telephones (if this is possible) to alert the prospective recipient.

The member of the Alianza de Médicos Mexicanos chiefly responsible for notifying physicians of impending meetings assured the interviewer that the post office had prevented delivery of hundreds of notices, making it necessary to use messengers to advise members. He had come to this conclusion when he discovered that many physicians failed to respond to a convocation sent by mail. He admitted, however, that the postal service had such a bad reputation that many physicians might have felt safe in claiming that they had never received their notices, when in fact they had done so but neglected to attend the meeting.

These remarks concerning telephone and postal service are not made for the purpose of impugning the judgment of those physicians who were convinced that their smallest move was the subject of surveillance and harassment by the government during the strikes. However, it seemed necessary to point out that evidence supporting their views was impossible to obtain and that in fact normal service and harassment are very difficult to distinguish in Mexico. The actual operating conditions of telephone and postal services, coupled with prevailing beliefs about their deficiencies, add further uncertainty to the already formidable problems of communication.

Anyone who has lived and worked in an economically underdeveloped country may have found the foregoing description of communications tiresomely familiar. Details may differ, but most of the general observations may be applicable to any Latin-American nation.

Mexicans delight in misleading each other, but they enjoy even more the opportunity of misleading foreign researchers. There can be little doubt about the problems caused by the lack of reliable data. A group of Mexican social scientists, meeting in Cuernavaca in April 1965, agreed that "one of the serious limitations in the achievement of an effective economic plan for Mexico is precisely the bad quality of information and statistics . . . with the grave series of implications that this has and which are well known." Even more pointedly, one of the participants in the discussion, remarking on the "vital problem of information," indicated that "much of it is mysterious and bad, and much else is nonexistent. We cannot make projections without a diagnosis of reality . . . when the most elementary data are lacking, when many of the data which we do possess are superficial [and] when others are considered secret or confidential." [82] An understanding of the communications system of Mexico should take these qualitative factors into account. Some of the political implications of these factors will be indicated in other chapters.

One of the conclusions that is obvious from this survey of communications is that the *consumers* of politically relevant information constitute a very small proportion of the total Mexican people. These consumers, constituting the sector that we have called the "concerned public," are principally urban, literate, Spanish-speaking mestizos. However, there are millions of Spanish-speaking urban mestizos who because of functional illiteracy, as well as other factors, are almost as marginal to the political process as are many rural mestizos and Indians. It is also apparent that the *producers* of information are comparatively limited in number, which is another way of saying that the Mexican political system is characterized by limited pluralism.

These limitations are almost as often imposed by the cultural context of Mexican society as they are by deliberate governmental policy. Official measures to limit dissemination of information are less frequently employed by the Mexican government than by some authoritarian regimes, mainly because in Mexico they have not been found necessary to protect the regime.

Limitations on the information disseminated by the mass media are counterbalanced by a proliferation of privately circulated information of even more dubious authenticity, thus contributing to the confusion and indecision of potentially active groups and individuals.

3 Information and Mobilization

In the same way that the visible part of an iceberg represents only a small percent of its total bulk, the mass media in Mexico are the most visible but by no means the only facilities for transmitting information. They are supplemented—perhaps overwhelmed would be a more accurate term—by a variety of formal and informal processes. At this time, fragmentary evidence indicates that the least public information channels are the most important, as far as decision making is concerned, and that the most public ones function only as official recognition of faits accomplis.

Political Parties

In the face of repeated assertions by other authors that political parties in Mexico are functionally superfluous, it takes some courage to insist that the parties *are* important components of the political system. One of their functions is to supplement the formal information channels, and they do this in a variety of ways. Because of its long-term preeminent position in the nation's political life—that is, its institutionalization as the party in power—the Partido Revolucionario Institucional (known popularly as the PRI) has evolved enormously complex mechanisms for performing the many tasks which it has taken upon itself. None of these tasks is unique to the PRI; many of them are performed by parties in a wide range of political systems, while others are peculiar to those parties whose long prepotency is a distinguishing characteristic of the system.

Mexico's PRI is able to implement both information transmission and mobilization activities, without bothering to trace the boundaries between the two functions. Unlike many other authoritarian systems, Mexico has provided through its only important opposition party, the Partido de

Acción Nacional, a supplementary information channel, while to a large extent excluding that part from the mobilization process.

During the doctors' strikes, Adolfo Christlieb Ibarrola, then president of the Partido de Acción Nacional, used his position as a member of the national Chamber of Deputies to present an analysis of the physicians' problems and recommendations for dealing with the situation. The daily newspapers reported the speech, and the PAN official organ published a lengthy analytical article on the problems of welfare-state medical care programs.[1] Informants from the doctors' movement stated that Christlieb's presentation of their case closely paralleled the position of the Alianza. Thus, the PAN made it possible for the same message to be directed at high-level decision makers in the government through four different channels: *viva voce* in the legislative chamber, and in print in the *Diario de Debates* (the congressional register), in the daily newspapers, and in the party organ. PAN deputies were outspoken in their criticism of the government's handling of the student movement and in 1971 formed their own investigating committee to inquire into the events of June of that year. The report of that committee condemned the repressions as stupid.

For many years, the Partido Popular Socialista (Popular Socialist Party, known by its acronym PPS) had also been a channel for criticism of Mexico's "turn to the right." The death of its leader, Vicente Lombardo Toledano, in 1968, hastened the decline of the party's prestige and influence.

By relegating the public transmission of this category of information to the opposition parties, decision makers were able to make use of it in their calculations without officially espousing it. Groups other than the PAN are sometimes utilized for this purpose.

Of all sectors of Mexico's population, the peasants present the greatest problems with respect to integration into the political system. A number of conditions contribute to blocking of messages or of potential messages, such as unfamiliarity with the Spanish language (by monolingual Indians), reticence in the presence of government officials, and—perhaps most important of all—the monopoly of important channels by the local bosses, the *caciques.* These individuals, inheritors of a long tradition of local strong men, often entrench themselves in the positions of *comisarios ejidales,* that is, administrators of and spokesmen for the presumably communal and democratically operated *ejidos.* Taking advantage of their position, the *caciques* often intimidate the peasants and administer the resources of the *ejidos* for personal profit.[2]

Among their powers, the *comisarios* are authorized to "represent the nucleus of population before the administrative and judicial authorities . . . administer the assets of the *ejido* . . . with power of attorney . . ." and "control the re-allotment of *ejido* lands. . . ."[3]

In theory, the peasants should be able to go over the heads of the *comisarios* to the next higher administrative level in the state government. In fact, several layers of government are often enmeshed in a network of reciprocal fear-and-favor relationships to the ultimate disadvantage of the peasants. When this happens, one outlet for frustration is the short-lived but violent *jacquerie* which is a familiar event in Mexican rural life.

Official propaganda points proudly to the fact that Mexico's constitution guarantees the Communist Party the right to exist and to recruit members. This is true, but it is also true that the CP (or PC, as it is known in Mexico) has for many years been a powerless organization that poses no threat to the regime.[4] Like the tame labor unions, the communists hold demonstrations when such activities will enhance the government's image with respect to its conduct of foreign relations. Few Mexican citizens take the party seriously; this comment, by a student leader, reflects the opinion of a large sector of the concerned public: the students, he recalls, knew what to expect from the PC. Twice a year, like clockwork, the party would hold a parade, once to condemn the United States for its actions in Vietnam and once to express solidarity with the Cuban revolution. The route of the march was always the same, and the speeches seemed to be tape recordings from previous years.[5]

The purpose of such demonstrations is to corroborate the Mexican government's boast that it courageously opposes attempts by the U.S. to dictate its foreign policy. The communist demonstrators, however, are not allowed to approach within stone-throwing distance of the American Embassy on the Paseo de la Reforma. In April of 1965, the rumor was circulated that a group of pacifist American students attempted to join forces with the Communist Party's demonstration against U.S. intervention in the Dominican Republic; the Americans, it was reported, were arrested and immediately deported. They had made the mistake of thinking that the demonstration was a genuine expression of protest.

The existence of the Communist Party in Mexico is an asset to the government when the latter needs justification for repressive action against almost any group of protesters. Whenever a dissident group begins to mobilize, "insidious foreign influences" are blamed and, almost as a reflex action, police raid the party headquarters, destroying office equipment and confiscating Marxist literature. The party's leadership complains about the injustice of the raid, disclaims any connection with the dissidents, and lapses into its comfortable routine, taking care not to challenge the government on domestic issues.

Among the parties, however, it is the PRI which developed the most elaborate framework for gathering politically relevant information, in the form of its Instituto de Estudios Políticos y Sociales. This activity evolved from the round tables conducted during the 1946, 1952, and 1958 electoral campaigns, during which the candidates met with representatives of local groups to discuss regional problems. By 1958 the evolution had progressed to the point where the Institute had become an accepted part of the PRI organization, with a national director and branch offices in all the states. In 1958, and again in 1964, these offices were active in organizing hundreds of meetings of local leaders for the purpose of listing and describing the problems of their areas. During the electoral campaign, it became established practice for PRI candidates, from presidential level down, to receive delegations of these leaders and listen to their statements.

The observer should not be misled by the Institute's electoral campaign activity into thinking that this represents an effort to involve the masses in the system's decision-making processes. The Institute's director admitted in an interview with the author that after the campaign the reports and recommendations were quietly stored in a warehouse in Mexico City, never to be used again.

If, as we have just seen, the Institute was not feeding the information it gathered into the decision-making components of the system, we shall have to look beyond its proclaimed purpose to decide whether it has performed any other useful function in the total scheme of things. What immediately comes to mind is the similarity between the

Institute's activities and those of President Lázaro Cárdenas in his perennial peregrinations in the Mexican hinterland, listening to the peasants' complaints, asking questions, and promising action to relieve their problems.[6] It is a tribute to Cárdenas's personal magnetism that the few instances in which remedial action was taken are enshrined by a grateful population in the heroic legend that has grown around the leader, while the innumerable instances of failure to take action are invariably forgotten. The PRI Institute which has moved in to fill the vacuum left by Cárdenas is a near-perfect example of what Weber calls the routinization of charisma.

During every election campaign, thousands of peasants are drawn into the Institute's activities. What do they get out of it? They derive satisfaction from symbolically participating in the political process. Although their appearance before the Institute's representatives may have no more real impact than that which a children's piano recital has on the world of music, it gratifies narcissistic impulses and enhances the individuals' prestige among their fellow villagers. But, above all, it defuses potential protests by providing a symbolic outlet for them. The Institute functions as a transmitter only in the sense that it informs the peasants that the Revolution for which their fathers fought is alive and well and listening to them.

It cannot be said that this is an inconsiderable contribution to the maintenance of the Mexican political system. While providing an example of the way in which a particular activity can actually function contrary to its proclaimed purpose, it also illustrates the present regime's preference for symbolic satisfaction wherever possible instead of the alternative course of repression. This latter course was the one adopted by the regime of Porfirio Díaz.

Another tool for defusing potential protest groups is the

spurious pluralism of highly visible organizations like labor unions. By now, an overwhelming chorus of testimony indicates that many of these organizations are a major element in the mass support of the regime. Politically sophisticated Mexicans are aware that the unions do not aggregate the interests of labor, as they often do in the North Atlantic group of industrialized nations, nor do they operate as autonomous pressure groups obliging the government to make important economic concessions to them. Instead, the

> majority of laborers (and employees) of the city and especially of the country do not belong to any union or belong to one "duly" controlled by the government and the employers, headed by some eternal, almost dynastic and completely dishonest leader. . . . It is understandable, therefore, that in spite of the fact that the number of laborers in all the urban activities is certainly more than 2.5 million, their political action as a social class is still weak. . . .[7]

Certain sectors of Mexico's labor force have derived limited economic benefits from this paternalistic relationship. Recent events indicate that some labor leaders are losing control of union membership and are being forced to negotiate more openly in behalf of the members. As industrialization increases, this development may be a major source of change.

As in the case of the Institute of Political Studies, the visible activities of the unions transmit a kind of information by informing the concerned public about the rewards enjoyed by groups that support the regime. The implied message is that while some groups may not yet be receiving an increased share of the available goods, they may hope to if they do not oppose the regime's program. While it is true that sophisticated Mexicans reject this as false, millions of others who are outside the charmed circle which we have called the concerned public are half convinced of its truth. They reflect the ambivalence so well exemplified by the Spanish saying, "I don't believe in ghosts, but they certainly exist."

By virtue of the fact that unions constitute most of the membership of the PRI's labor sector, their activities have been included in this section. An individual need not take any initiative to join; his membership in a union automatically makes him a member of the party, whether he likes it or not. Conceivably, an individual could remain a member of the union while expressly withdrawing from membership in the party, but I know of no such case. As it is, the definition of union membership is so flexible that many individuals benefit (or suffer) from the provisions of a collective bargaining agreement without paying union dues or attending meetings. This does not worry union leaders; they know that most of these individuals can usually be counted on to turn out for rallies in support of the regime or to vote for the PRI as long as they are paid a day's wages for their time.

The manpower for Mexico's rapid industrialization program is being drawn from rural areas whose social organization has not even completely recovered from the upheavals and bloodshed of the revolutionary period (1910–1925). That social organization had already been profoundly disrupted at the time of the Spanish conquest in the sixteenth century. As a result of this historical process, traditional modes of mutual assistance have disintegrated. They have not been replaced by privately financed charitable institutions, partly because endemic suspicion of strangers probably would have prevented people from accepting these institutions even if the initiative for their organization had been present. It might well be asked why Mexicans appear more willing to avail themselves of government services than of private charity. One explanation is that the government's motivation is above suspicion. The quid pro quo is clearly understood: services are rendered in exchange for massive acceptance of the regime.

The absence of a central coordinating agency has resulted in much duplication of effort by different governmental departments. In Mexico City, an attempt has been made to list the number and kinds of free social services available, not to reduce overlap but rather, according to one of the directors of the sponsoring group (personal interview), to provide impressive proof of "how much the government is doing for the people," and to instruct prospective voters concerning the location of voter registration centers. The thousands of bewildered and often illiterate in-migrants from rural areas or small towns to the large urban centers are almost invariably ignorant of the availability of such assistance, even in those cases where they fulfill the eligibility requirements. The political parties perform a valuable service by orienting these people and by acting as their intermediaries during the difficult transition from agrarian culture to industrial culture.[8] When all other resources fail, many emergency needs of individuals are handled by the dispensation of small amounts of cash from party funds.

The parties thus provide an important function in the socialization of the new masses of potential workers needed for the industrializing economy. They are often the only organizations to provide any continuity of experience, linking the rural past with the urban present. They performed a function similar to that of parties in cities of the United States during the period of massive European immigration, 1875–1914. In exchange for services rendered, they mobilize the masses of voters whose endorsement legitimizes the political institutions.

Hundreds of hours spent by the author in party offices and at party activities provide innumerable examples of this kind of reciprocal relationship. The PRI, being the dominant party, has the immense advantage of dispensing large amounts of money and patronage, but other parties engage in the same activities to the extent their resources permit. The author recalls attending a meeting at PAN headquarters in the fall of 1965 during which three sides of the assembly hall were lined with silent, motionless Indians in their traditional dress. Inquiry elicited the information that these spectators were waiting for the meeting to end so that they could spread their straw mats on the floor and sleep. Although there was no evidence of a formal compact, officials indicated to the author that they anticipated that in return for the use of these rudimentary dormitory facilities, the recent in-migrants would show their appreciation by casting their votes for the PAN in the next election.

A few months after the inauguration of a new president, the PRI holds a national assembly of delegates and workers in Mexico City. It is at this time that the party's platform and program of action for the six-year period is revealed, rather than at its nominating convention prior to the election campaign. Party bylaws require that the assembly undertake the following activities:

1. Receive and, when appropriate, ratify the report of the National Executive Committee.
2. Evaluate the national situation and that of the public administration in relation to the party's program, and formulate plans of action which it deems appropriate.
3. Establish the political and social norms which it considers necessary.[9]

The agenda of the assembly which was held on 28, 29, and 30 April 1965, showed the influence of the new technical cadres. Old-fashioned bombast still abounded, but for each of the major program proposals the orator was followed onto the platform by a matter-of-fact bureaucrat who summed up the problem and indicated the action recommended. These presentations were the result of studies initiated soon after President Díaz Ordaz's nomination by newly recruited party workers. Some of these workers stated in interviews carried out during the present study that they had been attracted to party militancy not by traditional partisan appeals but by the new possibility of applying rationalizing techniques to the solution of the nation's problems.

Shortly after the national convention, the National Executive Committee, headed by Carlos Madrazo, authorized Gonzalo Martínez Corbalá, chairman of the party's Federal District Section, to hold a series of round tables to discuss and propose solutions for problems peculiar to the nation's most congested urban area.[10] The preliminary agenda, subject to amendments or additions, included topics related to urban growth, low-cost housing, municipal services, traffic control, unemployment, enforcement of minimum wage laws (almost universally disregarded in Mexico), and expansion and improvement of the public school system.

Immediately following his appointment, Martínez Corbalá organized committees in all twenty-four wards of the Federal District for the purpose of gathering information on which to base preliminary reports. Public hearings were held in each of the wards, at which residents of the neighborhoods were encouraged to voice their opinions. Following these hearings, representatives of the ward committees met weekly, for three months, on the sixth floor of the party's national headquarters building. For these meetings Martínez Corbalá, himself an engineer by profession, was able to recruit a large number of technically trained individuals. The preliminary studies were of unusually high quality, in many cases providing data which clarified the recommended policy choices. I attended many of the meetings; these were no awed peasants, standing hat in hand before a visiting politician from the capital, stammering a timid request for a new road. The new breed, brought into the party by Madrazo, would not be satisfied with symbolic satisfactions.

There is reason to believe that at least some of the party's internal conflicts at that time were due to disagreement over the possible outcome of the activities just described, as well as to other liberalizing tendencies initiated by Madrazo (such as his attempts to bring about popular participation in party nominating procedures through local primary elections). It is quite likely that some sectors of the party feared that the PRI would be forced to admit new groups into the decision-making process, and that these groups would be difficult to control.

When the party began to suffer from serious internal conflicts in the fall of 1965, these meetings were suspended, and when the chairman, Martínez Corbalá, lost his position as a result of his close relationship with Carlos Madrazo, the whole effort was abandoned. Madrazo himself died in an airplane accident on 4 June 1969.[11]

The activities of the PRI are clearly distinguished from those of other parties and movements. Whereas the latter sometimes utilize the information they gather to propose intersystem change and even more often advocate goal reorientation within the system, the PRI always emphasizes that its recommendations are concerned with applications of the existing political system and implementation of established policy preferences. Its aim is to expand the techniques by which the system may maintain its equilibrium, while pursuing predetermined goals.

For this reason, perhaps, the PRI has been careful to avoid participating publicly in the decision-making process and has officially adopted an antiseptic attitude toward controversial issues. Policy is assumed to be given; the party mobilizes support for policy. This does not mean that party members are barred from shaping policy, but when they engage in that activity, it is because they occupy dual roles. Because there is no support for an equivalent of the Hatch Act in Mexico, most top echelon PRI officials have salaried positions in government agencies or institutions. They receive no salary as party officials, but the PRI pays all expenses they incur in the pursuit of their party duties. During my field work I became aware of innumerable cases of individuals who divided their time between government jobs and party jobs, not simply during campaign time, but on a year-round basis. In the privacy of party headquarters, these people compete with other party-government officials in trying to achieve adoption of their preferred policies, but once a policy has been adopted and made public—whether or not it was their original preference—they are obliged to act publicly, in their role of PRI officials, as though the policy were the most desirable one.

This duality is one of the elements which injects a certain flexibility into a system which might otherwise be isolated from important sources of information. The PRI official turned government official may use information obtained in his former role to support the arguments he advances in the latter role. The party acts in a fashion similar to that of some membranes in biological systems, which selectively allow certain substances to pass into cells and facilitate the elimination of other substances from those cells.

Individuals socialized in other types of political systems might find this duality confusing and unnerving, but many Mexicans accept it as both natural and desirable. For this reason it would be inappropriate to accuse them of insincerity when they insist, as they often do, that the PRI and the government are completely separate institutions.

The Legislature as an Information Transmitter

Members of Mexico's national congress are not confronted with the Burkean dilemma of trying to decide whether to obey the instructions of their constituents or follow the dictates of their consciences. To do either would be a breach of custom and party discipline. Since all of the senators, and an overwhelming majority of the deputies, belong to the same party as the president, and since he exercises decisive influence over their political present and future, they would not risk extinction by opposing any part of his legislative program. For this reason the congress has been described as a rubber stamp and its members dismissed as impotent.[12]

However, there have been recent indications that this body may actually be a part of the information-transmitting structure and may not deserve to be called functionally superfluous. It seems to be the launching site for trial balloons, by which the government is able to publicize the range of permissible actions on an issue and gauge the amount of support that can be mustered for each alternative. Such seemed to be the case in the debate about repeal of the antisubversive law in 1969.

In 1962, Mexico's constitution was amended to provide

representation of minority parties in the national Chamber of Deputies;[13] additional statutes enacted in 1971 and 1973 liberalized the bases for minority representation in that chamber, and lowered the age requirements for both deputies and senators.[14]

Under the electoral law as amended in 1973, an opposition party that obtains 1.5 percent of the total vote in the most recent national election can be represented in the Chamber of Deputies by as many as 25 at-large party deputies, the exact number corresponding to the percentage of the vote polled by that party. If, however, a minority party were to win a majority of votes in twenty-five or more electoral districts, it would lose its right to be represented and would, instead, send the deputies chosen through ordinary electoral procedures to the congress. Under this arrangement, a party might fail to win a majority of votes in any single electoral district and yet have as many as twenty-five party deputies admitted to the Chamber. As a result of the 1973 election the composition of the Chamber was:

PRI	189	elected
PAN	4	elected
PARM	1	elected
Total	194	elected

PAN was entitled to an additional 21 seats by reason of the number of votes cast for its candidates.

Since the 1964 elections, the expanded contingent of PAN representatives has seized many opportunities to force fuller discussion of important bills, such as the budget. On one occasion, the late Adolfo Christlieb Ibarrola, representing the caucus of PAN deputies, remarked from the floor:

> A few days ago we heard it said in this tribunal that the function of the Chamber in connection with the budget was not to examine its separate items but to approve or

disapprove the political tendency shown by the Executive in the annual plan of expenditures which he presents to the Congress.

And even further: with respect to the budget, it was pointed out that the decisive factors [should be] political solidarity and personal confidence in the Chief of State. . . .

Considering these statements, the deputies of Acción Nacional, after studying the budget for 1966, agreed on the convenience of presenting some orientations which might point to a different procedure, even though no result may be achieved by our views at this time. . . .[15]

He went on to criticize the proposal that the president be given authority to transfer surpluses from one category to another, at his discretion. This had been common practice in the past, without explicit legislative approval, but Christlieb Ibarrola insisted that it was not only unconstitutional but actually made the budgetary process meaningless. As he had predicted, the remarks had no effect on the final vote, but the publicity accorded the PAN's criticism made it necessary for the majority party to justify its procedure, which the leadership had not heretofore thought itself obliged to do.

The practice of giving legislative seats to minority parties without their having won them through the electoral process could have a narcotizing influence on those groups, causing them to relax their campaign efforts. Even without this factor, many observers believe that *all* minority parties are puppets of the PRI. There are numerous indications that this may be so in the case of parties other than the PAN, but it is my belief that the latter has retained some measure of autonomy. Its organization and behavior indicate that it resembles a nineteenth-century gentlemen's political club rather than a mass party like its overwhelming opponent, the PRI. There are elements within the PAN that are trying, in the face of determined resistance, to update its methods. After the 1970 national elections, PAN leaders felt that they would have won twenty seats in the Chamber of Deputies without the help of the party deputy clause, and insisted that by using the clause the Electoral Commission was hiding their strength from the public. Another PAN leader has contended that the definitive feature of a political party is its ability to wage a real campaign for the purpose of winning an election. "Let us not degenerate into a debating society," he pleaded at a meeting attended by the author.

Because of the preponderance of the Executive in Mexico, both the national and state legislatures often resemble oratory contests. A change in the direction of genuine debate might actually be a big step toward further development as a functional component of the information system. As the American senator John P. Hale remarked in 1858, "It is very rarely, sir, that a debate in the Senate is intended to influence the action of members here, but it is made to enlighten the country." [16] Governmental output of information, as "enlightenment of the country," might in turn stimulate greater inputs of information into the system.

Some theoreticians of the PRI were very much aware of this potentiality. The former director of the Institute of Political and Social Studies appeared to have this in mind when he commented:

> The consciousness of the strength of a Regime obliges it to meditate on its future almost as much [as would] its weakness. In the purest theory of democracy, an almost unanimous majority seems ideal, but historic experience has demonstrated that the best of political ideas, when they are overwhelmingly supported, begin to generate psychological uneasiness in society and run the risk of becoming rigid. . . . The political Regime . . . must be attentive to the smallest variations in the interplay of social expressions.[17]

Intelligence

Intelligence activities are conducted both by the secretaría de Gobernación (Ministry of Internal Affairs) and by the army, which also has a counterinsurgency section. There are many indications that the operations of the army and Gobernación are poorly coordinated, resulting in conflicts of authority and mistakes which sometimes have tragic consequences. Information about army activities is understandably unobtainable, but there are some clues about Gobernación.

Among the overt activities of this secretariat are those concerned with control of immigration and emigration; census and identification services; operation of prisons and reformatories; censorship of motion pictures, theater, radio and television, and publications; investigation of illegal gambling, and surveillance of religious activities (to prevent violations of constitutional restrictions).

Gobernación is an indispensable adjunct to the exercise of executive power, and a well-traveled route to high positions in the national government. Four recent presidents have come directly from service at the head of this ministry: Alemán, Ruiz Cortines, Díaz Ordaz, and Luis Echeverría. One explanation of this may be that experience in Gobernación enhances an aspirant's ability to evaluate information; an alternative explanation is that the incumbent secretary of Gobernación has already proved his expertness by his handling of this delicate job. The contribution of the agency to the successful exercise of presidential power has been described in these terms:

> With its channels of communications, *Gobernación* can transmit Presidential wishes to all levels of government. Through its intelligence functions, it enables the President to choose the most effective line of action to meet a

situation. Through its supervision of application of the Constitution, *Gobernación* offers the Executive an excuse for intervention in all stages of Mexican government. The power of the President is very much dependent on the operations of this agency.[18]

The ministry has a press and radio department which monitors media and prepares a digest of news and editorial comment for distribution to the president, cabinet ministers, and other high government officials every morning at nine o'clock.[19] Since the media are virtually echoes of government press releases, the digest's value as a carrier of new information is very low. The press practices autocensorship to such a degree that Gobernación is rarely required to intervene for the suppression of information.

The activities of some secret service agents are anything but secret; in fact, the assignment of agents to cover and report on a group's operations is tantamount to government recognition of the group's political existence. Over a period of months or years, group leaders get to know many of these agents by sight, and a mutually tolerant relationship sometimes develops between the watcher and the watched.

This kind of surveillance was very much in evidence during the doctors' strikes. One agent even posed for pictures with a group of physicians in front of one of the hospitals.[20] Other agents were assigned on a round-the-clock basis to the headquarters of the Alianza de Médicos Mexicanos in the old Medical School building on the Plaza Santo Domingo in Mexico City. On one of the author's frequent visits to this office, a group of AMMRI physicians introduced the agent then on duty. They later explained the symbiotic relationship which had developed. Knowing that anything they said in his presence would be reported to Gobernación, the physicians often planned their conversations so that they would constitute messages to the authorities about their intentions. In turn, the agent relayed advance information to the physicians about the government's intentions.

Members of protest groups did not seem suspicious or even surprised at the apparent generosity of government-connected organizations or institutions in lending them space for headquarters from which to conduct their activities. AMMRI and Alianza organizers found it quite natural that the University allowed them to settle into offices at the old Medical School building. They explained to an interviewer that as University alumni they had a right to use such facilities. A prominent Alianza member, ousted from his position in a government hospital, continued both his medical and his extracurricular organizational work in an annex of the hospital. "The government," he explained, could do nothing to prevent him from doing so, as the annex was technically the "property of the University."

During most of the student movement, the Universidad Nacional Autónoma de México (UNAM) campus was the headquarters for the protesters' activities, and preparatory school students often held strategy meetings in their schools. Thus, also, members of the Vallejo factions of the railroadmen's union, at the invitation of the "charro" faction, installed themselves in union headquarters in Mexico City. In all these cases, use of such facilities made it easier for Gobernación to exercise surveillance over the protesters' activities.

Politically active Mexicans are far more uncomfortable in the presence of strangers than they are with clearly identified government intelligence agents. It seems obvious to Mexicans that anyone who is present on the scene of political activity must have some stake in the outcome; there can be no such thing as "scientific curiosity." It therefore becomes necessary, as a matter of self-protection, to rapidly determine whether a newcomer is a friend, an enemy, or a spy for the enemy, so that he can be treated appropriately, with the ever-present caveat that an apparent friend may later prove to be a disguised enemy. After several months of continuous contact, two informants revealed that the Alianza governing council initially regarded the author as a C.I.A. agent and that a few members continued to regard her in this light. For this reason, the suspicious members had evaded requests for interviews.[21]

Informal Networks

In the presence of strangers, suspicion makes orators of most politically active Mexicans. Many of the statements quoted in American social science literature sound like excerpts from campaign speeches. They are not intended to reveal new aspects of political life to the visiting researcher; rather, they announce to fellow Mexicans that the stranger is being kept at an appropriate distance by a barrier of truisms and stereotypes. A key to the relative value of a statement can often be discovered in the volume and pitch of a speaker's voice: the louder and higher the voice, the less valuable is the information being conveyed. As suspicion evaporates, the tone begins to drop and the content of the message becomes more meaningful.

Because of the ever-present fear of betrayal, Mexicans assign great importance to the establishment of a network of reciprocal obligations which will ensure the loyalty of other individuals. The most reliable tie is blood kinship; at each step in their careers politicians carefully place as many members of their immediate and extended family as possible in positions which will enable them to gather information about the intentions of real or potential rivals.[22] Widespread nepotism, the inevitable result of such arrangements, is regarded as natural and necessary.

Another method of assuring faithfulness is ritual coparenthood (*compadrazgo*), preferably formalized through a religious ceremony.[23] In theory and very often in fact, the demands made by or upon a *compadre* (godfather of one's child or, conversely, parent of a child to whom one is a godfather) or *ahijado* (godchild) are regarded as sacred and must be complied with. Such demands may range from borrowing money to requesting physical protection against threat of violence. Foster, however, has indicated the possibility of heretofore unsuspected flexibility in these arrangements.[24] Because they are contractual rather than ascribed, an individual can choose which relationships are most advantageous and proceed to solidify them by appropriate action (for example, gift-giving), while ignoring the less advantageous ties. Without this flexibility, infers Foster, the burden of such relationships would soon become intolerable.

Friendship is the last of the classic triad of relationships upon which all Mexicans depend for security. Because the obligations of friendship are similar to those of the *compadrazgo*, an individual begins to choose his companions and potential friends in adolescence with great care. To be called a friend indicates that one has solidified the solemn bond by some overt act of service. In the urban industrial society that is the breeding place of most of modern Mexico's leaders, friendships formed among schoolmates or companions in work or political activity often become more important than *compadrazgo* ties. Sometimes these ties are reinforced by *compadrazgo* ritualization. By definition, the number of friends an individual has is limited

produce a cartoon showing the figure of a man in railroad worker's clothes trampling on the heads of many workers. The legend, "Guess the costumes of the quick-change artist . . . Colonel? Painter? Teacher? Railroadman?" referred to well-known opposition leaders like the painter David Alfaro Siqueiros and others prominent in recent protest movements.[29]

The strike at Ferrocarriles Nacionales began on schedule, Wednesday, 25 February, at noon, and was attended by a veritable blizzard of hostile press comment. *Excelsior* alone carried an eight-column banner headline on page 1, and over four main stories referred to the event. In addition, pages 6 and 7 carried derogatory cartoons, and half-page advertisements appeared on pages 12 and 16. One of these was signed by the trio of federal deputies who had previously subscribed to an anti-Vallejo attack; the other carried the names of the organizers of the Railroadmen's Liberation Movement.

Thursday's crop of press comment was even more extensive: two banner headlines, nine front-page stories, and a page 6 cartoon showing railroad tracks twisted into the shape of a hammer and sickle. In the same edition of *Excelsior*, a half-page advertisement of the Board of Conciliation and Arbitration announced its decision denying the legality of the strike.

By 10 P.M. Thursday a new contract had been signed—a victory for the union, according to Vallejo and his followers, a defeat according to their detractors. Among other benefits, the new agreement provided for the retroactive payment of the 16.6 percent of 215 pesos; free medical care for workers' families (to put them on a par with other Mexican workers covered by social security); and a contribution by the rail system of 30 million pesos for construction of low-cost rental units for railroad workers. Other clauses provided protection for union organizers against arbitrary dismissal by the government management company and against discriminatory hiring procedures.[30] It is of particular interest to note that the news and editorial columns of the major newspapers completely omitted reference to the provisions of the new contract, giving credence by their silence on this important matter to the allegations of the progovernment forces that the union had been forced to capitulate.

The newspaper blizzard gradually subsided and, for the first three weeks of March, remained at one or two news stories a day covering such aspects of the strike's aftermath as its effect on the tourist industry, the normalization of train service, and the possibilities of strikes on other lines of the nationwide system. The last became a probability on 19 March when a full-page advertisement signed by Vallejo and other officials of the STFRM called for a work stoppage on 25 March on the Ferrocarril Mexicano, the Ferrocarril del Pacífico, and the Ferrocarril de Veracruz, until such time as the expiring contracts would be replaced by acceptable new agreements.

Although it was to be expected that Vallejo would seek the same economic improvements for the workers of all lines of the system, progovernment groups responded to the new announcement as though it were a gratuitous insult. The first attack on the union from this quarter was spearheaded by the Bloque de Unidad Obrera, a government-sponsored confederation of unions, one of whose professed objectives was to expose and stamp out Communist influence in organized labor groups.

In 1959, Easter fell on Sunday, 29 March. To millions of Mexicans, Holy Week signifies the fact that all workers are given a week's vacation with pay. By a combination of meteorological conditions peculiar to the heavily populated central plateau of the country, Holy Week is the warmest time of the year and is characterized by intermittent dust storms which aggravate everyone. Panting at the end of the long dry season, parched Mexicans look forward to their vacation as an opportunity to join the lemminglike hordes in their annual stampede to the seacoasts. Like Paris in August, prepaschal Mexico City is a ghost town. The stranger, caught unawares, wanders down empty streets past shuttered shops in a forlorn attempt to obtain a meal or get his laundry done.

To reach the sea, fleeing Mexicans use every available means of transportation. Standard procedure for newspapers is to publish a photograph showing the main railroad station in Mexico City jammed with people trying to board a departing train, even if they must make the entire trip standing on the platforms or the steps of the coaches. Although every available piece of rolling stock is pressed into service at this time, the demand for space always outruns the supply. It is the one week of the year when the public cannot afford to be too critical of the deficiencies of the rail system, and the one week when the system's management can count on maximum passenger revenues.

Vallejo was undoubtedly aware of this when he planned the new strikes. The possibility of further immobilization of holiday travelers became a certainty when the governing boards of locals 15, 16, 17, and 18—all in the Federal District—approved a sympathy strike to coincide with the stoppage on the three struck lines.[31] Not all officers of these locals were in favor of this action; a few demurred, expressing fears that it would provide the government with precisely the justification it needed to break the strike.[32]

Counterattack

Their expectations were realized almost immediately. The strike began, on schedule, in the early morning of 25 March. On schedule also, the government mounted a two-pronged attack on the strikers, the first of which was a decision handed down by the Federal Conciliation Board to the effect that the strikes were illegal because the question had not been submitted to the union membership.[33] In this respect, the board appeared to be on firm ground, as there is no record, either in the pro-Vallejo published sources or in the interviews with strikers conducted for the present study, to contradict the allegation. In fact, some informants took the view that failure to submit the matter to a referendum had spared the members from conflicts and had promoted solidarity.

At any rate, it would have been difficult, perhaps even impossible, to have conducted a strike vote which would have satisfied the conditions laid down by the law and which, at the same time, would have given all the workers a voice. Under Article 264 of the Federal Labor Law in effect at that time, management, allied with *charro* leaders, could use the *claúsula de exclusión* in their labor contracts to discharge prostrike union men. This exclusion clause, originally fashioned as a device to guarantee a union shop, could be invoked between the time that the union filed formal notice of intent to renegotiate a collective bargaining agreement and the time that a strike vote would be taken.[34] In effect, this guaranteed that a majority of *charro* supporters would participate in the referendum and could be counted on to reject a strike.

The other prong of the government's attack began within hours of the strikes' onset. Army troops mounted guard over all rail installations in the country, and army telegraphers took over the wire communications, replacing union telegraphers who were sympathetic to the railroad men's cause. Soldiers accompanied by police and secret service men broke into strikers' homes and, at gunpoint, forced them to return to work. Engineers flanked by soldiers began moving trains out of the stations.

Although skeleton crews had been assembled through the use of military force, the strikes were not yet over. Thousands of union members evaded impressment in spite of published appeals and threats from management and the government. But the process of attrition had begun, with telegraphic communication cut off and mobility by rail suppressed through military vigilance.

"It is truly desperate," writes one veteran of the experience, "when one loses contact with the others and everything is reduced to guesswork in trying to reconstruct events from isolated news items that are broadcast or printed, in trying [also] to read between the lines or to deduce the truth from what is published." [35]

The newspaper storm had started again, the front pages crammed with antistrike stories topped by eight-column banner headlines. As early as 26 March, when the strike was only one day old, the editorials began to insinuate that the whole affair was "a maneuver of international communism." [36] On the following day, the pace was accelerated to include headlines calling the strikers terrorists and saboteurs, as well as a signed article stating that Demetrio Vallejo was a Moscow agent.[37] Predictably, this was followed by an editorial, appearing the next day, which demanded that the government intervene to protect the public interest.

By this time, many union leaders had correctly interpreted the message to mean that the government would soon begin a large-scale manhunt. Many veterans of previous conflicts went into hiding immediately, moving from place to place, never sleeping in the same house two nights in a row. This was a luxury not permitted to the national officers, who had to remain visible in order to reassure their followers and to try to negotiate with the rail system's management. On 28 March, Vallejo and several other leaders were taken into custody while they were lunching in a restaurant next door to union headquarters. Thousands of workers were imprisoned in the nationwide dragnet which followed. In Guadalajara alone, official accounts, confirmed by confidential informants, reported the arrest of at least seven hundred strikers.[38] As an extra precaution, the roundup included many leaders of the petroleum workers, the teachers' union, and telephone operators' union, known or suspected to be sympathetic with Vallejo. When the jails were full, the overflow was interned in military camps throughout the country.

In mass arrests of this nature, which have occurred several times in Mexico during the past twenty years, lists of names of those arrested are not published. Prisoners are often held incommunicado for several days before being arraigned. After the detention of the railroad workers, anguished relatives ran from jail to jail and made the rounds of the military camps, trying to locate their family members. The desperation of these people contributed to the confusion and isolation of the strikers who remained at large.

The vacuum created by the arrest of Vallejo and other officers was quickly filled by a group of anti-Vallejo men, hailed by the press as a "new leadership." Further indications of the government's strategy for eliminating the elected officers were soon made public. In announcing the arrest of an additional two hundred men on 30 March, the attorney general revealed that incriminating documents including a large quantity of subversive propaganda had been impounded. This material, never fully described by the press, apparently consisted at least in part of Marxist books and pamphlets whose possession and use were protected by constitutional guarantees. Vallejo and his followers, declared the attorney general, were part of an international plot.[39]

During the week that followed, the press was filled with stereotyped stories and advertisements heaping abuse on the railroad men and applauding the government for its prompt action to protect the public interest. The volume of such material was at its all-time peak for the periods covered in the present study. The most dramatic stories were concerned with the arrest and deportation of two members of the Russian Embassy. Although the government was under no compulsion to reveal its reasons for requesting the departure of these two men, the press reported that "this decision . . . was taken . . . after irrefutable proof had been obtained that Remisov and Aksenov [the two Russian aides] were abetting Demetrio Vallejo . . . aiding him with financial means." The story added that Vallejo had reported almost daily to the Russian Embassy.[40] The Soviet Union, which has frequently done the same sort of thing, did not protest.

By Thursday, 9 April, the strike had been broken, the trains were running, hundreds of railroad men had been released from jail, and all Vallejista union officials had been replaced by progovernment leaders. A page one newspaper story appeared, filled with words and phrases which in effect instructed readers how to evaluate the whole strike movement. An excerpt will illustrate the unequivocal nature of the message:

> *Arrogant* and at times *sarcastic* with the agents of the Attorney General's office, the *ex*-leader Demetrio Vallejo . . . did not *choose* to answer the prosecutor's questions, giving as his *pretext* that he has not been charged [with any crime]. The *number one agitator* of the railroadmen *ridiculed* the . . . authorized agents, for whom he had *defiant glances and in whose faces he threw* the incommunication in which they had held him.[41]

Vallejo and other union leaders were finally brought to trial in 1963 and were convicted of conspiracy and sabotage under the Law of Social Dissolution. Vallejo and Valentín Campa were sentenced to sixteen years in prison. Twenty-three other railroad union leaders were also found guilty and received long prison sentences.

The Doctors' Strikes of 1964–1965

5

A Chronology

When a need for concerted action arose in 1964, there was no formal structure for creating and sustaining feelings of occupational solidarity among Mexico's 20,000 physicians. In each of the hospitals or government health units where groups of doctors were regularly employed, a spirit of comradeship existed which rarely transcended the walls of the particular institution. In spite of this apparent isolation, numerous informal communication channels connected the seemingly discrete units in a network which facilitated the rapid transmission of messages.

Congenital ties incident to membership in the extended family structure provided important links between young people of the same generation and social class whose sense of kinship and mutual obligation remained strong even between cousins of fourth and fifth remove. Ritual coparenthood linked many married professionals, who often sought godfathers and godmothers for their children among members of their profession.

Probably more powerful, however, were the bonds of friendship forged among members of the same graduating class at the National University Medical School; the "generation" of the year of their graduation, as they called themselves. Each generation dispersed after graduation to take up their duties in the various government institutions, but for the rest of their lives many individuals would retain the relationship of intimacy and trust born of their years of work and study together. Because telephone directories were hopelessly incomplete, and the postal service was sometimes erratic, the most promising method of trying to locate a particular physician continued to be through the network of former classmates. This kind of arrangement undoubtedly facilitated communication when common interests required it. Only if this is understood can the initial events of the chronological account offered here be understood.

15 November 1964: At the Veinte de Noviembre Hospital—part of the web of welfare services provided for beneficiaries of the Instituto de Seguridad Social al Servicio de los Trabajadores del Estado (known as ISSSTE)—a rumor circulated to the effect that the customary Christmas bonus (known as an *aguinaldo*) would not be paid to the resident medical staff. This bonus was not part of any contractual fringe benefits. At most government hospitals a small amount was deducted from each paycheck of the salaried physicians—a kind of forced savings—and returned to them as a lump sum just before the Christmas holidays. No deduction was made from the residents' pay at the Veinte de Noviembre Hospital or other similar institutions, as their emolument was considered to be scholarship aid rather than a salary. However, it was a long-standing custom for the hospital administration to distribute cash gifts to this category of staff members, amounting to 1,500 pesos for each intern and 2,000 pesos for each resident. (At the existing rate of exchange, the Mexican peso was valued at eight cents in United States currency.) When the doctors became aware of the rumored withholding of the bonus, the four chief residents of the hospital formed a committee which visited the director of the hospital, Dr. Angel Gutiérrez, to obtain official information. Dr. Gutiérrez confirmed the rumor and expressed his regret, but did not hold out any hope that the policy would be changed.

15–25 November: The four chief residents, now joined by other hospital residents, discussed the problems occasioned by the unexpected withdrawal of the customary gift and the means available to them for appealing the decision. On four separate occasions they requested and were given appointments with Dr. Javier de la Riva, Chief of Medical Services of the ISSSTE, but Dr. de la Riva broke each of the appointments after having the group wait for long periods in the anteroom of his office.[1] On 25 November, the last of such appointments, the committee waited from 6 P.M. to 11 P.M., only to be told by Dr. de la Riva's secretary that he was "very tired" and could not receive them.

26 November: At a meeting in the auditorium of the Veinte de Noviembre Hospital Center, attended by approximately two hundred residents and interns, the residents' committee reported their failure to meet with Dr. de la Riva. By a majority vote, the assembly decided to remain "in permanent session"—amounting to a partial strike—until Dr. de la Riva would meet with their representatives. Provisions were made for coverage of emergency services, intensive therapy, obstetrics, and critical wards. Residents and interns not on duty in those special categories remained in the auditorium all night in what is described as a "festive atmosphere." A number of guitars appeared; group singing and impromptu speeches occupied much of the night.

27 November, 9 A.M.: Dr. de la Riva went to the Veinte de Noviembre Hospital and received the residents' committee in the office of the hospital director. He told the committee that as the residents and interns were scholarship students rather than employees, they would not be paid Christmas bonuses, to which the committee spokesman replied that long usage had created certain expectations almost as firm as legal rights. If these expectations were disappointed at this time, the spokesman indicated, what had begun as a permanent session, might develop into a full-fledged strike. Dr. de la Riva countered by saying that as of the moment all the residents and interns were fired and that they should leave the hospital immediately. (This terminology later gave rise to the first of many legalistic wrangles, none of which was resolved. In this case the controversy was to center on the problem of whether a nonemployee could be fired.) The committee reported the interview to the assembled interns and residents, the majority of whom decided to disregard Dr. de la Riva's orders and to remain in the auditorium.

27 November, afternoon: Each of the 206 residents and interns at the Veinte de Noviembre Hospital received an individual dismissal slip, properly made out and duly signed. The speed and accuracy with which names and positions were located on personnel lists, rechecked, and delivered demonstrates that the Mexican bureaucracy has, at least in some of its branches and in some situations, adequate means of information storage and retrieval.

27 November, evening: The residents and interns—still in the hospital auditorium—formed an association called Associación Mexicana de Médicos Residentes e Internos, Associación Civil (AMMRI). The act of incorporation was registered the same night before a notary public. This is a legalistic precaution often taken by Mexican groups to minimize the danger of having the name and sympathizers pirated by rival groups (often, it is alleged, sponsored by the government).

28 November: Envoys from the newly organized association were dispatched to other government hospitals to urge the interns and residents to join the movement. Some individuals walked off the job as a gesture of sympathy for the Veinte de Noviembre strikers.

29 November: A partial strike situation prevailed in seven hospitals. Members of the AMMRI met and adopted a five-point list of conditions as the basis for an end to the strike.

In deference to the style of Mexican verbal communications, this was entitled a 'petition' rather than 'demand.' The five points were:

1. Immediate rehiring of the doctors who were fired.
2. Conversion of the scholarship—contract to an annual, renewable work contract with provision for seniority and advancement in the ranking of residencies, with the hours of work and conditions characteristic of the different institutions and with the following wage scale:

Pregraduates	1,200 pesos monthly
Postgraduates	
First year	2,000
Second year	2,500
Third year	3,000
Fourth year	3,500
For each additional year	500

3. Preferential hiring of former resident physicians for permanent employment on full-time basis.
4. Active participation of residents and interns in the planning of teaching programs.
5. Satisfactory solution of the problems encountered in each hospital (improved housing, food, etc.).[2]

1 December: Inauguration of Gustavo Díaz Ordaz as president of Mexico, bringing about an almost complete turnover in top governmental posts.

Newspaper stories during the first week of December mentioned the doctors' movement, but there was no exact information as to just what had happened or when. There was a complete absence of names of the individuals involved. Excerpts from one such story show the editorial ambivalence characteristic of the treatment of the events by communications media during this stage of developments:

> The protest of the medical residents and *practicantes* is assuming a national aspect, which the nurses are also joining, to protest against the low wages which they receive in hospitals, clinics, and health institutions, both public and private.
>
> Personnel from hospitals in the different states are sending evidence of their support to the initiators of the movement in this Capital [Mexico City] . . . for the purpose of getting the Government to study carefully their problems and to seek more adequate solutions.
>
> . . . Directors of hospitals, medical services, and other institutions are interested in finding out if perhaps there is somebody behind this agitation . . . who is seeking some personal advantage . . . which some consider very probable.[3]

5 December: Dr. Rafael Moreno Valle, secretary of health and welfare, granted an interview to a group of members of the General Hospital Medical Society. This group explained the background of the doctors' protest with particular reference to the wages and working conditions of interns and residents at the different hospitals of the Ministry of Health (for example, General, Juárez, Neurology, and Women's hospitals). Dr. Moreno Valle assured the group that he would study the conditions carefully, with a view to correcting deficiencies "as soon as practicable." An atmosphere of cordiality reigned at this meeting.[4]

8 December: Members of AMMRI voted to hold a demonstration in the Plaza de la Constitución (known popularly as "El Zócalo," this is the centermost point in the city, flanked by the Cathedral, the colonial *intendencia,* and the presidential palace). A parade permit was requested from the office of Gobernación (internal affairs) of the Federal District, and was denied.

9 December: In spite of the denial of a parade permit, at 9

A.M., about 1,500 residents and interns made their appearance in the Plaza de la Constitución, facing the presidential palace. Picket signs and banners stressed two main themes: the need for favorable action on the five-point petition, and the desire for an interview with the president. At about noon, a fifteen-member committee was invited into the presidential palace. After receiving brief instructions on protocol, the group was asked to designate a spokesman who talked to the president for three minutes. Mr. Díaz Ordaz listened, then replied in a tone variously described as "angry," "brusque," "ill-humored," stating that the president was not a desk sergeant assigned to listen to petty complaints. There were, he said, proper channels through which to place their demands, and he advised them to use them in a peaceful manner. "He lectured us like schoolboys," observed one witness.

The committee went directly from the presidential palace to the huge auditorium of the Instituto Mexicano de Seguro Social (IMSS), followed by most of the physicians from the Zócalo demonstration. After listening to the committee's report, the group decided to continue the strike. At this point, two members of the original AMMRI governing council resigned without any explanation. One informant believes they had been intimidated, as many of the striking physicians had already been visited by secret service agents who had advised them to drop out of the movement.[5] Another informant felt that the resignations were a protest by moderates against strong-arm tactics of the extremist wing of the movement which succeeded in prolonging the strike.[6]

Sinister motives were attributed to the leaders of the doctors' movement by Dr. Sergio Novelo, president of the Federación Médica del Distrito Federal, a "company" union of doctors connected with the hospitals of the government of the Federal District. Dr. Novelo warned that the movement had "underground direction" whose "unspeakable purposes" were completely rejected by the doctors as a group and by society. Simultaneously, Rómulo Sánchez Mireles, head of the ISSSTE, declared that the problem of the doctors and residents at the Veinte de Noviembre Hospital could be considered "practically solved." [7]

16 December: By this date, the AMMRI was organized nationally, with active participation of representatives from forty-six hospitals in the Federal District and the states. After a heated discussion, these representatives decided by a close vote to end the partial strike.

17 December: By order of Rómulo Sánchez Mireles, the new director of the ISSSTE, the Christmas bonus was paid to all residents and interns at ISSSTE hospitals. The strike ended at 4 P.M. However, the AMMRI House of Representatives voted for a new strike on 26 December unless the other demands in the five-point petition were granted.

25 December: Date of new strike was postponed indefinitely as a result of assurances by various hospital and departmental officials that work was going forward to solve all problems in the petition.

1 September–1 December 1964: The three months just prior to the inauguration of a new president comprise a lame duck period in Mexican politics. On 1 September, the outgoing president makes his last public accounting of the nation's fiscal resources. When the new president follows this annual custom on the next 1st of September, he will report only on his first nine months of office, that is, from 1 December to 1 September. Thus there is a gap of ninety days for which neither president is held accountable. Without resorting to implications of wholesale malfeasance by officials of the outgoing administration (although such explanations abound, and there is little reason to reject them), some observers point out that it has been a tradition for Mexican presidents to spend all available funds in the initiation of public works to leave as monuments to their administration (political advertising). The mass media for this period are filled with pictures and stories of the president inaugurating new schools, hospitals, roads, and dams throughout the republic.[8]

As a by-product of this spree, money is often withdrawn from the operating budgets of existing public institutions which are usually forced to curtail all but skeletal services and must often default on financial commitments. All of those to whom the government owes money (for example, suppliers, contractors, government employees) are fairly confident that they will eventually collect what is due them, and for that reason they do not complain publicly.[9]

There is reason to believe that the suspension of payment of Christmas bonuses at the Veinte de Noviembre Hospital may have been due to the situation described above and to the need to cut cash expenditures wherever possible. Restitution might have been made in due course (some time after 1 January), even without a protest by the residents and interns, but probably not in time for their holiday celebration which traditionally culminates on Three Kings' Day (6 January).

The first three months of the new president's administration are expected to bring a massive change of personnel in top- and middle-level government positions. One observer estimates that "every incoming six-year administration brings with it a turnover of about 18,000 elective officials and 25,000 appointive posts" at the national, state, and municipal levels. Each of these new officeholders must receive the personal stamp of approval of the incoming president.[10]

There is always the chance that the new chief of state will request an incumbent to stay on in his post for the next six years. It is the remote but real possibility of winning this kind of political lottery which keeps thousands of officials at their desks during the lame duck period. They are deaf and blind to most incoming messages except those which relate directly to their job expectancy, and they bequeath a legacy of unresolved problems to their successors.

Díaz Ordaz was unusually slow in filling bureaucratic posts. Even when prompt action in extending appointments reduces the period of uncertainty to a minimum, the new appointees are in a poor position to take decisive action because they lack adequate means of evaluating information fed to them by their subordinates. Members of the new administration are aware that each six years they must laboriously forge their own links in the chain of communications. On taking possession of their new offices, they find no files, no data, no memoranda about past problems or future plans on which they can rely as accurate representations of reality. An academic administrator who was active as an intermediary between the government officials and the physicians' groups during the initial stage of the conflict observed:

> The government officials with whom we dealt were in the beginning completely ignorant about the most basic elements of the situation which caused the doctors' protest. . . . If there had been data-collecting and evaluating machinery set up in the different health agencies for the purpose of planning, a change of administration would not have affected it drastically. But the fact is that no such machinery existed. . . . When the emergency arose, the heads of the agencies did not even know which if any of their subordinates possessed any useful information.[11]

President Díaz Ordaz euphemistically referred to this situation in his remarks to the residents' committee on 9 December.[12]

7–29 December: On 7 December the president conferred

with the secretary of Gobernación (department of internal affairs, headquarters for the Mexican secret service); on 7, 15, and 29 December with the director general of the ISSSTE; on 14 and 15 December with the secretary of the treasury; and on 23 December with the secretary of health and assistance.[13] The activities of the residents and interns must have figured importantly in these conversations, but by his own admission the president sought information from other, unspecified, sources: "I have heard outside of official channels. . . ." [14] Having only recently vacated the post of secretary of Gobernación, he was in a better position than most to know how far he should or should not rely on official informants.

During this initial stage, the mass media contained unusually large amounts of information about the activities of the residents and interns. By making allowances for the style of Latin-American journalism, the reader can piece together a reasonably complete picture of the events of the period from the daily and weekly press. The reason for this atypical behavior is a paradoxical result of the role which has been assigned to the Mexican press and which has largely been accepted by it: that of a one-way purveyor of propaganda from the government to the literate public. (See Chapter 2 for a discussion of this subject.) In the confused situation prevailing during the first few weeks of the new administration, the nation's editors lacked clear-cut indicators as to the government's position on the hospital strike. They were therefore temporarily forced to report events as they occurred.

That there was not at that time any official antidoctor position with respect to the strike is apparent from these excerpts from the published version of the president's remarks: "I believe in your good faith; and that is why I wanted to listen to you personally. . . . I consider your desire [to be] fair, but I do not know whether it will be possible to grant you what you ask for. . . . I want it clearly understood that I am not offering a single cent of increase. . . ." [15]

Summary

By the end of December 1964, the residents and interns had organized a fairly efficient system of communications among their members, even including those located on the geographic periphery of the nation. They were able to establish a formal organization, convoke and attend meetings, inform absent members of the decisions reached, and solicit and elicit collective action. They had what appeared to be a well-defined and limited set of objectives (the five-point petition) and a powerful method of bringing their demands to the attention of government decision makers (the work stoppage).

Many decision makers, on the other hand, were forced at the beginning to operate in a relative vacuum of information. The organization of which they had so recently become a part suffered from an almost total lack of horizontal communication. Thus, for example, there was no way for the directors of two ISSSTE hospitals to exchange information about activities of residents and interns in their respective institutions except by going to (not through) the director general of the ISSSTE. And there was no way for the director general of the ISSSTE to communicate with his homologue, the secretary of health, or with the director of the IMSS except to go to (not through) the president.

Especially at the beginning of a new administration, it would have been an inadmissible confession of weakness to ask another government official for information. This lack of direct communications would be compensated later by information received through an intricate network of blood relatives, in-laws, *compadres, ahijados,* and political debtors, strategically located in other government agencies. But that kind of network takes time to build and must, to a considerable extent, be rebuilt each time a man changes positions.

At the outset, the doctors had no formal organization, no prescribed hierarchical system of information and decision making. Among them, the customary reticence of the Mexicans was shattered by the consciousness of a common grievance and enabled the rapid horizontal spread of information in somewhat the same fashion as a blotter absorbs water. Through 9 December, all communication was by word of mouth, and much of it was face to face. This was possible because the initial stage of organization was confined to the Federal District. But the kind of information thus transmitted among doctors was of a superficial nature. Attempts were made later to supplement the information, by formal and informal means, but were only successful in the Federal District.

When the medical director of the Veinte de Noviembre Hospital was faced with a group of indignant residents who wanted to know what had happened to their Christmas bonus, he was not confused by a wide range of choices of possible actions. There was one course of action open to him and he took it; he passed the buck.

Dr. de la Riva, director of medical services for the ISSSTE, was the next man up on the government ladder. His immediate superior, the director general of ISSSTE, was due to be replaced at the beginning of December by an appointee of the new president. If he could hold off until that time, he could then pass the problem on to the new incumbent. There is evidence that he tried to do so; the appointments with the residents' committee which were broken stemmed the flow of information for several days. But the doctors' work stoppage bypassed this block by bringing the situation to the attention of the literate public in general, and of the director general of the ISSSTE in particular, through the press.

Mexico does have a press, however underdeveloped it may seem by comparison with that of more industrialized countries such as France, Italy, and Great Britain. And this press is not under iron governmental control, that is, the government is sometimes unable to furnish directives as to what should or should not be published. Especially in the initial stages of conflict situations, this relative absence of control allows the press to act as virtually the only source of cues to the real situation.

Group Groping

AMMRI representatives who tried to contact government officials to learn what action had been taken on the five-point petition were told that the matter was under study and that nothing could be done until the study was completed. During this period, a number of holdover officials from the previous administration tried to obtain recognition as mediators between the government and the physicians. Best-known of such attempts was the one by Dr. Ignacio Chávez, rector of the Universidad Nacional Autónoma de México. Dr. Chávez, an internationally recognized cardiologist, invited a number of physicians to his home for an initial meeting; only one of those invited was in direct contact with the residents' and interns' groups. The others were older men whose careers and incomes were not affected by the conditions prevailing for the younger men.

Another offer of mediation was advanced by a young

lawyer, brother of one of the residents at IMSS Hospital Ginecobstétrico No. 3. This man appeared at a meeting of residents and interns alleging that he had had an intimate off-the-record chat with President Díaz Ordaz. The latter had assured him that if the strike movement were disbanded he would "see to it" that the demands in the petition were met "insofar as that was possible." [16] Some physicians regarded this offer with heightened mistrust because the IMSS doctors were remaining aloof from the conflict.

For reasons made clear in another chapter of this study, the professional staffs in the social security hospitals enjoyed better pay and better working conditions than those employed by other government health services. It was generally recognized that, compared with others, they had little cause for discontent. Arguments that they should join the strike were advanced chiefly on the grounds that they should give moral support to their less fortunate colleagues. The response to these appeals was discouraging; most of the IMSS doctors continued to work during all phases of the conflict.

The AMMRI rejected the above offers of mediation and many similar ones, holding that its own representatives were capable of dealing directly with the government officials to settle the conflict. In refusing to use the offices of mediators, the physicians made a significant departure from Mexican custom. In the past, similar situations were often attended by the frenzied comings and goings of swarms of go-betweens of varying degrees of real and fancied access to receptors of information in the government. Whatever the intentions of these go-betweens, their activity in such situations had softened the sharp outline of conflict and blurred the edges between the goals sought and the concessions granted. Public intransigence had thus been mitigated by private uncertainty as to the exact areas of agreement and disagreement.

The physicians' rejection of mediation clarified the picture and polarized the conflict. For many residents and interns this meant the difficult and possibly dangerous necessity of choosing sides.

Meanwhile, a loose grouping had begun to take shape among doctors who, although they had not been involved in the *aguinaldo* controversy, sympathized with the residents and interns. Many of these sympathizers were tenured staff members of government hospitals; a number of them had solidly-established reputations in their own specialties.

This group first met at the General Hospital of the Secretaría de Salubridad in Mexico City. It started as a movement to support AMMRI but rapidly became a movement aimed at airing the problems of physicians working for all branches of government health services. From the beginning, the members showed a tendency to advocate more moderate types of action than the members of the AMMRI, while at the same time insisting that the scope of negotiations be broadened.[17]

On 18 January 1965, a new association was formally organized, with the name of Alianza de Médicos Mexicanos (Alliance of Mexican Physicians). The Alianza membership included members of the already existing AMMRI, as well as doctors from the wider interest grouping mentioned above. AMMRI continued to exist and function separately but also had a voice in the formulation of Alianza policies.

The manifesto of the new organization reviewed the history of the doctors' troubles and pointed out that

> large sums have been invested by the Government and decentralized institutions to provide health services for the people; however, [this money] has been assigned almost

completely for construction of buildings and purchase of equipment and instruments, leaving the pay and fringe benefits of the medical personnel practically frozen. In spite of this, the work of the doctors has been efficient and inspired by the spirit of cooperation characteristic of our class. . . .

The present crisis developed more than twenty years ago when new techniques of diagnosis and treatment . . . made it necessary for doctors [to be affiliated with] hospitals having modern equipment. The increasing industrialization of the country gave rise to a demand by the workers for medical care, and the Social Security Institute was created to satisfy this demand. Later, to provide the same care for civil service workers, the Institute of Insurance and Social Services of the Civil Service Workers was organized.

The result has been that, in the long run, these institutions have almost completely deprived doctors of private patients, who would have provided additional income to supplement the inadequate salaries paid by the aforesaid institutions. Doctors are now practically obliged to work as employees of government agencies or decentralized bureaus. . . .

The adverse consequences for medical care consist of the bureaucratization of medical services; the demand for a greater quantity of service of ever-decreasing quality . . . the dehumanization of both the doctor and the patient and . . . the deprivation of the right of the patient to choose his own doctor.

The doctors are hired under disadvantageous conditions, at low salaries, exhausting work schedules and even in many cases without the protection which is required by our labor and social security laws. . . . In parallel fashion, the forty percent of [the nation's] physicians who are not on the government payroll are increasingly faced with unemployment. . . .

As a result of the lack of incentives the medical profession is threatened with decline; young people prefer other, better remunerated careers. . . .

We have grouped together . . . to seek the improvement of the social and economic position of the medical class of the country. . . .[18]

A temporary council of governors was elected for ninety days to direct the activities of the new Alianza and to prepare for the election of permanent officers. This board was composed of twelve members from the General Hospital, eight members from AMMRI, five members from the Gea González Hospital and Hospital Infantil, and ten members from hospitals located outside the Federal District. It was argued that this composition assured adequate representation of the two emerging attitudes toward medico-social problems: the activist views of AMMRI and the moderate views of other doctors.[19] What developed in fact was a conflict of views about both ends and means which made competing demands for loyalty and vitiated the organization's negotiating strength.

During the first weeks of the existence of this new organization, one of the principal topics of discussion at meetings was centered on a search for a truly democratic procedure. Members expressed concern that the organization would be taken over by doctors hoping to ingratiate themselves with government authorities by steering the activities of the Alianza into futile and meaningless gestures ending in complete capitulation. This kind of manipulator, known as a *gobiernista,* is a familiar figure in conflict situations in Mexico. To alleviate such fears, and to forestall the emergence of a *caudillo*—a Latin-American strong man—it was decided that there would be no permanent presiding officer. Much valuable time and energy were wasted in elaborate rituals aimed at demonstrating a lack of dictatorial tendencies which deprived the group of any possibility of effective leadership.

The rhetoric employed at this time showed striking similarity to the arguments advanced only a few years later by the advocates of participatory democracy in some of the loosely knit New Left groups in the United States, but the justification for such a stand was somewhat different in the

Mexican case. Rejection of formal organization by the American New Left was explained, in part, by insistence that the whole superstructure of liberal-democratic rules and procedures is rigged to assist the Establishment in maintaining its control. One of the most widely quoted expressions of this viewpoint states that "a comfortable, smooth, reasonable democratic unfreedom prevails in advanced industrial civilization. . . ." [20] That a number of Mexican intellectuals were familiar with Marcuse's argument can be concluded from the fact that he was a guest lecturer at the Universidad Nacional Autónoma de México shortly after the doctors' strikes.

Although some of the advocates of participatory democracy in the doctors' movement might answer the description of intellectuals (and by Latin-American standards, *all* physicians are considered intellectuals), few of them were lecture goers. Their reasons for opposing the election of officers were based on the belief that the "unfreedom" which they saw in their political system was neither comfortable and smooth nor based on democratic procedures. Elected officials, rather than appearing as dupes manipulated by the Establishment, seemed to be offering themselves for office solely to acquire a share of the Establishment's power. The suspicion toward such individuals by the doctors surpassed that of Sorel toward the *blanquistes* in France.

When a comfortable, smooth democracy is the accepted norm, the emergence of leaderless unstructured groups can be a profoundly disturbing, even revolutionary manifestation of the essence of guerrilla warfare. Under the circumstances, opposition movements enjoy almost as much anonymity and mobility as troops which employ the hit-and-run tactics of jungle fighting. Attempts to infiltrate such nonorganizations are largely nullified by the ephemeral nature of rapidly shifting coalitions. Predictions of intended actions are reduced to anxious guesswork by frequent last-minute changes in choices of targets. To function at all, a democratic system depends, as Truman in one context and Dahrendorf in another have observed, on a gentlemanly agreement by both sides to "fight fair," to telegraph their punches, or to announce their battle plans and to carry them through on schedule.

If it is true, as many Mexicans believe, that the government itself is an assiduous practitioner of guerrilla warfare against emergent opposition groups, then much of the psychological advantage of adopting the same methods might disappear for the opposition. In such an eventuality, insistence on leaderless action might result, at best, in loss of effectiveness and, at worst, in manipulation of the group by packing of the assemblies with adherents of an invisible but nevertheless powerful elite. Such were the risks courted by the doctors' movement early in 1965.

The modus operandi of the new organization was roughly as follows. The governing council was empowered only to propose actions. These proposals were then to be carried by council members to meetings of their respective organizations, whose members were to decide each issue by majority vote. A decision to call a new strike, however, could be adopted only by a majority of duly elected delegates from all sectors, assembled in plenary session.[21]

In spite of this cumbersome procedure, two decisions were made at the meeting of 18 January. The first authorized the Alianza to pool the mass resignations of doctors if the five-point petition of AMMRI was not dealt with to the satisfaction of the members. The second decision allowed the council of governors to request an interview with

President Díaz Ordaz to impress on him the breadth and depth of the nation's medico-social problems.

The first of these two measures was a belated attempt to confer an aura of solidarity on the wave of sit-down strikes which had begun on 13 January in a number of the government hospitals under the auspices of AMMRI. As of that date, the mass firing order of 27 November 1964, had not been rescinded, but was being selectively enforced against some residents and interns, while others had been allowed to resume work. Both categories showed a united front by refusing to work (except for manning emergency services) and remaining in their dormitories on hospital grounds in defiance of orders to vacate the premises.

Summit Meeting

On 20 January the temporary governing council of the newly organized Alianza implemented the second decision of 18 January by obtaining an interview with President Díaz Ordaz. The atmosphere was very different from the hurried extemporaneous meeting of 9 December. The group which was admitted to the chief executive's inner office on this occasion was composed partly of AMMRI men, but these were balanced by the addition of older doctors of established reputations from the Alianza group whose presence had the double effect of contributing experience and lending dignity and weight to the physicians' demands.

According to informants who were present, an almost unbelievable atmosphere of cordiality and permissiveness prevailed. Those who had had previous experience in interviews with former presidents were amazed at the lack of insistence on protocol and security measures. The president met with the doctors in complete privacy; no aides, advisers, secretaries, or secret service men were admitted. A guard was stationed outside the door and was summoned from time to time by President Díaz Ordaz to bring him documents needed to clarify points in the discussion. One doctor even took notes of the conversation; he was not told that this was usually strictly forbidden.[22]

The meeting lasted two hours, during which the president reiterated several times that he was talking off the record. Physicians at this conference who had also participated in the 9 December encounter were impressed by the rapidity with which Díaz Ordaz had mastered the intricacies of the medico-social problem. At the first meeting, only nine days after taking office, he had seemed ignorant of the prevailing hospital conditions, as indicated by his tendency to confuse the terms referring to various categories of medical workers. His brusqueness and irritability at that time were attributed partly to a feeling of insecurity and ignorance. On the second occasion, however, he spoke easily and expertly.

But there were no immediate concessions to the doctors. The president emphasized two points, the first being that he needed more time to study the economic demands put forward by the strikers. Although he did not doubt the justice of their request for pay raises, it was impossible in so short a time to examine the budget with a view to finding money for such raises. While this search for funds was being carried out, he insisted that the doctors call off their strike. The government, he said, could not afford to let it appear that it had been forced to make economic concessions, as this might trigger a wave of other strikes which would place an intolerable burden on the country's economy. Drawing an allegorical picture, he pointed out that if someone were to shove a gun into his stomach and demand his money, he would reply, "Please put the gun down so that I can see how much money I have in my pocket." [23]

The day following this interview, a plenary session of the Alianza met to hear the report from the council of governors and to decide what action to take. The meeting took place in the auditorium of the Social Security's National Medical Center, an impressive group of strikingly modern buildings which is often the seat of international scientific meetings. The main floor of the auditorium was occupied by delegates from the constituent sections of the Alianza, including AMMRI, and the balcony was filled with AMMRI sympathizers, medical students, and *pasantes.*

Almost at once, two opposing positions became manifest. The AMMRI doctors wanted to continue the strike, on the grounds that the president had promised nothing and that none of their demands had been met. The Alianza doctors argued that the president should be given a chance to prove his good faith.

The atmosphere was tumultuous; AMMRI-sponsored motions from the floor were supported by loud cheering from the balcony, while arguments against these motions were drowned out by booing. Dr. Mario Salazar Mallén, chairman pro tem, tried to keep the meeting in order but finally declared it adjourned without any decisions having been adopted.

The meeting resumed the following day, in an atmosphere of heightened tension. Chairman for the day was Dr. Ismael Cosío Villegas, director of the Huipulco tuberculosis hospital. Alleging that they had been threatened with physical violence if they opposed the AMMRI position, eighteen delegates handed in their resignations.[24] They were replaced by physicians of known AMMRI sympathies, after which a vote to continue the strike passed by a slight majority.[25]

On 29 January the situation with regard to the AMMRI

petition remained unchanged; none of the demands had been granted. Although the doctors were reluctant to admit it, the government had broken off communications with them at all levels, both formal and informal. Attempts to contact officials to determine what progress had been made were sidestepped with the excuse that the matter was under study and that until all the facts were gathered further discussion would be useless. Offers of mediation, so abundant only two weeks before, stopped almost completely. A disquieting silence settled over the strike scene. Baffled and uneasy, the doctors met again and voted to end the strike. They reported for duty on 30 January; the majority were admitted to the hospitals without opposition from governmental authorities.

Two weeks later the situation was the same, except that the doctors' nerves were more frayed. The AMMRI met again on 15 February and decided to try to force the government's hand by calling for a full-scale nationwide walkout to begin on 20 February. On 18 February, with no advance notice to the physicians, President Díaz Ordaz released to the press a copy of a decree which he had directed as of that date to the secretariat of health and assistance. He ordered an increase in the amount paid as scholarships to pregraduate *pasantes* and established certain fringe benefits for these student-workers. On 20 February, a supplementary decree was announced, making the provisions of 18 February retroactive to 1 February. It specified the wage scale which was to apply to other categories of doctors employed in federal dependencies, the ISSSTE, and the Mexican National Railroads. As to the Institute of Social Security, it was simply indicated that any action taken should conform to the measures outlined in the decree.[26]

The new scale of compensation was to be as follows:

Category	Monthly payment
Pregraduate *pasantes* (scholarships)	700 pesos (56 dollars)
Interns	1,500 pesos (120 dollars)
Subresidents (1st year)	1,750 pesos (140 dollars)
Subresidents (2nd year)	2,000 pesos (160 dollars)
Residents (1st year)	2,500 pesos (200 dollars)
Residents (2nd year)	3,000 pesos (240 dollars)
Residents (3rd year)	3,200 pesos (256 dollars)

In addition to the revised wage scale, the decree ordered the following measures:

1. Provision of proper working clothes and adequate diet for medical personnel;
2. Construction of new lodging facilities where necessary and renovation of existing facilities where feasible for medical personnel;
3. Revision of the teaching programs in all government hospitals to provide adequate continuing medical education;
4. Extension of all existing and new benefits to the medical personnel of ISSSTE not previously covered; and
5. Authorization for the ministries of health and welfare and finance and public credit to transfer funds in the authorized budget of the first-mentioned ministry to cover the expenditures required by these measures.[27]

Under date of 22 February, the Technical Council of IMSS approved a document which provided for exactly the same salary scale as the president's 20th February decree, except that no provision was made for *pasantes*, as this category did not exist in the IMSS organization.

These decrees were unilateral attempts to solve what the

government had now begun to call "the matter of the doctors." [28] The president had heard the doctors' petition, and this was his answer. But, untypically, the doctors refused to accept the decrees. Through the Alianza, the AMMRI made it known on 19 February that its members did not consider the new wage scale satisfactory, and advanced a counterproposition.[29] What they asked, for the purpose of standardizing nomenclature, was that the two categories of first- and second-year subresident, assigned wages of 1,750 and 2,000 pesos, respectively, be stricken from the schedule, and that these categories be subsumed under the titles of first- and second-year resident, with the pay scale corresponding to those ranks. This counterproposition was intended to obtain equal pay for equal work. It was alleged that for several years classifications and job descriptions for medical personnel were anarchic, resulting in obvious inequalities in pay and working conditions.[30]

On 25 February, Rómulo Sánchez Mireles, director of the ISSSTE, indicated that he had no objection to the proposed change. It was decided that, in deference to the supposed infallibility of the president, the change would be called an "interpretation" of the presidential decree, rather than a "counterproposition." [31] On 26 February, Dr. Rafael Moreno Valle, the secretary of health and welfare, informed a mixed committee of AMMRI and Alianza members that the president was willing to allow this interpretation to be made.

In view of this apparent victory, a plenary session of doctors' delegates met on 27 February and voted not only to call off the impending strike but also to send a delegation to the president to express their gratitude for his intervention. For the moment, they ignored the fact that this was only a partial solution to point 2 of their original five-point petition (the clause concerning individual work contracts was not mentioned in the decree) and that no action had been taken on points 3, 4, and 5.[32] A group of thirty-seven doctors visited President Díaz Ordaz in his official residence at Los Piños on the night of 17 March. Their spokesman, Dr. Norberto Treviño Zapata, summed up their satisfaction in these words: "Mr. President, you have carried out a real work of social justice and you can count on the enthusiasm, support, and friendship of Mexican doctors." [33]

Almost unnoticed in the general euphoria was a press conference held on 9 March by Sealtiel Alatriste, director of the IMSS. He revealed that the Institute was involved in considerable financial difficulties due to the fact that during the preceding administration, the Institute's building program had exhausted its capital and had made inroads on the operating reserves. This practice, he pointed out, would now make it necessary for the Institute to obtain long-term loans in order to cover its short-term obligations. In addition, there were twenty-eight uncompleted construction projects which had been halted; of these, priority would be given to the most needed projects as soon as funds became available.[34]

It is indicative of Mexican journalism that not one newspaper reporter at this press conference asked Alatriste *exactly* how much in debt the Institute was. To answer this unspoken question, he indicated that the figures would be released when the president authorized them. To the author's knowledge, they were not published during the next eleven months. No list of the suspended construction projects was requested and none was offered to the press, but during 1965 Mexicans returning to the capital from trips to the provinces contributed a number of stories about half-finished social security buildings being overrun by jungle growth, like the ancient Mayan temple cities.

The temporary financial difficulties of the IMSS may have been at the root of what the AMMRI representatives regarded as obstructive tactics, with regard to job security in the form of work contracts for medical personnel. To freeze the number of such workers at that time might deprive the Institute of much-needed flexibility in manipulating its resources. In the following months, no matter what the posture of other health agencies, social security officials adamantly refused to discuss contracts with the AMMRI, and very few of the IMSS doctors openly supported the AMMRI's demands, probably because they were unwilling to risk their favored financial position by seeking job tenure security.

Enter: The Unions

On the same day (17 March) that the president received the delegation of grateful doctors, physicians attached to the ISSSTE took steps to defend themselves from what they considered a new threat. For the first time in their attempts to secure interviews with ISSSTE officials, they were told that they were not the legitimate representatives of the doctors. Instead, they were informed, there existed a union local of the Federación de Sindicatos de Trabajadores al Servico del Estado (FSTSE) composed of professionals who were the only legitimately recognized bargaining agents.[35]

After hurried consultations, the ISSSTE group of AMMRI and Alianza members concluded that the heretofore unheard-of local was a hastily organized "company union" (known as a *sindicato blanco*), set up to bypass their attempts to negotiate. They voted to repudiate the local, to reject membership in it, and to continue to insist on their right to negotiate with the authorities on behalf of the physicians.[36]

Since the beginning of the conflict, AMMRI, and later the

Alianza, had made demands which concerned matters ordinarily subject to labor-management negotiations. In effect, they were claiming that physicians had the same rights to have a voice in regulating their working conditions as other sectors of the labor force. But neither AMMRI nor the Alianza was a labor union. AMMRI was in fact AMMRIAC, the two final letters of the acronym standing for Asociación Civil, nonprofit civic association. The Alianza was an even looser grouping, with less legal affinity to union status.

Strictly speaking, it was not necessary for the physicians to be grouped into a union in order to negotiate. Article 123 of the Mexican constitution, and the Federal Labor Law, which codifies the conduct of labor-management relations throughout the republic, recognize the right of any group of workers to present demands to their employers. This means that AMMRI or the Alianza could have legally engaged in bargaining on behalf of their members.

In practice, it is usually more convenient to organize a labor union to engage in collective bargaining. Syndicalism is a hallowed principle of the Mexican Revolution, almost automatically conferring legitimacy on any group which exhibits the appropriate stigmata of charter, membership, dues, and antimanagement rhetoric. Failure to organize as a union leaves a group vulnerable to preemption of collective bargaining activities by a rival group which, although organized later, has taken the precaution of calling itself a union. Nonunion groups experience great difficulty in trying to make use of the government's arbitration machinery.

In the past, physicians had shown a reluctance to consider themselves part of the working class.[37] In spite of this, some efforts had been made in the 1930s to found a union; in 1932 the Sindicato de Médicos del Distrito Federal was constituted, and similar groups sprang up in some of the states. Finally, in 1942, a Confederación de Sindicatos de Médicos grouped these unions together for more effective action. This confederation included only a very small proportion of the nation's physicians and never attained any importance. Its eventual disappearance has been directly attributed to two factors. The first of these was the enactment, in 1945, of a law "regulating the exercise of the professions" which authorized the creation of five medical guilds rather than a single authoritative body.[38] The second factor was the organization of a government-sponsored union called the Bloque Revolucionario de Médicos. Torn by rival claims on their loyalties, most physicians refused to commit themselves to either organization.

At that time, many doctors whose ideological orientations ranged from socialist on toward the left were ambivalent regarding the advantages and disadvantages of professional organizations. Several were familiar with the more publicized aspects of the American Medical Association and were unanimous in wanting to avoid the kind of pressure tactics which they believed were used by the United States organization. They saw this behavior as antipatriotic or against the public interest. On the other hand, they were aware of their weakness and helplessness without a solidly based association. Hastily organized groups like AMMRI and Alianza lacked precisely the "adaptability, complexity, autonomy, and coherence" which Samuel Huntington has seen as necessary for institutional strength.[39]

Less directly, but possibly more importantly, three obstacles had prevented the organization of doctors into a powerful labor group: (1) general fear of opposition by the government; (2) apathy of the physicians (unwillingness to attend meetings, serve on committees, pay dues); and (3) opposition by pharmaceutical companies.[40]

In 1965, the physicians had substantial reasons for mistrusting labor unions in general and the FSTSE in particular. The general justification for their attitude lay in the fact that Mexican labor leaders are a notoriously venal lot, "more interested in seeking union peace to assure themselves public office than in representing their followers." [41] In particular, the FSTSE, with a membership of over 300,000, is unequivocally branded a company union, "solidly committed to membership in the official party [PRI] . . . the pillar of the party's 'popular sector,' " [42] and therefore hardly neutral in any confrontation between the government and a group of aggrieved workers.

On the other hand, there was a powerful attraction in the notion of allowing an FSTSE local, however hastily organized for whatever ulterior motives, to negotiate for the physicians. It has been observed that "since possessing their own autonomous union [the FSTSE], the civil servants have unquestionably prospered more than any other single 'labor' union in Mexico. . . ." [43]

Shaken by these polarizing attractions, the governing council of the Alianza issued a no policy statement which read, in part:

> The *Alianza de Médicos Mexicanos,* in this particular matter, has decided not to act and even less to participate in such a challenge, considering that the medical organizations which make up the *Alianza,* according to the by-laws, have complete autonomy and sovereignty, to decide what is best for them in this matter, declaring also that it recognizes the organization of labor as an institution for the struggle and defense of workers, protected by the Constitution and labor laws of the Mexican Revolution.[44]

In the IMSS, the problem of company union manifested the same basic pattern but with certain variations of detail. There, the majority of physicians had refused to endanger their advantageous situation by espousing the AMMRI cause. The AMMRI responded by increasing its recruitment campaign, which bore fruit finally in small nuclei of sympathetic doctors in nineteen clinics and seven hospitals in the Federal District, as well as seven institutions in the provinces. These nuclei adopted the title of Asociación Nacional de Médicos del IMSS. Its organizers claimed that within a short time after its founding the meetings were infiltrated by hostile elements who gained control and undertook activities aimed at undermining the AMMRI purposes. Some of the frustrated original organizers claimed to discern discriminatory practices in the granting of time off to attend meetings of the new organization; individuals known to be active in the strikers' cause were denied permission to leave their posts, while progovernment doctors were given leave. The original organizers, seeing themselves outnumbered, withdrew into a rump congress, elected a temporary set of officers, and adopted a new name: Federación de Asociaciónes Médicas de las Clínicas y Hospitales del Seguro Social.

While the AMMRI members were thus regrouping to defeat this latest threat to their unity, the IMSS administration hastened to recognize the Asociación Nacional de Médicos del IMSS as the legitimate bargaining agent for the physicians, and proceeded to conclude a collective bargaining agreement with its representatives. The doctors were in a quandary: did these latest moves constitute legal justification for ISSSTE and IMSS to refuse to deal with their representatives? To reassure themselves on this point, they requested legal advice from attorney Mario de la Cueva, former rector of the National Autonomous University of Mexico, who concluded that

(1) The objectives of the *Alianza de Médicos Mexicanos* are

aimed at maintaining the dignity of man and work and at the achieving of fair working conditions;
(2) Joining a union is a right, not a duty;
(3) The standard contained in Article 69 of the Federal Law of Civil Service Workers is in conflict with the letter and the spirit of Article 123 of the Constitution in its clauses "A" and "B";
(4) Civil service workers have the right to detach themselves at any time from the union to which they belong;
(5) The "single union" principle is also in conflict with the letter and spirit of Article 123 of the Constitution;
(6) Mexican doctors may structure their organization in union form and request its recognition by the authorities.[45]

In spite of this reassurance, AMMRI-Alianza doctors in both ISSSTE and IMSS proceeded with badly undermined confidence to insist that they were the legitimate representatives of the physicians, but their tactics varied. The ISSSTE group accepted being party to a collective bargaining agreement; their only objection was to the encroachment of the company union on what they considered their right to negotiate from the labor side of the bargaining table. The IMSS men, on the other hand, feared that company unions were too entrenched to be dislodged; therefore, they insisted that each physician be allowed to enter into an individual work contract, renewable or revocable every year.

Confusion Compounded

This ambivalence damaged the doctors' cause. From December until the middle of March, the issues had appeared fairly simple: the physicians had presented a list of five demands and when the demands were not granted, they insisted on their right to strike. The simplicity was deceptive, however; the language of the demands provided no standards by which improvement in housing, diet, and continued medical education could be measured. Were the president's decrees of 18 and 20 February real concessions? How much time could be considered normal for their implementation? Were the seemingly endless meetings of advisory committees accomplishing anything toward satisfying the demands or were they simply delaying tactics? At this time, the problem for the decision makers in the doctors' movement was not one of lack of information; rather, it concerned the lack of a single authoritative yardstick by which that information could be evaluated. It was not strange that at least two different interpretations were made of events: the AMMRI leaders saw the actions of the government as clear evidence of intent to deny their demands, while the Alianza leaders believed that those actions indicated an effort to initiate the reforms demanded. From that time forward, although the Alianza continued publicly to support AMMRI actions, many of its leaders had private misgivings. "We began to suspect," stated one informant, "that AMMRI was using us for its own ends." [46]

In spite of those misgivings, the Alianza members voted to support the AMMRI doctors when the latter decided to call another strike beginning on 20 April. AMMRI spokesmen estimated that 4,500 interns and residents in eighty-five hospitals of the Federal District and the rest of the country obeyed the call to strike.[47]

With its leadership deeply divided on the interpretation of events, the doctors' movement had been suddenly flooded by new waves of information concerning company unions not directly connected with the original issues. Was this a kind of noise in the communications system? If so, could it drown out the signals they needed to hear in order to decide what to do next?

An example drawn from the daily press of that period is a half-page advertisement placed by the Federación de

Sindicatos de los Trabajadores al Servicio del Estado (FSTSE), addressed ostensibly "to civil service workers: to professional medical workers," which stated in part:

> Because a very important sector of professional medical workers are members of our unions, the National Executive Committee of the FSTSE considers it pertinent to express its viewpoint respecting the problems which they are now facing, and grasping their justified aspirations for collective improvement, it has formulated a program of action aimed at gratifying [these aspirations] without for a moment losing sight of the budgetary limitations of the Nation, the requirements of other professional, administrative, and manual workers, nor, least of all, the best interests of Mexico. . . .
>
> . . . it is proposed to put into effect the program presented by the Committee for the Organization of the Medical Branch, pressing for the inclusion of the proposals formulated in the Regulations of Working Conditions in the respective units. . . .
>
> It is convenient to apply measures tending to organize the Medical Branch within the union framework. . . .
>
> The FSTSE has recognized as worthwhile the interest of the doctors in organizing Alliances, Societies, *Colegios*, etc. as vehicles for the study of their technical and social problems within legal channels compatible with their participation in the organized syndicalism of Mexico, as our Federation maintains a permanent interest in the improvement of their living conditions. . . .[48]

In this disarming fashion, the National Executive Committee of the FSTSE made it clear that, while it did not object to the "technical and social" activities of the AMMRI and the Alianza, it reserved the right to represent the doctors in labor negotiations. About one-third of the remaining text of this advertisement outlined the benefits which the FSTSE claimed it would seek on behalf of the membership of its medical branches—branches which as of that date existed only on paper. These benefits were grouped into three classes: wages, economic fringe benefits, and cultural benefits (that is, scholarships, refresher courses, and so on). However, close examination of the advertisement reveals two important deficiencies: the description of the benefits is so vague as to be meaningless, and there is no date set for the accomplishment of any of the goals. To a hurried reader, these deficiencies would probably not become apparent; the impression given by the large type of the heading and signatories, as well as the boldfaced subtitles, is that of a long-established union's announcement of negotiations in progress on behalf of its members.

A similar approach was employed by Sealtiel Alatriste in a press release which stated that

> the relations between the Mexican Institute of Social Security and its workers are covered by a collective bargaining agreement which has just been revised to the satisfaction of both parties, a revision in which important benefits were granted to more than fifty thousand workers of the Institute, among whom are more than seven thousand doctors.[49]

These allegations were flatly denied by the AMMRI in a large display advertisement. In particular, with reference to work contracts, the AMMRI had this to say:

> The individual work contract has only been granted to the residents of the Medical Services of the Federal District and the English Hospital [American British Cowdray Hospital, a privately supported institution].
>
> Conversations are being held with the authorities of the SSA, ISSSTE, [and] decentralized and private [institutions]. In the IMSS there is a flat refusal to accept contracts because, in spite of the fact that our legal advisers have demonstrated that there are legal bases for not belonging to the Union, without [by this refusal] violating the juridical statute which covers that Institution, the union leaders refuse to recognize this.[50]

AMMRI and the Alianza made strenuous efforts to inform

their members that the FSTSE and IMSS claims were false, but only those doctors who took the time to attend frequent meetings were able to keep abreast of events. Many others—the majority, in fact—became increasingly confused by the rumors they heard and the information they saw in the newspapers.

The two items excerpted above mark an important change in the kind of information published about the doctors' movement. Toward the end of April, the daily newspapers began to be flooded with full- and half-page advertisements sponsored by previously unknown groups such as the Comité Pro Defensa de la Dignificación de la Clase Médica (Committee for the Defense of the Dignification of the Medical Class) and Asociación Nacional de Profesionistas e Intelectuales, A.C. (National Association of Professionals and Intellectuals, Civic Association). These advertisements uniformly condemned the activities of the strikers who, the apocryphal signatories alleged, were a troublesome minority in the ranks of the largely contented professionals. One such half-page advertisement was headed by the question, "Scholarship holders, Interns, and Residents: What are you after?" It went on to state that the first strike had presented justifiable demands, all of which had been granted, but that the present strike was capricious and malicious, and ended by stating, "Your attitude is undignified, unworthy and immoral, and the disrepute which you have brought [upon the medical profession] affects us as well as you. . . . You may return to your posts or not, as you choose . . . we can get along without you." [51]

Another full-page advertisement used the guilt by association approach; why, it asked, were certain "key" members (three names were mentioned) known communist sympathizers, and why were the most favorable accounts of the strikers' activities published by the writers and journals known to be "rabidly communist?" [52]

Consistency, however, did not characterize the advertisements sponsored by the above group. A week later another half-page display accused the AMMRI of perpetrating "a fascistoid attack which hides obscure political motives," and further declared that "the fascistoid attitude of the members of the *Asociación Mexicana de Médicos Residentes e Internos* is also revealed by the fact that they are trying to form a privileged caste outside of and above the common people." [53]

Although the financial supporters of these advertisements advised "the young doctors" not to worry, that "in due time you will learn our names and where we work," [54] this promise was never kept. Instead, other individuals and groups joined the paid condemnations. ABC, for example, accused the strikers of stabbing the nation in the back.[55]

In the midst of this crescendo of condemnation, the heads of the government departments, agencies, and bureaus which provided the bulk of health services made a joint public statement which contained an ultimatum for the striking doctors. After reviewing the official version of events leading up to the prevailing situation, and stating that "the relief of pain, the care and safeguarding of the health and lives of our fellow humans is above the small differences which might prevent the reaching of an agreement," the advertisement announced that the following steps would be taken:

1. The strikers must return to work on Monday, 17 May, at the latest;
2. A job registry would be opened to offer to all qualified applicants any positions left vacant by doctors who failed to return to duty under the deadline;

3. The strikers would forfeit all pay from 17 May forward;
4. No more conciliatory meetings would be held between health officials and doctors until work was resumed in all hospitals;
5. After resumption of a normal work schedule, conciliation meetings might be renewed on the initiative of either side;
6. The legal points on which there was disagreement between medical workers and government authorities [that is, jurisdiction of government-sponsored unions and the new doctors' groups] would be submitted to the constitutionally authorized courts for decisions;
7. Steps would be taken to gradually restore the normal operation of health services and academic, scientific, and administrative discipline in all institutions.

This full-page advertisement carried as sponsors the names of Rafael Moreno Valle, secretary of health and welfare; José Antonio Padilla Segura, secretary of communications and transport; Ernesto P. Uruchurtu, head of the city government of the Federal District; Rómulo Sánchez Mireles, director of the ISSSTE; Sealtiel Alatriste, director of the IMSS, and Eufrasio Sandoval, manager of the National Railways of Mexico.[56]

In the light of this governmental decision to stop temporizing with the strikers, the fast-multiplying number of advertisements condemning the doctors could be seen as public protestations of loyalty to the government. In the days that followed, the rush to climb on the bandwagon—or perhaps to clamber down from the tumbrils—accelerated.

The heights of rhetoric were scaled by one advertiser signing himself "Luis del Toro," who began his full-page diatribe with this paragraph:

With resplendent aureole of fierce disrepute, the illegal strike of doctors (!) residents and interns has reached a scant month of existence. Nevertheless, in that lapse, it has accomplished a formidable task. An apotheotic task, [sic] majestically directed against society but, in a very particular way, against the poorest classes of the nation.

In another outbreak of verbal fireworks, the author of this advertisement exclaimed, "The culture of the university [is] on its knees before the savage Moloch of the flaming belly, to sacrifice children to him in the same way as did thousands of years ago the monstrous fanaticism of Carthage and Phoenicia!" [57]

This was an obvious reference to an accusation launched against the strikers to the effect that two children had died owing to lack of medical attention at one of the struck hospitals. Physicians questioned on this point vigorously denied the accusation, which was not supported by data specific enough to permit an independent investigation. At any rate, there is no evidence that emergency services were left unattended in any hospital during the strike. They were covered, by arrangement, with the full-time physicians and with volunteers from the IMSS hospitals. Both of these categories worked during some of their normal off-duty hours, and were paid double time for their services. Whether substantiated in fact or not, the accusation of contributing to the death of sick people through negligence hung in the air for some time and provided material for public attack.

The Comité Pro Defensa de la Dignificación de la Clase Médica published a half-page display advertisement urging the government to take energetic measures to protect "the thousands of patients who are suffering because of the egotistical and irresponsible attitude of the young doctors of the *Asociación Mexicana de Médicos Residentes e Internos*." The text stated:

Public opinion . . . contemplates with real alarm the conditions which prevail in the hospitals. There, the situation is becoming progressively worse, to the extreme that the most seriously ill of the patients are dying for lack of timely medical attention because, as it is easy to understand, the full-time doctors are insufficient to take care of all who need their attention, even though they are making prodigious efforts.[58]

A cartoon by "Ric y Rac" published under the caption "The Insane Strike" showed a mob of rabid young "men in white" railing at a larger than human-sized figure of Hippocrates, who is warding them off with outflung hand and quoting from the Hippocratic Oath, *"Primum non nocere,"* while an older doctor strives desperately to succor a dying woman.[59]

By the middle of May the prolonged absence from work of an undetermined but substantial number of residents and interns made it necessary to curtail some of the government's hospital services. Without these workers to perform the preliminary screening of patients, taking of medical histories, making physical examinations, and carrying out some of the laboratory tests, it was undoubtedly necessary to postpone all elective procedures in the affected hospitals and to provide service only for the most urgently needy cases. The Mexican government's chief claim to legitimacy rests on constantly presenting the image of a revolutionary socialistic state. One of the features most often cited to support this claim is the widespread system of health and welfare services, prolonged suspension of which might materially alter the image. Although the IMSS hospitals were hardly affected by the strike, a vastly greater proportion of the population depended on services provided by the hospitals staffed by the strikers. These doctors could not totally paralyze the nation's medical services, but they could—and did—make their absence painfully obvious in both the literal and figurative senses.

To restore normal health services, the government needed

the residents and interns. The AMMRI had shown that its members would not go back to work on the basis of promises alone, and the organization had refused to bargain or compromise on any of its five original demands. In addition, it had responded to attempts to outflank it (for example, the ISSSTE and IMSS union activities) by increased militance. Short of acceding to all the AMMRI demands which, as will be seen in another chapter, may not have been possible, the government would soon have to find a way to force the physicians to return to their duties. Indications of how this might be accomplished began to emerge.

One of the first hints appeared in a half-page advertisement published under the sponsorship of "Manuel M. Reynoso," which concluded by predicting:

> it should come as no surprise to the ungrateful, insatiable and traitorous physicians . . . that in the future they will receive harsher treatment . . . [t]hey will receive the just and severe punishment which they and those who manipulate them are bringing upon themselves.[60]

In the same vein, but in milder language, a later advertisement sponsored by "Dr. Miguel Necochea A." stated that

> the Government, in our opinion, has been fair, has taken pains, and has done everything possible to alleviate the physicians' economic situation. . . . Let us not push it to the brink of taking other measures, in spite of the fact that it would have the right to do so in defense of the public welfare. . . . We respectfully exhort the Government to take the measures which it believes necessary . . . to put an end to this chaotic situation, created and provoked by a group of physicians who, although fortunately their number is dwindling, are ill advised.[61]

On the day this advertisement was published, union leaders

of the FSTSE, Bloque Unido de Obreros (BUO), and Confederación de Trabajadores Mexicanos (CTM) called a joint meeting of their members which began at 11 A.M. Following established custom, those who attended were given leave with pay for the whole working day, and were provided with free transportation to and from the meeting place. In this fashion the government is able to mobilize an impressive show of support for its policies whenever such a manifestation is judged useful. Union leaders addressed the group, reported at a thousand persons, in speeches condemning the attitudes and actions of the physicians.[62]

Three days later another newspaper, ordinarily somewhat more critical of government actions than the largest metropolitan dailies, published an article in which the notion was advanced that the physicians' strike was a conspiracy to destroy the hospital services of the Social Security System.[63]

Another meeting of union members, consisting this time of an estimated 4,000 garbage collectors and street cleaners, was held on 17 May in the main square of the city, to hear union leaders condemn the strike. Gilberto Aceves Alcocer, secretary of the Sindicato Unico de Trabajadores del Gobierno del Distrito Federal, Rafael Argüelles, an official of the FSTSE, and Felix Cortés of the Sindicato Nacional de Trabajadores de la Industria Militar were the speakers.[64] The assembled workers were excused from listening to more speeches when a persistent drizzle forced the speakers to seek shelter.

The next public statement, reviving the accusation of manslaughter through negligence, stated:

> The Residents and Interns . . . have committed a crime against Society, and they also want to destroy laws, institutions and the rights of others. . . . Mr. Prosecuting

> Attorney for the Federal District and Territories; the time has come to act energetically; the health of the people must be protected . . . the authorities should know that human patience can endure no more. If they [the authorities] do not wish the people to take justice into their own hands, they must act energetically to suppress the strikers.[65]

Since the beginning of May, very little had appeared in the newspapers defending the physicians. The news and editorial columns carried only material supporting the government's position, echoed by advertising whose large bulk evidenced a heavy outlay of money.

On only three occasions was the silence broken by advertisements favoring the strikers. The first was a half-page display placed by the AMMRI which insisted that its original five-point petition had not been implemented, and challenged government spokesmen to a public debate.[66]

The Alianza de Médicos Mexicanos spoke up to express its concern against the "campaign of insults and calumnies against the physicians, creating . . . a climate of tension and veiled threats. . . ." [67] Finally, the Asociación Médica de la República Mexicana, a scholarly body of physicians, paid for space to "repudiate publications contrary to the movement for unification and socioeconomic improvement of Mexican physicians." [68] However, this last advertisement was worded in such a way that it could be interpreted either as defending the AMMRI and Alianza activities or supporting the IMSS and FSTSE unions. This kind of verbal fence-straddling is commonplace in Mexico; in this case it safeguarded the amicable relationships between the older physicians (the members of the Asociación Médica) and their younger colleagues (the AMMRI and Alianza members) and at the same time reassured government health officers of the Association's noncombatant status.

During the first weeks of May, much publicity had been

devoted to an event apparently unrelated to the physicians' strike. News stories and radio and television programs reported the imminent unification of the two major labor organizations in the nation: the BUO and the CNT (Central Nacional de Trabajadores). Each of these organizations grouped a number of unions under its aegis; BUO, for example, was made up of the CTM, FSTSE, STMMSRM (Sindicato de Trabajadores Mineros, Metalúrgicos y Similares de la República Mexicana), CGT (Confederación General de Trabajadores), CROM (Confederación Regional Obrera Mexicana), and several smaller unions; while the CNT covered SNTIMSS (Sindicato Nacional de Trabajadores del Instituto Mexicano del Seguro Social), STFRM (Sindicato de Trabajadores Ferrocarrileros de la República Mexicana), CROC (Confederación Revolucionaria de Obreros y Campesinos), and others.

The steps leading up to this "solemn pact of national unity of the labor movement" and the events of its subsequent existence are not of direct concern here. On 18 May, however, the pact was made the occasion of a celebration banquet in the Club Imperial, organized by the leaders of the component unions and attended by President Díaz Ordaz as guest of honor; senators and representatives of the national congress; Salamón González Blanco, the secretary of labor; and Carlos Madrazo, the chairman of the National Executive Committee of the PRI.[69] Of the three major speeches made on this occasion, two attacked the physicians' movement and affirmed union support for the government's actions in dealing with the strikers.

One of the speeches contained a new threat. Luis Gómez Zepeda, a PRI member of the national Senate, speaking as secretary general of the Sindicato de Trabajadores Ferrocarrileros de la República Mexicana, proposed that in retaliation for the curtailment of medical services, members of utility and public service unions should cut off the electricity, water, and telephone services of the strikers.[70]

On 18 May the government ultimatum was scheduled to go into effect. On 19 and 20 May, the leading newspapers carried front-page stories about the firing of the strikers and their replacement by applicants for the positions left vacant. The ISSSTE supplied the newspapers with a photograph of two lines of men, all with their backs turned to the camera, who were allegedly signing the register of applications for medical positions. The picture was so obviously spurious that the usually complaisant newspapers labeled it government propaganda and refrained from vouching for its authenticity.[71]

Whether or not replacements were available, an undetermined number of AMMRI and Alianza physicians received dismissal notices at this time. The Veinte de Noviembre Hospital, scene of the original *aguinaldo* controversy, was the hardest hit, with 203 firings. The main hospital of Ferrocarriles Nacionales in Mexico City, as well as its smaller counterparts in Monterrey, San Luis Potosí, and Chihuahua, accounted for an additional 49 displaced medical workers, and 33 interns lost their posts in the health department installations in Jalapa, in the state of Veracruz.[72]

These firings produced panic among AMMRI officers, who sent a committee to Dr. Norberto Treviño Zapata, the newly elected president of the Alianza de Médicos Mexicanos, to urge the Alianza to act as intermediary and try to obtain another interview with President Díaz Ordaz. What they wanted to tell the president was that, contrary to the stories published and broadcast in the mass media, they were not making new demands. They insisted that they were simply holding out until the president's decrees of 18 and 20 February were implemented in good faith.

The physicians must have known that the ultimatum of 14 May had the president's approval. In spite of this, Dr. Treviño Zapata contacted Joaquín Cisneros, the president's private secretary, and conveyed the AMMRI request to him. The reply was predictable: the president would have nothing to do with the physicians until after the strike.[73]

With Dr. Treviño Zapata as spokesman, the Mediation Committee made a total of four visits to Cisneros, ending on 25 May. At each encounter, he was courteous, but unyielding. They could not get past him to see the president, who, Cisneros reiterated, had nothing to say to them at that time. AMMRI leaders circulated a memorandum to its membership calling for a united front in the crisis, and then decided to call for a march of white-uniformed physicians and nurses, starting at the Monument to the Revolution and terminating in the main square in front of the presidential palace. Reluctantly, Alianza leadership was persuaded to lend its support to this effort; 26 May was the date set for the parade.

The March to the Zócalo

On that date an estimated five thousand doctors and nurses marched silently through the center of the city.[74] Organized groups of hecklers made halfhearted attempts to force the marchers to break ranks, but the number of these hecklers was relatively small and their lack of enthusiasm was evident. In Mexico, unions are sometimes called on to mobilize their members for demonstrations of this kind, to give an impression of public disapproval of the actions of dissenting groups. In the 26 May march, knowledgeable observers believed that Antonio Bernal, head of the FSTSE, was responsible for organizing the harassers, but he denied this.[75] To refute this protestation of innocence, the Alianza published nine photographs of hecklers along the line of march. Well-known union officials can be seen in three of the photographs.[76] One observer, a reporter for a large daily newspaper, interpreted the light turnout of hecklers as a repudiation by most union members of the government's treatment of the doctors.[77]

In spite of the physicians' show of strength, their leaders knew that they had no choice but to call off the strike. One of the AMMRI leaders, in summing up the reasons for ending the strike, felt that it had gone on so long that many doctors had exhausted their financial resources and were becoming desperate.[78]

On 29 May, AMMRI voted to return to work on 3 June. Late that night the Alianza seconded the decision.[79] Spokesmen for both organizations, searching for some positive result of the strike with which to console their members, hailed as a moral victory Cisneros's assurances that the president recognized their constitutional right not to join the company unions, and the president's promise that strikers who had been fired would be reinstated in their positions. The five demands contained in the original petition were as far as ever from being granted.

The inconclusiveness of the first and second strikes was followed by a reaction similar to that of the positive feedback mechanism in a control system. By 20 June, delegates to a national convention of the Alianza advocated a third strike, in view of the "frankly negative, intransigent, and even insolent attitude" assumed by officials of the health and welfare agencies.[80] While some Alianza delegates pointed out that a third strike was unlikely to succeed, AMMRI delegates insisted that such a strike would be a continuation of past efforts which, they contended, should not be given up until the original goals had been achieved. In support of this view, a militant member emphasized that since the end of the second strike,

> there has been *NO* progress on the pending points, and it really seems that only when the physicians are on strike are they listened to adequately. . . . The position of the residents and interns is quite simple: *AT NO TIME DO THEY PLAN TO DESIST FROM THEIR ORIGINAL PETITION* (*OF NOV., 1964*) . . . and if it is necessary again to have recourse to more active measures, they will not hesitate to do so.[81]

True to his promise of a meeting after the end of the strike, President Díaz Ordaz granted an interview to the Alianza governing council on 23 June in his official residence at Los Piños.[82] They described the widespread dissatisfaction among the doctors because of the failure of health and welfare officials to take any steps to implement his instructions. In reply, he merely asked them to be patient. The doctors emerged from the interview with the feeling that they and the president had been talking past each other.[83] This was the last time that they had any personal contact with Díaz Ordaz.

The initiative again clearly belonged to the government, a fact which the president did not ignore for long. On 9 July, with no advance notice to the Alianza, Díaz Ordaz made public a new decree, granting what appeared to be flat across-the-board increases to full-time physicians in the employ of the federal government (the department of health and welfare and the Coordinated Rural Medical Services). A codicil specified that the decentralized health services and federally subsidized organisms such as Petróleos

Mexicanos, ISSSTE, National Railroads of Mexico, and others, could adopt the new salary schedule if their governing boards voted to do so.[84]

In this decree was inserted a curiously worded paragraph which seemed to indicate that the president considered the interns' and residents' problems had already been satisfactorily dealt with. This passage read:

> This sector of the medical profession which also comprehends medical students and recently graduated doctors who expect to devote themselves to hospital work, as well as those who are known as scholarship holders, interns, and residents, has very special peculiarities. The first of these [categories] are in reality finishing their university studies, as many of their classes are held in the hospitals themselves; while the residents are practically taking postgraduate courses aimed at specialization, usually in surgery.[85]

This statement ignored the fact that it was these categories of doctors who continued to insist that their original five-point petition of November 1964 had not yet been satisfactorily dealt with. Those who worked in the health and welfare institutions and the hospitals of the Federal District were especially enraged by this bland dismissal of their plight. They insisted that the president's decree of 18 February granting them salary increases had done them no good.

The new decree, like the first one, overlooked the fact that in order for the physicians to benefit from salary increases, a thorough revision of health and welfare payroll practices would have to be instituted. In their interviews with the president, the AMMRI-Alianza representatives had repeatedly emphasized that large numbers of the department of health doctors (allegedly as high as 80 percent of the total employed) were listed on payrolls as orderlies, stretcher-bearers, ambulance drivers, and other nonprofessional categories.

A parallel practice, affecting an alleged 600 general practitioners employed part-time in outpatient clinics of the Federal District health services system, classified these full-fledged doctors as residents, thus making them eligible only for pay at that level, instead of placing them on a standard hourly fee basis. These were the doctors who dealt daily with long lines of people presenting the whole catalog of minor complaints, including headaches, colds, and gastrointestinal upsets, interspersed with occasional cases of more serious symptoms. It was the doctors' duty to dispense medicines to the patients with minor ills and to refer the more seriously ill to specialists in the Federal District hospitals. On their diligence depended the feasibility of keeping the hospitals' load down to manageable proportions. For this category of physician, the AMMRI and Alianza representatives had proposed a fee schedule of 1,500 pesos per "month-hour" worked.[86]

Within three days of the publication of the new decree, the recently organized doctors' union of the ISSSTE held a meeting at which union leaders lauded the president's action in terms which implied that it had been taken as a result of union activities on behalf of the doctors.[87] To emphasize that this was the officially approved interpretation of his action, the president, on 15 July, granted the union leaders a much publicized interview during which he congratulated them because

> they do not take shelter in selfishness but rather . . . accept the process of socialization [of medicine] in spite of the prejudicial effect which that process might have on their personal economic condition, because [it] aims fundamentally at benefitting the majority of individuals who make up society.[88]

Again a committee of Alianza doctors tried to obtain an interview with the president. Again they were rebuffed by Cisneros. Without waiting for formal approval by Alianza delegates, 87 interns and residents from Federal District hospitals, and nearly 300 general practitioners from the clinics, walked off the job on 16 August.[89]

A week later, the Alianza delegates met in a general assembly and, in an atmosphere of high tension, voted for a new strike. For a time it appeared possible that the large and influential delegation from the department of health's General Hospital would remain aloof from the strike until 2 September.[90] A motion to that effect had already been approved, but heated discussion continued, in the midst of which a woman delegate sprang to her feet and shouted an obscene reference to the male delegates' alleged lack of virility.[91] In the ensuing uproar, a show of hands was interpreted by the chair as a majority in favor of the strike. The date set was 24 August.[92]

Uproar approached riot proportions at the Veinte de Noviembre Hospital of the ISSSTE, where one faction of doctors took matters into their own hands by shunting all emergencies to the Social Security Hospital (whose doctors were not on strike). Another faction at the Veinte de Noviembre Hospital refused to recognize the legitimacy of this action, and continued to work as long as circumstances permitted. For the first time in the history of the strike movement, conflict between groups of doctors was as deep and bitter as conflict between doctors and health officials. The hospital corridors became platforms for debaters while many patients went unattended.

If the government had needed a reason for armed intervention, this was it. On 26 August, Rómulo Sánchez Mireles, director of the ISSSTE, led a contingent of grenadiers (Federal District riot police, so called because of the tear gas grenades they clip to their belts) into the hospital and ordered all doctors to vacate the premises within ten minutes.[93] Some 300 nurses who had met in the hospital's auditorium to protest the police action were also ordered to leave.

As soon as the building had been cleared of strikers, forty doctors and forty nurses from the army medical corps under the command of Colonel Alberto Gallegos Domínguez were escorted into the building and began improvising arrangements for providing skeletal services. Cases which could not be handled with the minimal personnel thus available were shifted by ambulance to the large military hospital on the outskirts of the city.[94]

Elsewhere in the nation, the response to the AMMRI's call for sympathy strikes was disappointing. The only group which reacted in a coordinated manner was that of Pachuca, in the state of Hidalgo, where all regular hospital activities were shut down in the ISSSTE hospital, Coordinated Rural Services, and Children's Hospital, and emergency cases ordinarily routed to those institutions were cared for by social security doctors.[95] On 28 August, two Pachuca doctors, Alfredo Ortega Rivera and Alberto Hernández, were jailed by state authorities for participating in the strike.[96] To the author's knowledge, these were the only two individuals who were jailed during the entire period covered by the strikes, on charges directly connected with the strikes.

The evacuation of the Veinte de Noviembre Hospital began at 5 P.M., and was followed at 9 P.M. by a bulletin from Antonio Bernal, secretary general of the FSTSE. He applauded the action taken by Sánchez Mireles and indicated that the union had requested him to do so to protect the lives of the patients by making it possible for the strikers to be replaced by noninvolved physicians.[97]

The attention of the concerned public now turned from the strikers to President Díaz ordaz's impending state of the nation address, scheduled for 1 September. In view of the events of the last week of August, it was generally expected that the president could not avoid making a public statement clarifying the government position with respect to the doctors.

These expectations were not disappointed. In a speech lasting two and a half hours (brief by comparison with those of his predecessors), the president reported on national problems and steps taken toward their solution during the nine months of his incumbency. All radio stations carried the speech live, and all major newspapers carried the complete text later. It was divided into four main parts: (1) national politics (state gubernatorial elections, important appointments, and administration of the Federal District); (2) fiscal and economic matters; (3) health, education, and welfare; and (4) foreign policy. Under section (3), the strikes were the topic which received major emphasis. Díaz Ordaz spent thirty minutes on this subject, in contrast with twenty minutes dedicated to the entire subject of foreign policy. He outlined the government's position at length, insisting that everything possible had been done to satisfy the doctors' demands, and assuring his listeners that as a result of his decrees of 18 February and 9 July, the doctors were better off in every way than they had ever been before.

After reviewing the recent events at the Veinte de Noviembre Hospital and reiterating the government's view that the doctors had been delinquent in their duty of caring for the sick, Díaz Ordaz outlined the four alternatives which, according to him, were available to the government. These were:

1. To grant "another" raise in pay to the doctors. This, he predicted, would only satisfy them for a few weeks or months, after which they would make fresh demands. This ignored the fact that the new strike, like the two preceding ones, had been called precisely because the physicians claimed that no action had been taken to implement the presidential decrees.

2. To grant the demand for a compensation schedule of 1,500 pesos per month-hour.[98] This, he pointed out, would require the expenditure of "many hundreds of millions of pesos every year, billions destined exclusively to pay the salaries of doctors, which is completely beyond the limits of the budget." Such an expenditure would require heavy new taxes which he was sure the people would not tolerate. The manner of presenting this alternative ignored the doctors' contention that standardization of salaries *and* work schedules would eliminate much payroll duplication and result in an overall savings of manpower and money to the government.

3. To force the doctors to return to work. This alternative was expressly forbidden by Article 5 of the constitution.

4. To reduce the government's health and medical services to the level of those available four of five years before the present time, that is, before the existence of the social security Medical Center and the Veinte de Noviembre Hospital. This ignored the fact that the social security doctors were not, and had never been, on strike.

The government was thus practically forced, the president indicated, to implement the fourth alternative. But it was determined that the doctors should pay dearly for their actions which had been prejudicial to the public interest. "Already," he assured his listeners, "steps are being taken in connection with the different misdemeanors which are possibly being committed, which may include homicide due to neglect of duty, association for criminal purposes, intimidation of officials, desertion from their jobs, and resisting arrest. . . . We shall proceed prudently but vigorously against those who are responsible." [99]

After voicing this threat, Díaz Ordaz made a last appeal to the physicians. "Your jobs are waiting for you in the hospitals, in the clinics, in the laboratories, in the operating rooms. I invoke your feeling of human solidarity so that you will return immediately to the [bed]sides of your patients [who are] innocent victims poised between pain and death." [100]

The Mexican public is rarely left in doubt as to how it is expected to react to specific governmental actions. In this case, the members of congress, gathered in the Chamber of Deputies to hear the president's speech, provided the cues. On two occasions, the assembled legislators rose to their feet and accorded Díaz Ordaz enthusiastic and prolonged applause. One such occasion was the reiteration of the government's refusal to participate in the creation of an Inter-American Peace Force (proposed to the Organization of American States by the United States after the uprising in the Dominican Republic). The other occasion was the president's threat of reprisals against the doctors; this received the longest and loudest applause of all.

For the striking doctors, gathered around television sets or radio receivers, the signs were unmistakable. The strike was at an end; so too were their hopes of negotiating with health officials. The latter, in view of the president's public proclamation of hostility to the physicians could, from that time on, safely refuse to deal with them. Nor could they expect protection from the courts if they were jailed or fired from their jobs.[101]

Under the circumstances, the decision taken by the Alianza general assembly to end the strike was a lugubrious formality. The motion which was approved specified that the physicians would return to their jobs provided that no retaliatory measures were taken against them. The effect of this provision was, in the words of a popular Spanish saying, "to threaten a lion with a stick."

On 6 September 1965, the Monday following the president's speech, all physicians reported for work at their respective hospitals and clinics. Government health and medical services rapidly reverted to normal.

As the doctors had feared, reprisals were instituted almost immediately. The department of justice of the Federal District issued orders for the arrest of an undetermined number of doctors and nurses, and approximately 500 others were verbally notified that they had been fired.[102] Subsequently, 206 doctors received written confirmation of termination of employment.

On 20 November 1965, a hardy little band of veterans gathered in the old Medical School building in Mexico City to celebrate what is officially known in Mexico as "Physicians' Day." Celebrate? It would be more appropriate to say that they held a wake. About seventy-five persons were present, including the orators and the inevitable secret service agents. Instead of referring to past grievances or demanding immediate government action of one kind or another, the speeches referred somewhat vaguely to the need for restructuring Mexico's medical services. The hope was expressed that the government, perceiving the constructive attitude of the physicians, would now be ready to engage in a dialogue with them, with a view to solving national health care problems. After gathering in the school patio to have their pictures taken together, the group dispersed, never to meet in public again.

The Student Strike of 1968

6

Friday, 26 July 1968 "Mamá, I'll be home late. There's been a *bola* here."

The voice was that of a stenographer in a telephone booth at Sanborn's Madero, within sight of Avenida Juárez and the Alameda, in Mexico City. *Bola* is the Mexican slang word for trouble, for an unpleasant complication, a nasty mess.

On the day in question, there had indeed been a *bola* whose origin and development are still surrounded with uncertainty. Because this was the initial incident of what was to prove the most serious political disturbance since the Mexican Revolution and its violent aftermath (1910–1928), it is important to have some idea of the sequence of events on that day.[1]

Two groups of students were involved in the 26 July incident. One of them, the Federación Nacional de Estudiantes Técnicos (hereinafter referred to as FNET) had applied for and received a city government permit to hold a march to protest police roughness with some rowdy students at a brawl that had taken place on 23 July. The other group, led by members of the Communist Youth Organization, had also obtained a permit to parade in celebration of the anniversary of Fidel Castro's assault on Moncada Barracks.[2] This parade ended with a brief ceremony in front of the statue of the hero of Mexico's reform movement, Benito Juárez, which was in sight of Avenida Madero, where the stenographer made her telephone call.

The demonstrations took place at widely separated locations but after they dispersed, some members of both groups made their way toward the Zócalo, the traditional center of Mexico's religious and political life. At some point—probably at the corner of Avenida Madero and Palma Street—the converging groups were met by a contingent of

Mexico City riot police. Accounts differ widely as to why the police intervened and what occurred as a result. Shots were fired, heads were cracked, and the students retreated down the narrow street toward the open space of the Alameda. Those who were able to scattered across the park or slipped down side streets and made their way home, or took refuge in Preparatory Schools 1, 2, and 3 near the city's center.

By the time the downtown shops had closed for the day, calm had apparently returned to the area. Vehicular traffic flowed normally; pedestrians hurried homeward for their evening meal, oblivious of the fact that the opening chapter had just been written for a violent drama. Before that drama was to end, hundreds of persons would be dead; other hundreds would be in prison, and the comfortable fiction of peaceful progress would evaporate in the hot wind of impassioned protest.

While millions of adult Mexicans were drinking their evening chocolate, several hundred adolescents were barricaded in school buildings near the Ciudadela plaza, about five blocks south of the Alameda, where they were under attack by the riot police. Some of these boys, whose ages ranged from twelve to sixteen, had participated in one or the other of the two demonstrations which had taken place earlier.[3] The majority, however, were students who had been on their way home from school when the disturbance erupted. The police, in no mood to distinguish between participants and passersby, had pursued them all indiscriminately, forcing many of them to take shelter in the schools.

The siege lasted until well after midnight, ending when one of the school principals persuaded the police to withdraw. By that time, however, the city's hospitals had received more than thirty individuals—a few police, some spectators, and many students—who had been injured in the melee. Almost before the last beleaguered boy reached home, the mass media had begun placing the blame for the disturbance on "outside agitators" and "extremist elements." Unlike the two other cases reported in this book, there was no lag between the initial event and condemnation of civilian participants by press, radio, and television.

Morning newspapers, which had gone to press before the last of the schoolboys was safely in bed, announced that secret service men had raided the headquarters of the Union of Mexican Communists, a mile away from the disturbed area, and had confiscated "at least a half ton" of printed material some of which, it was stated, was to have been distributed to the students. Five men were arrested in the Union office and were held as indirectly responsible for the day's violence.[4] Headquarters of the central committee of the Mexican Communist Party was also raided, and employees of the party newspaper, *La Voz de México*, were arrested.[5]

Thus ended an apparently unimportant incident—one, like many that had preceded it, which involved students, law enforcers, and alleged outside agitators. The traditional propensity of Mexican students to demonstrate, as often as not disorderly, had prompted President Miguel Alemán in 1952 to relocate the National University from the center of the city to its southern outskirts. In the 1960s, five of the nine professional schools of the Polytechnic Institute were relocated at Zacatenco, a new campus on the northern periphery of Mexico City, perhaps in the hope that this geographic marginality would help quarantine some of the effects of student activism. By 1968, the National University's enrollment was above 80,000. This figure included students enrolled in various preparatory schools. The figure for the

Polytechnic Institute, including enrollment in several vocational schools scattered around the city, was well over 50,000.

Schools and Students

The differences between the National University and the Polytechnic Institute went deeper than the division of subject matter might indicate. The National University (UNAM) and its affiliated preparatory schools had decentralized status, which meant that it was an autonomous public corporation whose academic and administrative self-government were stipulated by law. This freedom from overt government interference was a cherished tradition of UNAM and "prepa" students.

The Polytechnic Institute and its affiiliated vocational schools, on the other hand, were centralized institutions with only limited self-government, while the federal government actively intervened in many aspects of its operation. The significance of this distinction can be appreciated when it is recalled that in the 1950s government troops invaded the "Poli" campus, evicted students from dormitories, and closed the school for several months.

An advantage derived from admission to the National University was the opportunity to serve a political apprenticeship which could bring rewards in later life. On a smaller scale, the same was true of the several state universities, which also enjoyed de jure autonomy. For many years, the university campuses had been miniature battlegrounds on which the contending factions within the officially monolithic PRI could test their strength. Thus, what often appeared as student government disputes proved to be attempts to gauge the influence of potential candidates for the presidency of the nation, or attempts to challenge the existing distribution of power within the party. This seems to have been the case during the student strike of 1966, as a result of which President Díaz Ordaz's claim to PRI leadership was drastically eroded.[6]

Student leaders who allied themselves with the right party factions could count on a chance at working their way up in the party after graduation. My interviews with upper echelon PRI officials revealed that many of them entered the political mainstream via this route.

In addition to supporters of PRI factions, every element of contemporary Mexican political thought was represented on the National Autonomous University of Mexico (UNAM) campus. MURO (Movimiento Universitario de Renovadora Orientación), the campus arm of the ultrareactionary PRI faction, was strong and well organized. Minority opposition parties had their groups of loyal sympathizers, and the bulletin boards of the different university departments (known as *facultades* in Mexico) reflected as well a microcosm of past and current world leftist movements. Here one could see the manifestos of Trotskyists, Leninists, Maoists, Castroists, and others. An observer was prompted to comment that "young Marxists never die; they just organize student groups at UNAM." Every issue of national and international political life was passionately discussed, often followed by policy proclamations and adoption of action programs. Students of the different *facultades* tended to sort themselves out along the political spectrum, with many from the Medical School and the Department of Philosophy and Literature (located at opposite ends of the campus) showing an affinity for New Left viewpoints, while those of Business Administration and Law (next door to each other) tended to be conservative.[7]

If the national government had hoped to end student

disturbances by removing the institutions of higher learning from the center of the city, it soon perceived the error of its premature optimism. Four professional schools were still located on the Santo Tomás campus of the Polytechnic Institute, a short distance north of Mexico City's center. In addition, nine preparatory schools and seven vocational schools remained at previously established locations, some of them in the heart of the densely populated urban area. The "prepas" were part of a system which channeled its graduates into the National University, while the "vocas" prepared graduates for the Polytechnic Institute. Both of these groups showed strong loyalty to their respective parent institutions.

"Prepa" students were regarded as the elite of the public secondary school system; they who could look forward to an education in the humanities, social sciences, or "liberal" professions (for example, law, medicine, architecture), and to positions of prestige. For many parents, the ability to state "I have a son [or daughter] at the University" enhanced their status in the community. Because opportunities for economic and social mobility were still limited, the marginal differentiation provided by the right kind of education was an important advantage.

"Voca" students, on the other hand, could not hope for such prestigious careers. Created by President Lázaro Cárdenas to upgrade the technological skills of the manpower required for industrial growth, the Polytechnic Institute shared the reputation of similar institutions in some other countries. As in pre-1968 France, the selection process separated students at an early age into prepreparatory or prevocational groups, with the parents' socioeconomic status an important indicator of probable career opportunities. Once the initial selection was made, it was extremely difficult for an individual to change from the vocational group to the preparatory group. The alternatives were even further reduced by the fact that the number of privately supported institutions of higher education in Mexico could be counted on the fingers of one hand, and their tuition charges effectively barred children from working-class families. This rigidity had prompted a group of activist students at UNAM and the Polytechnic Institute to initiate, in the summer of 1968, a campaign in favor of liberalizing the University's admission policies so that more "voca" graduates would be admitted to the University.

For some time after its founding, the "Poli" reflected the prevailing educational philosophy of the Cárdenas period. Referring derogatorily to "academic" education as effete and inappropriate for a socialist nation, the Cardenistas advocated greater prestige for technical training. By the 1960s, however, many students of both institutions shared left-oriented activist and antiestablishment attitudes.

Student Activism

The populist orientation of many UNAM students had shown itself in repeated efforts to support those labor groups which were not part of the conservatively oriented power structure of the PRI's labor sector. A favored subject of campus rhetoric was the mythical establishment of a student-worker alliance. To promote this alliance, student groups often declared sympathy strikes in support of demands by independent unions. In 1965, they had shown their solidarity with bus drivers by capturing a number of buses and holding them in the campus esplanade until a new contract was signed. To the disappointment of the most idealistic members of the campus community, the relationship between the bus drivers and the student body did not improve as a result of this gesture.

Another incident involving the bus service occurred in July 1968, showing again the populist sympathies of many students. For many of them, the buses were the only way of getting back and forth between home or boarding house and class. The trip had to be made four times a day, because all academic and administrative business was suspended between 2 P.M. and 4 P.M. for the dinner period, and then resumed from 4 P.M. to 8 P.M.

Mexico City and its environs were served by more than ninety independent bus lines, each plying a different route. The buses that converged on the University from various sections of the city entered the campus, traveled a perimeter road dropping off students at the separate *facultad* buildings, and then stopped in a large paved terminal area near the administration building where passengers were lined up for the return trip to town. On the day in question, one of the buses made too rapid a turn in the terminal; out of control, it jumped the curb and pinned a young woman against a pillar. She survived the impact, but both her legs were crushed and had to be amputated.

Other accidents had occurred at the same place on previous occasions. The students blamed the bus companies, most of which operated on a shoestring and did not keep their vehicles in safe condition. Few of the companies carried casualty insurance, and previous victims had not been adequately indemnified for their injuries. Indignant at what they saw as callous negligence, student leaders organized a committee to visit the bus company officers and demand compensation for the latest victim. When they were turned away with evasive answers, they rallied a segment of the student body and sequestered all buses entering the campus, without regard for the fact that they belonged to several different companies. To show all of the company owners that nonpayment of indemnity could be very costly, they inflicted as much damage on the buses as they could. On 9 July, I counted more than thirty buses in the terminal area with smashed windows and slashed tires. A few had actually been burned. Within a few days, the company that owned the bus involved in the accident had paid the injured woman a cash sum which the students regarded as sufficient, and the sequestration of vehicles ceased. When asked why they had resorted to violence instead of seeking legal remedies, student leaders answered that in the past the courts had favored the companies' interests.

During the summer of 1968, other evidence of student restlessness could be seen. Flyers were being circulated, asking for support of the jailed labor leader, Demetrio Vallejo, who was about to initiate a hunger strike to protest the parole board's continued refusal to grant his release. Student leaders had a long memory in spite of their youth; they included the railroad strike and the doctors' strike in an impressive list of grievances against the government, which they titled "Ten Years of Repression" and which they posted on the wall of the *facultad* of Philosophy and Literature.

At the time the student strike attracted international attention in 1968, many Mexicans were astounded at the number of sympathizers it attracted, and at the intensity of feelings manifested by the participants. The whole affair seemed to have blown up in a few hours, like a great natural disaster such as a tornado or volcanic eruption. That the student volcano had already emitted many warning rumbles was ignored even by most of the concerned public, and this was due in good measure to the failure of the mass media to devote adequate coverage to the preliminary events.

For the past two decades, Mexican newspapers have adopted a practice which seems to reflect the attitude that "the least said the better," with regard to protest group activities. Whenever possible, information about disturbances is confined to a one- or two-paragraph story, relegated to one of the back pages, and couched in such ambiguous terms that it is impossible to understand the significance of the events. Spanish newspapers employ the same technique, especially when such stories are compared with the lengthy and prominent display given to the activities and speeches of government officials. In both political systems, stories about protests are sometimes held for a week or two and then published with a lead sentence announcing that a number of agitators have been arrested, and the matter is under control.

In 1956, a prolonged student strike at the Polytechnic Institute, supported by many faculty members, was broken when government troops occupied the campus, evicted students from dormitories, and closed the institution for several months. After the Institute was reopened, the Federación Nacional de Estudiantes Técnicos became a powerful campus organization, receiving support from the government and acting, according to many observers, as a company union to implement government policies while giving the appearance of independent action. In response to this development, remnants of the campus organizations that had participated in the 1956 strike made efforts to regroup and recruit new members. They worked at a disadvantage, however; many of the former leaders were in jail, and all meetings were infiltrated by secret service men.

In 1960, the university of the state of Guerrero had been the setting for a student strike; others had taken place in 1966 at the University of Morelia and at the UNAM, and, in 1967, at the University of Sonora. At Morelia, the long-standing tension between the student body and the state government took on an ominous aspect when a student leader, Everardo Rodríguez Orbe, was killed in police headquarters. Rodríguez Orbe was a member of a student delegation that had been invited by the police to recover a loudspeaker from police headquarters which had been confiscated during a rally held to protest a rise in bus fares.[8]

All of these disturbances, except the 1966 UNAM strike, had been quelled by government troops. One of Mexico's most astute political analysts believes that troops were not called in to crush the 1966 disturbance because that event had been instigated by "high administrative officials" who saw the university's rector as a possible source of opposition to a PRI faction which was working to dominate the party.[9] These events indicate that during the late 1950s, and all through the 1960s, students' grievances against the law enforcers, especially the army paratroopers and the police grenadiers, had been mounting, and that the tension was not confined to the Federal District area.

Most of the concerns that had moved Mexican students to active protest had been parochial in nature, centering largely on matters whose impact was felt immediately and personally in their daily lives. Sometimes these problems were involved with or even the result of political quarrels arising in the town or state where the university was located, but there was rarely any involvement with the wider national scene. While some of the student activists may have been troubled by ideological preoccupations, the majority seem to have been interested only in bread and butter issues. The common bond, if there was one, between students of different campuses was a lively resentment at the unresponsiveness shown by governmental authorities toward their demands for what often amounted to small concessions. It was not so much that the demands were not satisfied as the fact that the demanders were ignored. This resentment, and the strong antagonism toward the often brutal law enforcers, were the two elements which provided the emotional momentum for later events.

Involved in at least three of the serious student disturbances of the 1960s was the increasingly troublesome problem of internal democracy in the dominant political party, the PRI. In the sense that this affected the career opportunities of many student politicians, it can be regarded as a parochial problem although, as we shall see, the effects on national decision making soon became very important.

Because the campuses had been made miniature arenas for the party's factional fights, many students became sensitized to the growth of oligarchical tendencies in the PRI's conservative sector. Carlos Madrazo, chosen by President Díaz Ordaz to head the PRI (as chairman of the National Executive Committee of the party), had been ousted in late 1965 by the conservatives. This was the first time in more than thirty years that the president's choice of party leader was repudiated. The importance of this event in national politics was of the first magnitude. Madrazo's expulsion signified a drastic deflation of the president's power to dictate party policy. Díaz Ordaz could no longer count on enough support from the more liberal elements of the PRI, including the young technocrats, to make binding decisions. It is even possible that as of that moment he lost the power to name his successor. This view of the internal dynamics of the party permits us to speculate that whatever actions Díaz Ordaz was subsequently to take with respect to the student strike resulted from the necessity to reassure the party's dominant conservative element that he had the situation under control.

In the few months in which Madrazo was party chief, he had waged a vigorous campaign to abolish the old system of secret consultations (called "auscultations") through which party nominees were selected, and to replace that system with public primary elections. For many students, Madrazo's defeat thus became a symbol of the party's obstinate elitism and ended their hopes for upward mobility. Before his death in the spring of 1969, he had talked about organizing a new opposition party, and there is little doubt that he could have counted on strong student support.

The continuing tension further cemented the solidarity which already existed among the students, extending beyond actual presence on the campus to include alumni who felt that their years of study entitled them to membership in the nation's intellectual elite. Their exclusion from influential positions in the PRI, contrasted with the rapid rise of some of their former classmates who had picked the winning faction, may have embittered them even further. For many, belonging to this ill-defined group of "outs" was the nearest thing to membership in an autonomous secondary type of association. Almost all other secondary associations, such as large labor unions, chambers of commerce and industry, professional groups, and the few existing civic or cultural associations, had long ago been co-opted by the government. Outside of family ties, the friendships formed during their student days were likely to be the deepest emotional commitments many Mexicans would make during their whole lives. As we have seen, this was an important factor in mobilizing the residents and interns in the doctors' strikes.

unity ✱

On the night of 26 July 1968, the preparatory and vocational students were attacked by a common enemy, and the sensation of solidarity not only transcended the rivalry between those two groups, but also bridged the age gap between them and the university students. During that night, student leaders in the besieged schools were in touch with each other by telephone, planning a protest strike that would demonstrate their newfound solidarity.

Prelude to Tragedy

First fruit of the new militancy was the strike announced, on 12 July, by students of schools 1, 2, 4, 5, 6, and 8, and of the Polytechnic's High School of Economics. On Sunday, 28 July, a group of students from the Polytechnic Institute, the National University, and the National Agricultural School of Chapingo met on the "Poli" campus and issued a set of conditions for ending the strike. These included indemnization for injured students and for the families of a number of students said to have been killed; release of all students jailed during the fracas; abolition of Article 145 of the Penal Code (the ill-famed antisubversive law), and abolition of the grenadiers and other special police forces. It was announced that if these demands were not met, a general student strike would be called throughout the nation.[10]

Daily newspapers immediately began playing on the themes of extremist agitation and intervention of foreign agents. As an example of the publishers' Pavlovian reflexes, the first information published by *Excelsior* on 27 July had begun: "About three thousand students—egged on by leftist agitators—yesterday created a disturbance in the center of the city. . . ." A bulletin from the office of the Attorney General, released on 28 July, accused the Central Nacional de Estudiantes Democráticos (CNED), the student arm of the Communist Party, of having planned and executed a provocation to elicit police intervention. The bulletin also announced the arrest of sixteen persons, three of whom were listed as foreigners. The CNED retaliated by accusing the police of having sent in a group of agents provocateurs, disguised as students, to break store windows and thus justify police intervention.

Excelsior's lead editorial on 29 July was entitled "The Work of Provocateurs." On the facing page a column, under the byline of Froylán M. López Narváez, offered two explanations of the disturbances, neither of which ruled out the other. This provided leaders with a "do-it-yourself" political analysis kit, and absolved the writer from the responsibility of pronouncing judgment. The first explanation was that "un-Mexican" interests had instigated the disturbance; the other hypothesis was that some unspecified group or agency had got the jump on radical groups by bringing the matter to a head so as to repress the discontent before it got out of hand. This second possibility was never mentioned again in the nation's "big press," but the first theme was constantly repeated in the months that followed. It was to be the basis of the government's case against the hundreds of individuals who were arrested and eventually brought to trial.

Monday, 29 July: Faced with a strike, educational authorities closed all the institutions under their jurisdiction in the Federal District. For the secretariat of public education, this meant closing all vocational schools and the Polytechnic Institute. The National University, under the charter which conceded its autonomy, took separate action to suspend classes not only at University City but also in the preparatory schools which were included in the autonomous jurisdiction.

Two areas in the city were the scenes of tumult since the early morning of that day. One of these was the district around the secretariat of Education, a few blocks north of the Zócalo; the other was the huge high-rise public housing complex known as Nonoalco-Tlatelolco, less than a mile north of the Paseo de la Reforma. In both of these areas, vocational students had captured buses, overturning them and setting fire to them, effectively blocking the streets. Riot police poured into the areas, accompanied by regular police and army paratroopers. By nightfall, the uniformed forces had surrounded the areas and were closing in on the trouble spots, clubbing students and firing tear gas grenades. Photographs of soldiers clubbing students with rifle butts did not appear in the Mexican media, but two such pictures were printed in the *New York Times* of 30 July, together with a story stating that the *Times* correspondent had seen a soldier break his rifle butt over the head of a student, who was then carried off to an ambulance.

Tuesday, 30 July: This is the date which has become enshrined in student folklore as *el día del bazukazo* (the day of the bazooka blast). Shortly before 1 A.M., infantry and parachute troops moved in on the students barricaded in the San Ildefonso preparatory school, not far from the secretariat of education. By this time, most of the boys who had taken refuge there were injured. The school is in a very poor area of the city, where buildings 150 and 200 years old teem with families submerged in poverty. From these buildings some of the tenants, enraged by the army attack on the school, did what they could to delay the final victory by pouring boiling water on the heads of the troops from the upstairs windows.[11]

Finally, the troops positioned a bazooka at the main entrance of the school and blasted open the massive baroque doors. They occupied the school and herded the boys into police wagons, military vehicles, and ambulances.

Newspaper stories about the event only confused the reading public. It would seem that some reporters must have been in the vicinity of an event of such magnitude, in the center of the city, but the published accounts do not reflect this. Details which could have been supplied by eyewitnesses were absent; instead, official government versions of what happened were offered to the public without additional comment. Even in these versions, there were confusions, contradictions, denials, and retractions. Alfonso Corona del Rosal, regent of the Federal District (often mistakenly called the mayor of Mexico City, but actually appointed by the president of Mexico and serving at the pleasure of the chief executive) responded to rumors about the bazooka blast by insisting that schools had not been invaded by the police or military. A defense department bulletin, on the other hand, stated that the army had intervened at the request of the regent. According to the secretary of defense, 180 students were arrested; the bulletin issued by the secret service (an arm of Gobernación) announced that 500 arrests had been made by the time the newspapers went to press, with more arrests still being carried out. An afternoon newspaper reported 1,606 detentions and 65 hospitalized injured persons, all except one of whom were listed as students.

At the time of these disturbances President Díaz Ordaz was out of the city, mending political fences and gathering information which would be useful in making decisions. Since the time of Lázaro Cárdenas, this "riding circuit" has been a frequent practice of Mexican presidents. Even if he had been in Mexico City, however, it is doubtful that Díaz Ordaz would have intervened. Luis Echeverría, secretary of

Gobernación (later elected president of Mexico for the term 1970–1976), stated that "a tiny minority of selfish interests is trying to detour the upward march of the Revolution," [12] At the same time General Marcelino Barragán, the secretary of defense, insisted that there was no conspiracy against the government.[13] One newspaper headline proclaimed that "in the UNAM and the Poli there is absolute repudiation of the provocateurs," while the accompanying article reproduced a bowdlerized version of a speech made by the rector of the National University in which he had declared a day of mourning for the invasion of schools by the armed forces.[14] Editing made it appear that a small gang of hoodlums, not representing any sector of student opinion, had caused all the trouble.

31 July: With troops still occupying the schools, and the students locked out, the press concentrated on familiar themes. Members of the national congress condemned the students and applauded the Executive Branch of the government for using stern measures. "[The students] shouldn't stick their noses into our business," stated one legislator.[15] The defense secretary announced that order would be preserved at all costs. While the news columns ignored the bazooka blast entirely, and only the slightest hint of it crept into some bylined columns, editorials pursued the themes of foreign intervention, Castroist plots, and student violence. "These fifteen-year-old kids [*chamaquitos*]," stated one editorial writer, were "pushed" into the disturbance by "foreigners who had planned" it. It was these "subversive foreigners and gangs of provocateurs" who should be blamed for the affair, concluded the writer.[16]

On this day the first half-page advertisement appeared, addressed "to the Studious Youth of Mexico," blaming "alien influences" and "foreign interests" for the recent tumult, and calling upon the students to desist from their disruptive behavior in order to cooperate with the government's program of peaceful progress.[17]

An FNET delegation visited the regent of the Federal District to present a "petition for the solution of the conflict." This petition consisted of seven demands: dismissal of police chiefs, dismissal of those responsible for actions at Vocational School No. 5, indemnization of injured students, regulation of actions by police and military forces, erasure of names of arrested students from police dockets, release of all arrested students, and immediate evacuation of schools by armed forces and police.

While the delegation was presenting this petition, police invaded the School of Dramatic Art of the National Institute of Fine Arts and arrested 73 students. All were released later that day. During the following months, students from that school participated in events in ways for which their training had particularly suited them.

Readers who have observed the unfolding of events in the two previous case studies can predict the next development. On 1 August, in what became known as the "outstretched hand" speech, President Díaz Ordaz voiced a conciliatory note: "Public peace and tranquility must be restored," he declared. "A hand is stretched out; Mexicans will say whether that hand will find a response. I have been deeply grieved by these deplorable and shameful events. Let us not further accentuate our differences. . . ."

This was the kind of rhetoric which Mexicans loved, and which made newspaper headlines. The mass media took up the theme of the outstretched hand and elaborated on it in editorials, cartoons, signed columns of exegesis, display advertisements, and news broadcasts. Students also took it up: picket signs declared, "The outstretched hand has a pistol in it," "The outstretched arm wears a swastika," and "The dead cannot shake hands." [18]

In spite of the rhetoric, the government made no attempt to negotiate directly with the student leadership. For their part, the students were in no mood to accept platitudes. In 1965, they had seen the striking doctors beguiled into thinking that they could negotiate with the president, only to be disillusioned after a protracted and futile struggle.[19]

About this time, students began to capture buses and to use them in getting around the huge city, to join other groups and to hold strike meetings. In another chapter, we observed that Mexicans had universally manifested reticence in criticizing the president; for over thirty years, citizens refrained from attacking the chief executive directly, and instead had heaped the blame on his subordinates for any governmental malfunctioning. Suddenly, the old rules no longer applied. I saw buses speeding down the avenues, their sides painted with the slogan "Death to Díaz Ordaz." This marked a radical change of mood. In addition, the "filthy speech" revolution which had erupted on the Berkeley campus in the spring of 1965 apparently had spread to Mexican campuses. Profanity and obscenity emerged in the discourse of the protesters, with the expected effect on their elders. The literature produced as a by-product of the student movement is filled with words and phrases which were formerly excluded from published material as unfit for respectable Mexican readers.

August: "In 1958 the railroadmen were alone. Not so with us." Public support for the students, first manifested on the night of the bazooka blast, grew rapidly during the next few weeks. The students themselves were chiefly responsible for mobilizing sympathy. They had found ways to bypass the intricate communication blocks which, in the past, had kept different sectors of the population isolated and ignorant.

During the railroad strikes and the doctors' strikes, the mass media had reacted, after initial confusion, by closing ranks and presenting an unfavorable version of the strikers' actions. Even sophisticated people who had learned to take the news with a grain of salt were handicapped by lack of reliable information. In the case of the doctors, there had been so much noise in the communication system that many strikers became suspicious of each other, lost their sense of unity, and finally withdrew from the movement. If the students had simply been aware of that situation, they would have been as helpless as the doctors had been, but they took steps to prevent a recurrence.

Apart from occasional broadsides in the form of newspaper advertisements, the railroad men had given a low priority to appealing their case to the public. Too late, they found themselves cut off from the herd, hunted down, and overcome. The doctors with their parades and their "to the Honorable Public Opinion" advertisements had made a greater effort to keep communication channels open, but, in the end, they were defeated by their own small numbers and by the unwillingness of the newspapers to publish their side of the story.

In 1968, a whole new era of protest publicity took shape in an amazingly short time, based on the assumption that every student was responsible for carrying the strikers' arguments directly to the public. While government officials held press conferences to condemn them as a bunch of rowdies, students by the thousands were on the streets, talking with people, asking for their understanding and support. They used a wide repertoire of techniques for getting their message across.

We have already seen that bus hijacking by students had been so frequently resorted to for many years that it was almost regarded as a sport. As far as the public record testifies, it would appear that bus drivers did not put up any resistance, and no one appears to have been injured during these incidents. On previous occasions, captured buses had usually been held only to pressure the owners or the government, but during the 1968 movement, they became an important element, not only in moving the strikers around the city, but also in bearing their messages, painted crudely on the vehicles' sides.

Probably the most effective method of transmitting the students' message was the development of people-to-people brigades. These were mobile groups of eight to fifteen students who visited slums, working-class neighborhoods, and factories, distributing flyers, talking with people, explaining their point of view, and answering questions. Other brigades visited marketplaces and department stores. Very soon, someone thought of doing the same thing on trolley cars and buses—not the ones which had been hijacked, but those which had remained in regular service throughout the city. In Mexico City it had been the custom for beggars and newspaper vendors to board public vehicles as fare-paying passengers, working their way from the front to the rear, asking for money or offering their wares. When they had finished their canvassing they would alight and board a vehicle traveling in the opposite direction, so that they covered a limited, well-defined territory. The people who made their living in that way had worked out a rough route schedule so that they did not conflict with each other. Now the students copied their methods, passing out flyers and asking for donations to finance further activities.

Other brigades held "lightning meetings" on street corners in densely populated neighborhoods. Using the roof of a hijacked bus as a platform, such a brigade would pull up to the curb, invite a dialogue with the public, and present their propaganda. If the lookout detected the police, the speakers clambered down from the roof and the bus rolled away. The Polytechnic Institute owned a small fleet of buses, which the students appropriated for the duration of the strike and used for this purpose.

Students from the School of Dramatic Art of the National Institute of Fine Arts, with the assistance of a few professionals, developed their own variant of this technique which, for lack of an adequate term in Spanish, they christened with the English name of "happening." One participant gives the following account of such an event: A middle-class "matron," dressed for a shopping trip, would stop at a newsstand and buy one of the progovernment daily papers. Glancing at the headlines, she would comment aloud, "Those crazy students, always raising a fuss about something . . . now, what on earth are they after this time? . . . They're all a bunch of communists, that's what they are." At that juncture, a passing "student," attired in miniskirt and boots, would pause and interrupt the "matron," snapping, "Take that remark back señora. You don't know what you're talking about!" The two would soon be engaged in a heated argument, drawing passersby into the discussion. Often the unsuspecting bystanders would defend the students and warn the "matron" to be on her way.[20]

Throughout the 1968 movement, it was a cherished objective to establish a united front of students and workers. It was a morale-sustaining fiction, like Sorel's myth of the general strike. A student-worker force, they were sure, could bring such overwhelming pressure on the government that the latter would be obliged to concede their demands. To this end, brigades visited factories and talked with workers during their lunch hour, trying to persuade them to hold sympathy strikes. The net result of this activity was very discouraging; although a few small independent unions gave some support, the bulk of the labor sector refused to identify its interests with those of the students. It was not simply that labor leaders acted as executors of government policy; the rank-and-file workers were frightened of anything that threatened the loss of a day's pay. In the lugubrious postmortems conducted after the strike, even the most stubbornly optimistic of the movement veterans had to admit failure on this score.

Although the buildings and grounds of some of the closed schools became meeting places for many "prepa" and "voca" students, the main centers of organizational activity were the Poli and the UNAM campuses. For weeks, these places served as home base for tens of thousands of young men and women, who felt safe from police detention as soon as they entered the academic precincts. On the UNAM esplanade, the parochialism and reserve so characteristic of Mexicans gave way to a discreet and decorous version of the Woodstock spirit. The campuses were the assembly points for the brigade workers; funds collected in the city's streets were brought back to the central committee for administration. According to the accounts of several members of this committee, most of the money was used to buy paper for mimeographing propaganda flyers. Duplicating machines belonging to the University were commandeered for the daily production of these materials. Some money was also spent on the insertion of quarter-page advertisements in the daily newspapers until they were no longer accepted for publication. Other students were engaged in hand-lettering picket signs which were carried during the "lightning meetings" and which were often changed to fit the latest developments into easily understood slogans and demands.

Overriding all of these campus-based activities, however, was the one which occupied the time and attention of most of the students most of the time: discussion. Night and day, in small committee sessions and huge mass meetings, the talk went on and on. Surely never before had so many individuals focused their attention on Mexico's political problems for so long a time and from so many different ideological viewpoints. Almost from the beginning, a difference could be noted between the orientation of the UNAM group and that of the Poli group. In broad terms, it can be said that many members of the first group thought of themselves as the theoreticians of the movement, while most of the latter preferred more active roles.

In the interminable and inconclusive talk fests, Mao, Marcuse, Sartre, Guevara, Debray, and every other major revolutionary theorist or practitioner of the twentieth century, was the subject of earnest and sometimes violent argument. In their newfound solidarity, young Mexicans who had been taught never to disagree openly with anyone about anything felt safe enough to challenge each other's ideas and even to experiment gingerly with "self-criticism" sessions. It was an exhilarating experience, one which may have left some permanent impression on a significant sector of this generation.

One of the most important aspects of the new feeling of trust was seen in the changing perceptions of male and female roles. Mestizo Mexicans, like their counterparts in other Latin-American countries, have developed a pattern of expectations based on certain ideal attributes of men and women. *Machismo,* the cult of virility, places great value on aggressive and intransigent behavior in male-to-male interpersonal relationships and on arrogance and sexual aggression in male-to-female relationships.[21] *Marianismo* is the cult of feminine spiritual superiority which teaches that women are semidivine, morally superior to and spiritually stronger than men.[22] The dynamic interplay between the two patterns of expectation provides the leitmotif of mestizo social relationships throughout Latin America. Full attainment of feminine superiority comes only through motherhood, reaching its highest level after middle age, when grown children can render homage to the mother-cult object. As a result, the only universally approved male-female relationships have been oedipal ones. The most damaging criticism that can be made of a man is to say that he is a bad son to his mother. This idealized mother-child relationship has, in large part, been responsible for the hostility underlying heterosexual contacts among peers. Young men regard young women as opportunities for exploitation and the latter, knowing that they cannot displace the mothers in the men's affections, view men as the instruments by which they hope to achieve eventual sainthood through martyrdom.

Mexican university students surveyed before 1968 showed that they expected their amorous relationships to bring them unhappiness. Pessimistic expectations were much more prevalent among the Mexican students than among a control group of American students in Texas.[23] These forebodings not only made courtship a stormy affair, but also prevented the development of any genuine spirit of comradeship among classmates of the opposite sex.

The events of 1968 had an unmistakable impact on this

aspect of Mexican behavior. Soon after the initial incident of 26 July, large numbers of girls began to share the work and risks connected with constant participation in the movement and, as a leadership group emerged, several feminine figures were clearly discernible. One of the most prominent figures, in both the literal and figurative senses, was Roberta Avendaño Martínez, a law student known as "Tita." She weighed 244 pounds.

Among the slogans painted on the walls of UNAM buildings, many referred to sexual liberation. During the meetings held on the campus esplanade, groups would often shout, "Down with papal encyclicals, up with The Pill!" To join and remain active in the strike, thousands of girls made a radical break with urban middle-class mestizo tradition, defying their parents' authority.

It was the second time in this century that Mexican women had gone to war. The first time was during the most violent phase of the Revolution (1910–1920). During that period, the peasant *soldaderas,* celebrated in countless Mexican songs, had followed the guerrilla bands of Villa, Zapata, and others, acting as cooks, nurses, and bedmates of the men, and occasionally participating in the actual fighting. The difference in 1968 was in the social class from which the girl student strikers emerged. Not only were there girls from the UNAM and Poli in the movement; there was even a contingent from the Universidad Iberoamericana, the private coeducational Catholic school where young ladies from wealthy families attended classes "to pick up a little culture" while waiting to find a husband. All of them—from the UNAM, the Poli, and the "Ibero"—found emotional support for their actions not so much in the precedent of the *soldaderas* as in the more recent Cuban revolutionaries.

During the week that followed the initial incident, an

important development took place on the Polytechnic campus. The FNET, recognized by the government as the voice of Poli student opinion, and ipso facto under suspicion by most of the student body, was challenged by another group. On Saturday, 3 August, José Cebreros, the president of FNET, announced a strike at the Institute which would continue until the demands of the FNET petition were met. But two days later, a group of professors and students held a meeting, repudiated the FNET, and led an estimated 100,000 students and sympathizers on an orderly four-mile march, from the Institute's Center for Scientific Research to the main campus, known popularly as the Casco de Santo Tomás, where they dispersed peacefully. Guillermo Massieu, director of the Institute, refused to participate in the march, on the grounds that it was not composed exclusively of his students.

After this demonstration, a new and powerful group emerged, calling itself the Coordinating Committee of the Polytechnic Institute General Strike Movement. FNET influence was rapidly eliminated; within two weeks, Cebreros issued a rather plaintive statement saying that hostile elements had taken over the movement. After that, the FNET ceased to play an important part.

According to one account, there were at least forty-seven separate student demonstrations between 23 July and 10 August.[24] Most of these were small, hastily improvised affairs, but a few reached truly impressive proportions. Compared with the months of preparation, the nationwide network of communications, and the hypermobility of the students who organized the large antiwar demonstrations in the United States, it must be admitted that the Mexican students did a superbly efficient job in spite of serious obstacles.

The Poli march of 5 August has already been mentioned; on 1 August, the rector of the UNAM, Justo Barros Sierra, had led 80,000 students and sympathizers on a "funeral" march into the southern section of the city, along Insurgentes Sur Avenue, to manifest their dismay at the invasion of schools by the police and military.

"August 12–27 was the Golden Age of our movement," reminisced one student leader, long after the strike had come to an end. All accounts, including that of the government secret service agents, seem to confirm this appraisal.

Students from provincial universities and the National Agricultural School at Chapingo joined Poli and UNAM students, professors, and sympathizers on 13 August for a march from the Poli campus to the Zócalo. About 150,000 people participated in this event. Alerted by rumors that hostile groups might try to provoke a riot, the organizers recruited a squad of peace-keepers who stood on both sides of the street and, joining hands, prevented spectators from breaking through. The students had borrowed the technique from the doctors' movement of 1965, when the silent march, protected by men in white suits, had proved very effective.

At intervals the spectators chanted, *"Díaz Ordaz, dónde estás? Díaz Ordaz, saca los dientes."* (Díaz Ordaz, where are you? Díaz Ordaz, get your teeth pulled.)[25] The reference was to the president's distinguishing facial characteristic, his buck teeth. This is a sample of the kind of behavior which caused an observer to comment that "the attacks on the president . . . were direct and mordant, something without precedent in the modern history of Mexico." [26]

Police chief Cueto and a grenadier were burned in effigy, while a group of students pranced about bearing a coffin labeled "dead government." In spite of the raucousness, there was no violence; the crowd was in excellent humor, in a mood to find each incident hilariously funny, as at a circus. Newspaper stories and editorials found nothing ominous about the evening's events. In general, however, the first two weeks of August had witnessed a tremendous mobilization of support for the government by all organized sectors of the political system. A survey of newspaper space devoted to the subject during that period shows that 85 percent was aimed at showing how unified the people were and how bad the students were. Compared to the other two case studies, we find an unusually large number of antistudent advertisements for such an early stage of the conflict, indicating that some influential sectors of high-level decision makers had already made up their minds about the need for justifying any action that might be taken in the future. Some of the earliest arrivals at the antistudent advertising front were groups long active on the campus, with memberships reputed to be very conservative. There was a quarter-page broadside from MURO headed "[University] Autonomy, yes! Communism, no!" and ending, "Communist provocateurs, get out of the UNAM! Let's get back to our classes and to academic order! Autonomy, yes! Communism, no!" [27] A half-page advertisement from FUM (*Frente Universitario Mexicano*) on the same day, proclaimed: "It's now or never, Mr. President! The time has come to crush the communist plot!" [28]

Of all the demonstrations, however, the most impressive, and one of the largest in Mexico's history, was the one on 27 August, in which most sources estimate that approximately 300,000 people participated, marching from Chapultepec Park down the Paseo de la Reforma and terminating in the Zócalo at 9:30 P.M. There was a festive atmosphere. Just as on the great national holiday, the fifteenth of September, spectators and participants mingled, consuming enormous quantities of chile-coated peanuts and carbonated drinks. Two medical students, in their white uniforms, climbed the bell tower of the Cathedral and, with the permission of the priest, rang the great bells. There were speeches, more speeches, and then speeches about speeches; the public did not tire of them. There were songs composed especially for the occasion, poetry declamations, derisive jingles—parodies of radio and television singing commercials—and shouted slogans. One of these, directed at the president (who neither on that nor any other occasion during the strike made an appearance before the students): "Bigmouth, come out on the balcony. Where is your outstretched hand?" [29]

At some point in the evening's festivities, an unidentified person raised a Maoist flag on the pole usually reserved for the Mexican flag. Finally, not long after midnight, the crowd began to disperse; by 1 A.M. only about 5,000 students remained, declaring that they would keep a vigil in front of the presidential palace until the first of September. Soldiers and police advanced on the group, scattering them and forcing them to quit the square.

If the mass media had found nothing ominous in the 13 August and 27 August demonstrations, neither did they see cause for alarm in the events which took place soon after that. On 29 August, an unidentified group fired on Vocational School No. 7, near Tlatelolco. On the same day, a group of masked individuals attacked "Voca" No. 4, invading the premises with lead pipes and sections of steel construction rods. Two days later, about 200 armed persons arrived at "Voca" No. 7 in automobiles. Jumping out, they assaulted students and passersby, injuring about 50 persons. The terrorists also invaded the nearest buildings of the Nonoalco-Tlatelolco housing complex, destroying property and breaking windows. The residents retaliated by pouring water on them and tossing flower pots from upper-story windows.

The student strike committee blamed MURO (when used as a word, the acronym means wall). Subsequent events indicated that these attacks marked the first public appearance of subsidized street gangs whose mode of operation was disquietingly reminiscent of the "Hitler Youth" of the mid-1930s.

For three weeks, the president's offer of 1 August remained a photogenic and rhetorical gesture, nothing more. Losing its patience, student leadership took matters into its own hands by inviting (perhaps challenging would be a more appropriate word) members of the national congress to participate in a teach-in, modeled on the Berkeley prototype, to be held on 20 August in front of the UNAM administration building. No legislator appeared, of course, and the occasion was devoted to speeches demanding that the Federal District police chiefs be summarily dismissed, that the grenadier unit be disbanded, that all political prisoners be freed, and that Article 145 of the Penal Code be repealed.[30]

Luis Echeverría, secretary of Gobernación, sent an oblique reply to the 20 August teach-in two days later, indicating the government's willingness to receive a committee of students to present their complaints and "exchange views . . . with the object of definitely solving . . . the conflict." [31] The statement expressed a long-standing rule that the Executive Branch does not negotiate with protesters; it may choose to listen to them, but it retains absolute autonomy in the decision-making process. On the same date, the regent of the Federal District promised an exhaustive investigation "to establish the truth about the disturbances."

For several days excited groups of students discussed these statements and tried to decipher their implications. On one thing they agreed: any encounter with government officials must be witnessed by as many people as possible. They were not going to repeat the innumerable cozy little chats behind closed doors from which the striking doctors of 1965 had emerged with the impression that at last the government was going to take decisive action, only to be disillusioned time after time. No: the students wanted all Mexico to know exactly what was said by both parties. But how to achieve this objective? They agreed to demand that the promised meeting be broadcast live by radio and television, and that a full complement of newspaper reporters and magazine writers be present to take notes. The students' choice of time and place for the "dialogue" was announced during the gigantic demonstration of 27 August; they proposed that it be in the Zócalo at 10 A.M. *on 1 September!* The choice produced maximum consternation; on that date and at that hour, the custom of every president during the past thirty years had been to leave the presidential palace, drive to the seat of congress, and present his annual state of the nation address to a joint session of senators and deputies.[32]

Whether the proposal had been presented as an elaborate joke is not known. Whatever its motives, the student leaders retracted the proposal on 30 August and urged all students to avoid clashes with the police and the army. Perhaps they were momentarily intimidated by the threatening atmosphere which was now being translated into overt acts. The day before had seen the beginning of terrorist attacks on schools in the city. On the thirtieth itself, the UNAM campus was surrounded by army tanks and police began large-scale arrests of students who ventured off the campus. Many of them were arrested at factories, where brigades were haranguing the workers to join a united student-labor front.

Who had been speaking for that vast amorphous body known as "the students" and by what right did they do so? Given the populist sympathies of many of the participants, it might have been anticipated that a kind of marathon mass meeting would discuss each proposal until a Rousseauan "will of all" was achieved—an exhausting, if not impossible, procedure, given the number of people involved. Actually, the student leaders quickly worked out an organizational structure which avoided the frustrating stalemate the doctors experienced in 1965.

The essential feature of the 1968 structure was the Consejo Nacional de Huelga (The National Strike Council, hereafter referred to as the CNH), a body consisting of a representative from each of about 150 schools, including the UNAM, the Polytechnic Institute, the National Agricultural School at Chapingo, the Colegio de México (a private university of international prestige), the Normal School, the National Music Conservatory, the National Institute of Fine Arts, the National School of Anthropology and History, the few existing private universities and high schools, the "prepas" and the "vocas," the Industrial Workers' Training Centers, and the state universities. Each institution was empowered to send a voting delegate to meetings of the CNH; these delegates were chosen by the "combat committees" which had been formed in the institutions and which consisted in all except the largest institutions of two or three members. Together, all of the members of the combat committees, numbering about 600, formed the Coordinating Committee as a check on the power of the CNH.[33]

Even from this brief description, it is clear that neither the CNH nor the Coordinating Committee represented the full range of student opinion on any of the campuses. The word "strike" in the Council's name reflected the members' orientation so that those persons who were opposed to the use of strike tactics could stay away from the meetings. Representatives from the more militant *facultades* (for example, law, philosophy and literature, medicine) had more influence on the outcome of the deliberations than those from less enthusiastic units, mainly because participants knew that they would have to rely heavily on those combat committees for implementing decisions.

The CNH attained its organizational structure on 8 August, less than two weeks after the initial incident had given rise to protest activity. The Council's formal debut was marked by announcing six demands for ending the strike. These demands, the platform on which all future strike activities were supposedly based, were: "Freeing of all political prisoners; repeal of Article 145 of the Federal Penal Code; abolition of the 'grenadier' corps; dismissal of police chiefs Luis Cueto, Raúl Mendiolea, and A. Frías; indemnization for the families of all those killed or wounded since the beginning of the conflict; and clarification of the roles played by the officials guilty of perpetrating the bloody deeds."[34]

While the first three demands had been the topic of impassioned student discussions for several years, the last three were specifically related to the recent incidents. All six demands reflected the conviction of many students and intellectuals that since the end of Lázaro Cárdenas's presidency in 1940, a tacit antipopulist bias had been increasingly evident in the repressive measures adopted by the government. These were the demands that the CNH wanted to make the subject of a "dialogue" with government representatives. The railroad men had discussed their demands with company officials and the doctors had obtained two audiences with the president, but the student leaders wanted much more than this. They intended to press for a public airing of the discrepancy between the regime's rhetoric about its revolutionary aims and what the students saw as increasing unresponsiveness to popular aspirations. The complaints that fostered the six demands were thus symbolic to the students of the growing repressiveness of Mexico's elite, determined to exclude the masses from any share in formulating national goals. Some student speakers left little doubt that they favored a reallocation of available economic resources in the direction of a wider share for the lower classes. On campus, many of them talked with varying degrees of sophistication about socialism. But the most characteristic formulation of the CNH's main goal, reflected in endless discussions, can be described as populism. For this reason, they decided to concentrate on the demand for a public dialogue, to show that they rejected the behind-the-scenes maneuvering which had traditionally characterized Mexican political activity.

One of the CNH members expressed the students' orientation in these words:

> We insist on the principle that all discussion must be public. All of the sectors which have a stake in the dialogue should be aware of all the arguments. . . . We want to end the corrupt practice of smoke-filled rooms or little groups, where the give and take excludes the masses from any participation. We know that our six point petition does not signify an essential change in society. But the Movement that presents it has an objective . . . to give to the people

confidence in their own strength. We are not so much interested in convincing the people that things are bad as we are [in convincing them] that correcting the evils depends on popular participation.[35]

For nearly forty years Mexico's post-Revolutionary leaders had been building a political system that would deflect the pressures of mass participation; the decision makers of 1968 were not anxious to scrap this achievement. If any of them had been so naïve as to ignore the social and economic consequences of the proposed changes, they did not lack articulate observers to disabuse them of their illusory security. One of the clearest warnings was this:

If the government accepts the [public] dialogue, it will have to initiate a new political style and change the ways of governing which have prevailed in this country since the era of [Plutarco Elías] Calles, which presupposes for the government a series of risks concerning the control of governmental organizations and the apparatus of power, including the PRI, the Confederación de Trabajadores Mexicanos, and the Confederación Nacional de Campesinos [i.e., the labor and the peasant sectors of the Party]. The apparatus would have to readjust very seriously for a political struggle in which the importance of other political parties and mass organizations and unions would be increased. In addition, to accept the dialogue . . . would . . . encourage other movements and popular demands, not only for democratization but also for social justice . . . [including] expansion of the internal market, supply and demand of goods and services, of employment and, finally, a much more stable development and a relatively long term capitalization.[36]

After the flurry caused by the ambiguous overture to the students on 22 August by the secretary of Gobernación, the nation awaited the president's 1 September speech, knowing that they could expect a statement concerning the government's future course of action toward the strikers. If there was a special aura of urgency surrounding the president's pronouncement, it was undoubtedly due to the pressure of time. In less than six weeks, Mexico would host more than 100 countries during the nineteenth Olympiad.

Crews had been working around the clock to finish preparations for the 12 October opening. It was the first time that the Olympic games would be held in Latin America and the first time, too, in a country which was considered to still be in the process of achieving full economic development. In the Olympic Village, construction was continuing on competitor's dormitories, a Press Center, an International Club, and an Administration Building. To avoid traffic problems, magnificent buildings such as the Sports Palace, the Olympic swimming pool, the Velodrome, the firing range, a canoe and rowing canal, and several other facilities were scattered around the edge of the city. Young men and women with some knowledge of foreign languages were being trained as interpreters. Many of these were university students, and some of them participated in the strike.

As early as 1965, city planners had taken advantage of the great surge of national pride, which had been generated by the decision to hold the Olympiad in Mexico, to propose construction of a subway system to help solve the serious transportation problems that had almost paralyzed the citizenry. It was first thought that the marshy, sinking ground on which the city is built might prove an insuperable obstacle to the realization of this dream, but French engineers called into consultation pronounced the plan feasible. On the day the president was presenting his message, three shifts of hardhat workers were swarming around the project, racing against the calendar to have the first of three planned routes in operation by the time the main contingent of Olympic visitors started to arrive. Since the start of construction, a weekly newsmagazine had been reporting on its progress in a column titled *"El Metro, metro a metro"* (The Metro [subway], meter by meter).

By 1 September, the investment in projects related to the Olympiad had already passed the 100-million-dollar mark, with the end not yet in sight. Much of the construction could be used for other purposes after the Olympiad, and there were possibilities that some structures might even pay for themselves in the long run, by being converted into salable apartment buildings. It was apparent to everyone, however, that the gesture of national pride would severely drain Mexico's scarce resources for some time to come.

Student leaders spoke frequently about the paradoxical contrast between these heavy expenditures and the poverty in which most Mexicans dwelt. On repeated occasions, before large audiences, they insisted that the incumbent elite was spending too much for circuses and not enough for bread. They said the government should never have invited the Olympic Committee to hold the games in Mexico but, having committed the initial error, should have realized the magnitude of the commitment and retracted the invitation. While condemning Mexico's participation, the responsible student leaders—at least in public—reiterated that they did not advocate student action for the purpose of obstructing the celebration of the games. On the other hand, they saw no reason why they should not take advantage of the leverage provided by the situation to try to pressure the government into making concessions before the capital city would be flooded with foreign observers and athletes. Other student speakers, however, were impatient with this moderate stand and called for more militant action to prevent the Olympics. The attorney general was later to allege a conspiracy by the students to sabotage the games, and would point to those intemperate speeches as evidence of intent.

1 September: The public's expectations were not disappointed. More than one-third of the president's traditional state of the nation speech was devoted to the student protest. He left no doubt as to the conspiratorial nature of the student leadership and the government's firm intention to suppress illegal or subversive activities "with all the elements that the people have placed in our hands." [37] This was the authority, the attitude of intransigence, that Mexicans had expected of their president as the highest exponent of the *machismo* ideal.

And now the rationale behind the early campaign of denunciatory advertising and editorializing was unequivocally revealed. An informant interviewed for another case study had stated that "the government does not listen to demands from the public unless they are demands created and promoted by the government itself." Now the president seemed to confirm this observation as he proclaimed,

> Our confidence . . . is based . . . fundamentally on [the fact] that there will be such a widespread and indignant repudiation by millions of Mexicans that it will force those who thought of [obstructing the Olympiad] to reconsider, and it seems to us that under such circumstances a small group cannot achieve its objectives.

This was whistling into the wind; the demonstrations of 13 August and 27 August indicated that the students had already elicited, if not militant public support, at least an impressive show of sympathetic interest. If the claim were to be made that an alarmed citizenry demanded official intervention to suppress the students' activities, more evidence of such a demand was required. The president's statement was a frank appeal for a manifestation of that demand from all quarters. Company unions (*sindicatos blancos*), organized sectors of the party, apocryphal groups, government officials large and small, journalists on the government payroll, and countless others who depended directly or indirectly on the continued stability of the prevailing economic and social structure, were expected to wait no longer to join the denunciatory campaign against the allegedly subversive agitators.

A tone of reasonableness and willingness to compromise seemed to suffuse the chief executive's rhetoric. He chided the students for not having presented a single written document formulating any concrete demands, but after proclaiming, "I shall take the first step," he fell back on platitudes laced together with excerpts from earlier speeches such as those he had made during the doctors' strikes. Reaffirming that the government was willing to engage in a dialogue, he cautioned that such an exchange was impossible when each side was speaking a different language and "when one side insists on remaining deaf. . . ."

Far from being deaf, thousands of students were gathered around television sets or radios, straining their ears to catch a phrase or a sentence that would specify the government's conditions for meeting and talking with a student delegation. They waited in vain, as had the doctors on 1 September 1965. But the doctors, much fewer in number than the students, had comprehended the hopelessness of their situation and had capitulated. The president undoubtedly hoped that his speech would have the same effect in 1968. In the first days following the speech, the movement lost some adherents, the kind who for reasons of personal safety or other powerful motivations, could not afford to be caught on the losing side of the conflict. A group called the Coalition of Graduating Classes of Teachers of the Polytechnic Institute appealed to the students to cancel future demonstrations in order to provide a peaceful atmosphere for solving the conflict. On the other hand, the movement did not collapse, nor did a righteously indignant public turn against the students as the president had predicted.

Retreating somewhat from the high point of militancy that had been reached on 27 August, the CNH suggested, on 4 September, that the dialogue mentioned in the president's speech be held in the main auditorium of the National Medical Center. The auditorium, with a seating capacity of 2,145, is an ultramodern facility which has housed many international scientific meetings since its opening in 1963. Reducing their demands for guarantees of good faith, the CNH insisted on only two conditions: that the dialogue be public, and that student repression cease.

Although the president had announced that he would take the first step, that step was not taken; instead, government spokesmen, from highest to lowest, lapsed into the same sort of sinister silence that had prevailed during a crucial period of the doctors' strikes. In the case of the doctors, the freeze had set in fifty-three days after the first outbreak of protest; there were only thirty-seven days between the first student demonstration and the stoppage of communication. CNH leaders were quick to sense the significance of the silence. At a meeting on 7 September, attended by about 25,000 people, speakers announced that if satisfactory progress were not made by the Olympiad, the students would make sure that foreign visitors were fully informed about the conflict.

The setting of this meeting has special significance, as it will acquire added prominence during the rest of our chronicle. We have already caught a glimpse of the Nonoalco-Tlatelolco housing project when it was invaded by antistudent terrorists on 29 August, but it is time to take a closer look at the area. Hereafter, the housing project will be referred to by its short name, Tlatelolco, as it is more generally called by Mexicans.

The multistoried apartment complex had originally been planned to provide low-cost housing for working class families. By the date of its opening, these plans had been changed and the majority of the tenants were middle class: government employees, teachers, and other professionals of moderate incomes. Stretching over a mile from east to west, the area is occupied by buildings named for the various states of the Republic which, in addition to the apartments, contain convenient shopping facilities.

Tucked into the southeast corner of the area is the Plaza of Three Cultures, so called because the three major epochs of Mexican history are represented by authentic original structures. The apartment buildings on two sides are the modern manifestation, while the restored sixteenth-century church of Santiago Tlatelolco represents the colonial epoch. Legend has it that the peasant Juan Diego was a neophyte of this church when the Virgin of Guadalupe, later the patron saint of Mexico and of all Latin America, appeared to him in a vision in 1531. The earliest cultural epoch, that of pre-Columbian Mexico, is evident in the restored remains of a massive stone structure originally built by the Aztecs. Because of this historic juncture, the plaza is visited by thousands of tourists each year.

The president had called for a massive popular repudiation of the student movement, but all he got in response to the meeting in the Plaza of Three Cultures was a counterdemonstration on 8 September made up of MURO militants, boy scouts, and some peasants.

Although the student movement was centered in the Federal District, like almost every important political manifestation since the Revolution, the students were well organized and active in a number of other places. The government prosecutor later cited this fact as proof of a widespread conspiracy against the constitutional order. That left little choice for the protesters: either remain small and powerless or organize and be accused of subversion. It is not in our province to ascertain whether, as the government later alleged, the movement was part of a revolutionary plot. It is difficult to arrive at such a conclusion from the reports of secret service agents on meetings which took place during the last week of August in Morelia, Oaxaca, Sinaloa, and Monterrey. These reports only indicate that the students were well organized in their support of the CNH.[38]

Nevertheless, on 10 September, the Mexican senate empowered the president to use the army, navy, and air force "in defense of the internal and external security of Mexico." As the president already had that power under the constitution and had used it many times, the gesture can probably best be interpreted as a warning to the students that a crackdown was imminent.

Eight days later the warning was translated into action when the army moved onto the UNAM campus. Working closely with police, they loaded 334 persons onto military vehicles and took them to the Preventive Jail for detention until charges could be verified or dismissed. The action was repeated on 24 September at the Poli campus where students, forewarned by events at the UNAM, put up a stiff fight against the police.

Even before the occupation of the two campuses, the focus of student activity had been shifting to another location. Tlatelolco, and particularly the Plaza of Three Cultures, had proved to be a convenient meeting place for both UNAM and Poli students. Only a mile north of the Alameda, it was easily accessible by bus. Although it was close to the Poli, its physical separation from both campuses helped to alleviate fears that students from either one of the institutions might be gaining control of the movement. The Plaza was an excellent open-air auditorium, and Vocational School No. 7, on the west side of it, was a good meeting place for smaller groups. As the month progressed, hardly a day passed without some student activity in or near the Plaza. Police surveillance increased accordingly, giving rise to an air of tension and slowly escalating hostility between the grenadiers, on the one hand, and the students, abetted by some apartment tenants, on the other.[39]

Coinciding with these events, an enormous barrage of publicity attacked the University, its rector, students of all ages, and any person who sympathized with the movement. The advertisements, news stories, editorials, and cartoons surpassed, both in volume and vehemence, any other campaign studied by this author. Still the "millions of Mexicans" referred to in the president's speech failed to rally to the government's support. The campaign of slander and increasing police pressure had some effects. The UNAM rector tendered his resignation, but it was rejected by the University Governing Board. The agriculture students at Chapingo, believing their cause to be lost, capitulated. The Teachers' Coalition, which had supported the movement, stood by helplessly as the police arrested some of its most prominent members on charges of being Communist agitators. Fear, discouragement, and suspicion began to take their toll among some of the adherents.

Many citizens were confused by what they read in the newspapers, saw on television, or heard over the radio, but student brigades—often only a few steps ahead of the police—were busy counteracting such influences by addressing groups on street corners and distributing news bulletins in heavily populated areas. Speakers at the "lightning meetings," as the students called them, stressed the allegation that nearly a hundred youths had already been killed by the police, and that the invasion of the campuses violated university autonomy. The first charge was never substantiated or denied. Luis Echeverría, the secretary of Gobernación, replied indirectly to the second charge by announcing that the troops would be withdrawn whenever the educational authorities requested such action.

During September, an undetermined number of students had been killed by the police.[40] On the last day of the month, the troops were withdrawn. Now, with twelve days remaining before the start of the Olympiad, with foreign athletes, tourists, and journalists pouring off every arriving plane and crowding into the capital, the stage was set for one of the bloodiest dramas of Mexico's dark history.

October: As the month began, observers searching for clues on which to base predictions were confused by apparently contradictory signals emanating from official sources. On one hand, the president had finally appointed a committee to meet with CNH representatives for a preliminary discussion. On 1 October, administrative employees of the UNAM went back to work, but troops still occupied the Poli campus.

Echeverría emerged from a meeting with the president on the morning of 2 October and stated to the press, "I think that . . . something more than . . . a truce is in sight, that is, a path toward the solution of the problems." [41] But that afternoon, three prominent members of the CNH were taken into custody by the police. What emerges from an examination of the available sources is an impression that no clear decision had been made as to how the regime would proceed; no unequivocal directive had emerged from the president or from his nearest advisers. "According to some sources," comments an observer, there was a debate within the government "over the issue of how to respond to the student challenge." [42]

More than two months had passed since the outbreak of protest; an unprecedented attack by the mass media had pictured the student leadership as violent revolutionaries, trained and financed by the Cuban and Russian governments. If the Mexican secret service had been able to gather any convincing evidence to substantiate such accusations, it would seem to have been sufficient to end the controversy within the ranks of those who contributed to the formulation of policy. The continued indecision of the president may be interpreted as a sign that no such evidence had been obtained. The situation begged for an authoritative indication of guidelines, but none was forthcoming. The Olympics were scheduled to begin; events were creating their own pressure. The failure of the upper-echelon decision makers to agree on a course of action left the lower-level implementers of policy in a potentially disastrous position, in which there were too many panic buttons within reach of too many fingers. It was a good illustration of the observation that "not to decide is to make a decision." Everyone agreed that the situation must be resolved before 12 October, but *how* to resolve it was the troublesome question.

On one thing even some of the severest critics of the regime are agreed: what happened next resulted partly from the confusion just described.

The New Sad Night

In the history of the conquest of Mexico, the night of 30 June 1520, is known as *la noche triste* to commemorate the massacre of Hernán Cortés's troops as they retreated from the Aztec capital of Tenochtitlán. The story of that night is highlighted by details vividly recalled by witnesses of the events of 1968, and which inspired some observers to refer to 2 October of that year as *la nueva noche triste.* On the earlier date, Cortés and his men found themselves in a cul-de-sac, overwhelmingly outnumbered by Montezuma's heavily armed warriors. Trying to force their way out of the city, the Spaniards were caught in a deluge of arrows; many were killed, others were captured and later offered as sacrifices to the Aztec gods. The decimated survivors straggled to safety, later to return with reinforcements to complete the conquest so inauspiciously initiated.

Despite the confusion at the beginning of the month, there was no indication that the gathering scheduled for 5:30 of the afternoon of 2 October in the Plaza of Three Cultures would be markedly different from the dozens of other meetings held since 26 July. The tenants of Tlatelolco were accustomed to seeing the students, often amused by the bombast of the speakers, and occasionally annoyed by the noise of the loudspeakers. Still, the event occurred at a slack time, when housewives had finished tidying their kitchens after the heaviest meal of the day (the *comida,* or dinner, usually served between 2 and 4 P.M. The *cena,* or supper, would not be served until 8–9 P.M.). The spectacle the students offered might prove an antidote to the afternoon doldrums. Children returning home from school loitered at the edge of the crowd, estimated at between five and ten thousand people. Mingling with the spectators were members of the elite army battalion known as the Batallón Olimpia, created to perform special duties during the Olympics. These individuals were dressed as civilians but wore white gloves on their left hands for identification. A cordon of police surrounded the area.[43]

The orators, accompanied by local journalists and foreign correspondents, took their places on the third-floor balcony of the Chihuahua apartment building. It had been rumored that some of the speakers would urge the crowd to march to the Poli campus to dislodge the army unit that occupied the grounds, but this did not materialize. Instead, the speeches were quite tame, consisting mainly of warmed-over rhetoric from previous meetings: denunciations of the regime, exhortations to the students to continue their strike, reading of messages from sympathizers, and pleas for nonviolence.[44] While the orators declaimed and gesticulated, army vehicles filled with helmeted and bayonet-bearing soldiers began to fill the surrounding streets. A helicopter passed lazily back and forth above the plaza.

What happened next is difficult to determine, because of conflicting reports offered by eyewitnesses. According to some, they saw a green light, like that of a roman candle, flash from the helicopter, followed almost immediately by the roar of gunfire at the ground level.[45] Others insist that at a signal from the white-gloved men, the army closed in, in a pincer movement, firing as they advanced.[46] The secretary of defense, General Marcelino García Barragán, explained the next day that the army had responded to a call for help from the police "when shooting broke out among the students," but this was denied by the police chief, who stated that the police had merely *informed* the army about their activities and the army made the decision to intervene.[47] The military press release also mentioned rooftop snipers, but in such an ambiguous way that this possibility was not pursued in subsequent dispatches. The responsibility for firing the first shot was never determined, but a number of foreign correspondents who were present have either categorically denied that the students took the initiative or have affirmed emphatically that the military fired first.[48]

From the welter of accusations and denials which raged for months after the event, it seems probable that some students had guns and used them at some time during the confused action of that night. But no attempt was made to separate the noncombatants, who were the overwhelming majority of those present, and to isolate possible foci of resistance. The orders received by the military officers at Tlatelolco that day will probably remain unknown. It seems apparent, however, that the orders did not provide for the protection of the spectators.

When the gunfire broke out, panic swept the crowd, as people tried to flee in all directions. At their backs stood the old church of Santiago Tlatelolco; facing them was the Chihuahua building, while to the right and left the troops were firing directly at them. Like the followers of Cortés, they were in a cul-de-sac. Witnesses have described the wavelike movement of the crowd. Apparently, they fled first toward one side of the plaza, trying to escape the bullets coming from the other side; as they were met by fresh bursts of fire, they retreated in the opposite direction. Those who tried to take refuge in the Chihuahua building found the entrances blocked by soldiers. Those who sought sanctuary in the church found it locked and dark.[49]

Heavy fire continued for about an hour, and burst out intermittently thereafter until past midnight, with the soldiers aiming at anyone who moved. Actions of the several participating armed units were uncoordinated and, once the shooting started, out of control. Gunfire by members of one unit was met by fire from another, possibly in the belief that they were being attacked. Two soldiers were killed in the cross fire. Witnesses reported that at intervals they could hear shouts of "Olimpia Batallón here. Stop shooting! Cease fire! Who has a walkie-talkie? Somebody find a walkie-talkie!" Later, police began rounding up all boys and men who appeared to be of student age, herding them into trucks to take them to jail. Some students took the precaution of chewing up their identification cards and swallowing them. One tried unsuccessfully to masquerade as a Chilean newspaper reporter, on hand for the Olympics. Platoons of soldiers accompanied police in an apartment-by-apartment search of the Chihuahua building and other nearby buildings, rounding up all the student-age males and females they discovered.

The Plaza itself presented a nightmare spectacle of uncounted dead and wounded, of lost shoes, torn clothing, and abandoned placards on the bloodstained pavement. For several hours, Red Cross and Green Cross stretcher bearers had been prevented from carrying out their work by the heavy firing, but about 11 P.M. they began to remove the wounded to the emergency clinics, where police detachments had been stationed since 9 P.M. to prevent the entry of people who were searching for missing family members. While it is true that this measure was necessary in order to enable the doctors to carry out their work, it also effectively barred inquirers from accumulating statistics on the number of victims. Bodies of those already dead were taken to police station morgues. Autopsy reports appearing in the press during the first few days after the event attributed a number of deaths to bayonet wounds.

At least 2,000 persons were arrested and confined in three locations: the Santa Marta Acatitla penitentiary, the Preventive Jail, and Military Camp No. 1, on the western outskirts of the city. Mass arrests had made their debut as a feature of Mexican law enforcement during the railroad strikes of 1958–1959. As the police stations and jails were not big enough to accommodate a large number of prisoners, the practice had been adopted of housing some of them in military camps located in or near the major cities.

Arrested persons are held incommunicado until they are photographed, fingerprinted, and often questioned before they are booked. The Mexican constitution places a 72-hour limit on this initial detention period, but the time is counted from the moment that the police acknowledge that they have a named individual in custody. For this reason, they are often reluctant to acknowledge the identity of detained persons. After Tlatelolco, some people remained in jail for ten days or more before they were booked. During that time, they were invisible, that is, their names did not appear on the official lists.

These conditions added to the anguish of families who tried to locate missing members. About 4 A.M., after the shooting had definitely stopped, the procession of searching relatives began: from the Balbuena first aid station to the Red Cross, to the Green Cross, to the Rubén Leñero hospital, to Precinct Station No. 3, to Precinct Station No. 9, to Military Camp No. 1, to the Preventive Jail, to Santa Marta

Acatitla, and back again to the beginning; asking, waiting, exchanging scraps of information with other searchers. Those whose pilgrimage was the shortest were the ones whose search ended in the morgue. Many returned home without knowing if the missing persons were dead or alive, arrested, or in hiding. Some of them never obtained definite information.

For these reasons, it is impossible to cite with confidence any figures on the number of people who were killed at Tlatelolco or who later died as a result of wounds. Photographers who had tried to photograph the bodies at the Plaza were prevented by soldiers from doing so. A soldier smashed one photographer's camera and another soldier wounded his hand with a bayonet as he tried to rescue the camera.[50] Because the tight security around the prisons and hospitals prevented reporters and others from making independent death counts, the published figures were received with skepticism which was fed by ugly rumors. Understandably enough, newspaper headlines of 3 October gave confused and sometimes contradictory accounts of the casualties. A survey of the major Mexico City daily papers on that first day shows that the lowest number of deaths reported was 20, while other stories gave figures ranging up to 29. In the next few days, the figure was revised upward to 49; after that, newspaper coverage dwindled and disappeared, as stories about the Olympic games occupied most of the space. The officially acknowledged toll has remained at 49, but the *New York Times* correspondent estimated that 200 would be a more accurate figure.[51]

Epilogue

The trick of consciousness which transforms those facts that seem intolerable into a nightmare that is later forgotten, is an act which we commit naturally, precisely because of the intolerable nature of the facts. Those who participated in and those who were victims of what has come to be called 'the events of '68', have been saved from [the] fate . . . of having perished . . . in events which were *not* recorded in history. . . . Things have changed since the night of Tlatelolco.[52]

Whatever changes had occurred or might later take place were not yet apparent to the thousands of tourists who attended the Olympic games in Mexico City. The "night of Tlatelolco," the "new sad night," marked the end of student demonstrations. The following day, the Mexican Senate officially applauded the police and military intervention, calling it constitutionally valid and practically justified in order to "protect not only the life and tranquility of the citizens but also . . . the integrity of the nation's institutions." [52] The next day, the Chamber of Deputies followed suit by condemning the events which had occurred since July 26 as "a subversive action . . . perpetrated by foreign elements." [53] Minority deputies from the Partido de Acción Nacional and the Partido Popular Socialista voted against this resolution.

To support the contention that the demonstrations were part of a conspiracy to destroy the government, the police on 5 October announced that Socrates Amado Campos Lemus, one of the student leaders, had confessed to complicity and had implicated a number of prominent intellectuals and political figures who, he alleged, had given financial aid and encouragement to the movement. Among those named were Carlos Madrazo (the ousted former head of the PRI), Braulio Maldonado, Humberto Romero, Elena Garro (former wife of the poet Octavio Paz), and Víctor Urquidi. All of these people immediately denied the accusation.

News about the events of 2 October soon reached around the world. Octavio Paz, who had been serving as Mexico's ambassador to India, submitted his resignation, stating that under such circumstances he was no longer willing to continue in his post. In accepting his resignation, the secretary of foreign relations expressed disappointment that Paz had criticized his government without waiting to receive an official version of the events.

The Olympic games were a great success, attracting many favorable comments in the world press, especially with regard to the Mexican government's efficient handling of the logistic problems involved in housing, feeding, transporting, and entertaining the thousands of athletes and spectators.

On 29 October, the troops were pulled out of the Polytechnic Institute campus, and it was announced that classes would begin again in all educational institutions on 4 November. But on that date the reconstituted student leadership (replacing the CNH original members, most of whom were in jail) announced that the strike would continue until such time as the six points raised in the original petition were satisfactorily resolved. That time never came. Finally—if such a word can be used in this context—on 4 December the CNH declared the end of the strike and announced its own dissolution, calling on students to ally themselves whenever possible with workers and peasants in a continued effort to force the regime to become more democratic.

Three months after "the new sad night," a road company of the American musical comedy *Hair* arrived in Acapulco for what was advertised as a short engagement. The opening night crowd consisted of well-known figures from Mexican political, social, and entertainment circles, whose photographs filled the next day's newspapers in Mexico City.

At sixteen dollars for each ticket, it was unlikely that many students were present.

It was indeed a short engagement. The government closed the show after its initial performance and deported the actors. The official explanation was that the obscene language was an offense to Mexican decency. A member of the audience recalls that in the scene where the cast came on stage carrying picket signs, one of those signs bore the legend, "Remember October 2."

The Life and Death of Protest Movements

7

Epilogue

It has been thrilling, and at the same time moving to observe this group of young people struggle in so many different ways to avoid suffering, to affirm themselves, and to try to achieve something authentically positive in life, and yet wasting so much energy in pursuing mistaken paths. . . .[1]

These lines were written in 1967 by a team of psychologists who had carried out a five-year study of 100 members of the 1956 freshman class of the Medical School of the National Autonomous University of Mexico. The authors had undertaken their study hoping that their findings would determine whether there is a constellation of personality characteristics which can serve as a guide for predicting future professional achievements of medical students. While we might disagree with the adjective "mistaken," the above quote is of particular interest to us because the class of 1956 produced many of the young physicians who were active in the doctors' strikes of 1964–1965, including some of the leaders of AMMRI.

When I returned to Mexico in 1968 one of my objectives was to try to find out, not what the professional achievements of the physicians had been, but what, if any, the political and economic achievements of the doctors' strikes had been. I therefore intended to reinterview some of my 1965 informants, as well as to pursue the research along other lines.

The first name on the reinterview list was a physician who had been a tireless worker at Alianza headquarters during the strikes. As a letter asking him for an appointment had not been answered, it became necessary for me to try to locate him after I arrived in Mexico City. Not surprisingly, his name was not listed in the telephone book. Nor was he at the address to which my letter had been sent. Although, to my positive knowledge, the man had lived at that address only two years before, neighbors answered inquiries about him with *"No lo conozco. No sé nada."* ("I don't know him. I don't know anything.") Again, this was not surprising; a stranger in the neighborhood, inquiring about a man who had been involved in "the matter of the doctors" could be a secret service investigator or even a CIA agent. During my last interview with him in 1966, the informant had revealed that he and some of his companions had had grave suspicions about my motives in studying their organization and their movements.

A storekeeper in his old neighborhood finally remembered that a doctor of that name had lived nearby. The name and address of a relative were provided, and the search was transferred to a district on the other side of the huge city. But the doctor was not there; his relative explained that he no longer lived in Mexico. Blacklisted for his part in the strikes, he had been dismissed from his post in a government hospital and, in spite of the chronic doctor shortage, had been refused employment by all government health agencies. Unable to obtain telephone service, having no savings to support himself and his wife while trying to establish a private practice, the only courses of action open to him were abandonment of his profession and emigration. Faced with these alternatives, he accepted a residency from a foreign hospital, which paid his plane fare.

The hospitals of Canada, England, and the United States, to name only three outstanding examples, experienced an acute shortage of professional personnel during the 1960s. Figuring among the efforts to solve this problem was a widespread campaign to recruit physicians from underdeveloped countries in order to repopulate institutional staffs. Although these physicians were usually designated as residents, their duties were often identical with those of house staff doctors, and they received little or none of the on-the-job training which is associated with residency. It was precisely this lack of a teaching program in Mexican hospitals which had been the subject of one of the complaints during the doctors' strikes. Some of the blacklisted Mexican physicians who were able to pass the minimum language and professional requirements availed themselves of the opportunity to wait out the difficult period in a foreign country. They were counting on the 1970 presidential elections to bring about a more permissive atmosphere. It has been noted elsewhere that a distinguishing feature of Mexican political calculations is the hope that the high turnover of government officials accompanying the installation of a new president will favor the aspirations of the presently disadvantaged. "Just wait; it will be our turn at bat in the next *sexenio* (six-year term of office)," is a familiar statement. The election in 1970 of Luis Echeverría as president of Mexico was not encouraging, however. During the doctors' strikes, Echeverría had been secretary of Gobernación, the ministry in charge of internal intelligence operations for the whole Republic. It was his secret service men who had shadowed the strike leaders.

Another of the original informants, whose nationalistic pride had once prompted him to boast of his monolingualism, was less fortunate than the émigrés. Also blacklisted, he made a living by peddling encyclopedias and textbooks, which at least enabled him to maintain some contacts with other professionals. His hopes for the future were based not on the presidential elections but on structural changes which he believed would be brought about by growing pressures from protest groups.

In the struggle for survival, the most disadvantaged

physicians were those whose limited resources restricted their options. More fortunate were the men who had obtained advanced training. One doctor, a specialist in an important field of medicine, had been chief of service in a government hospital for several years. Discharged peremptorily, he was able to expand the private practice which he had formerly carried on as a sideline. Although he missed the wealth of clinical material which had been available to him, he found himself in a more comfortable financial situation. During the reinterview, when asked what he would do if given the opportunity, he responded immediately that he would abandon his private practice in order to return to his government hospital position.

When a government health service had urgent need of the special skills possessed by one of the strike organizers, ways were sometimes found to retain his services. A specialist who had been very active in the Alianza was demoted from his post in a well-equipped hospital and assigned to an outpatient clinic in an outlying neighborhood, where he carried on his work (at much less pay) through the cumbersome process of referring the patients to the main hospital, miles away across the city, for all laboratory tests.

Even though they lost their jobs and could not get other professional employment in any of the government health agencies, some doctors continued to live in low-rent government housing projects. Others were reinstated, after periods of six to eighteen months, in positions comparable to those they had held before the strikes. But the mass petition for a writ of *amparo* as a first-step to mass reinstatement, signed by nearly 200 doctors, was denied by the courts.[2]

Some doctors seemed not to have suffered at all as a result of their connection with the strikes. An older man—

regarded by some physicians as almost the patron saint of their movement—had counseled the strikers and had attended many of their meetings during the first stage of activities, but had refused to accept an office in the Alianza and did not join the walkout from his hospital. He remained at his post as head of one of the clinical services throughout the strikes, and retains that position at the present time.

Another doctor, about forty-five years of age, who had given encouragement to the strikers, suddenly left Mexico several weeks before the final strike and returned a month after the president's state of the nation speech, when hospitals had resumed normal activities. In my interview with him, he first explained that he had gone to Europe because government agents had advised him to leave the country. Later, in the same interview, he said that he had won a large amount of money in the national lottery, enabling him to take the extended trip. When he agreed to a follow-up interview in 1968, he was living in a luxuriously appointed house in a fashionable district of Mexico City. At that time he said he was writing a book about the doctors' strikes and would appreciate reading my notes on the subject; he did not reciprocate by showing me his material.

A curious facet of behavior in some Mexican communities, as reported by an anthropologist, may throw some light on the doctor's explanation of his sudden affluence. Where chronic economic deprivation is the rule, it is assumed that economic status is a zero sum game, that is, that enrichment of one individual can only take place at the cost of further impoverishing other individuals. A man who has been able to amass more wealth than his neighbors often hides this fact, for fear of arousing envy or suspicion. If he wants to improve his standard of living, he may safely do so only if he explains that his new wealth comes from a source *outside* the community and therefore represents no threat to his neighbors. Stories reported by the anthropologist centering on the discovery of buried treasure, or the cheating of a wealthy American tourist, seem to satisfy people's curiosity and allay suspicion.[3] The inclusion of a lottery story in this category was suggested by the anthropologist in a personal conversation.

A few of the most active strike leaders were later arrested and convicted on charges apparently unrelated to the physicians' movement. The most widely publicized case of this nature included the detention of doctors Rolf Mainers Huebner, Yolanda Ortiz, Miguel Cruz Ruiz, and Gilberto Balam Pereira, together with forty-two others allegedly involved in a plot to overthrow the government.[4] The chronology of the case may be relevant: On Monday, 6 September 1965, the fourth and last of the physicians' strikes came to an end; on Wednesday, 17 August 1966, police in various sections of Mexico City took forty-six individuals into custody for arraignment and interrogation. Twenty-six secret service agents presented the evidence against them. A newspaper columnist commented at that time, "Surely in the annals of Mexican criminal investigation there exists no other case of an inquiry which has been carried on night and day for ten months in such a secret and careful manner. . . . The three [men] physicians figured prominently, it is repeated, among the agitators of the medical conflict in 1965."[5]

The young woman physician was soon released, together with a number of other individuals, but the three male physicians as well as twelve others were denied the writ of *amparo* and held in jail until their conviction, sixteen months later, of the crimes of incitement to rebellion, conspiracy, and illicit stockpiling of weapons.[6] They were given long jail terms.

These sample case histories demonstrate that the hand of reprisal did not fall with equal weight on all the doctors. The unequal treatment may have been the result of lack of coordination between different government agencies, or it may have been caused by neat discriminations among doctors whose degree of participation in the conflict had varied widely.

Varieties of Activism

On the basis of available information, a number of characteristics of various groups of doctors can be observed. First, there appears to be a correlation between age and militancy. The most intransigent strikers, those who held out for continued application of a hard line, were fifth-year medical students, interns, and first-year residents. This group provided the numerical strength and unity for dominating the balloting at meetings held during the strikes.

Most of the dependable organizational workers were in the group of physicians from thirty to forty-five years old. They tended to be less sure of their policy preferences, more fearful of the future, and more conciliatory toward the government than their younger colleagues.

The oldest group included doctors from forty-five to sixty-five. Numerically, this was the smallest of the protest groups, and presents no clear-cut characteristics. A considerable number, in spite of their age, could be classified as dependable workers, cautious as compared to the most militant sector, but willing to identify with the movement to the extent of risking their own professional futures in order to help achieve limited objectives.

Probably some of the apparent militants, organizers, and sympathizers were playing dual roles. Again, evidence is insufficient to warrant firm conclusions, but circumstances indicate that some older men were useful as government informers, while some very young physicians, circulating freely at large meetings, were more successful as agents provocateurs.

Many of the newer government hospital buildings contain large, well-furnished auditoriums to house lectures and meetings of the institution's professional personnel. During the initial stages of the strike movement, in late 1964 and early 1965, protest meetings held in these facilities had resulted in the organization of the AMMRI and the Alianza. The most significant landmark of this kind was the auditorium of the Veinte de Noviembre Hospital, where, it will be recalled, the first sit-in took place the night of 26 November 1964. On 20 July 1968, the hall presented a changed aspect to the visitor. Access to the area, by means of two stairways, was now barred by large iron gates secured by padlocks. Doctors were no longer allowed to enter the area unless by express invitation of the administration. Permission to hold meetings had been granted to government-approved doctors' unions, but a request by a group of interns and residents for use of the hall to show recreational films to personnel on standby duty was refused. The hospital director, in denying the request, told the *cine* club's representatives that he feared the group might seize such an opportunity for other purposes. A check of several other government hospitals confirmed that similar restrictions had been placed on use of the facilities.

One last effort to find some sign of the continued existence of the AMMRI or the Alianza took the visitor back to the old Medical School building, on the Plaza Santo Domingo in the center of the city. Entrance was difficult because of the heap of construction materials lying just inside the door leading to the large courtyard. There, a plaque erected by the class of 1954—the last class of doctors to graduate from this location[7]—detailed the history of the building, which had been originally constructed as headquarters for the Spanish Inquisition in the seventeenth century. On one side of the court, the door leading to the former offices of the Alianza was now sealed off by concrete blocks and further obscured by sacks of cement piled five feet high. The doors to the auditorium—where, on 26 November 1965, a dismal little group of survivors had commemorated the first anniversary of the strike movement—were closed, but through them could be heard a chamber music group rehearsing. The concierge was a new man who denied any knowledge of the Alianza or its possible new location.

The Price of Progress

"The organization of doctors is smashed. It will be many years before they will attempt to reorganize. The attempt to establish a dialogue between the physicians and the government has been truncated." This was the way one informant evaluated the situation.[8]

Were there no positive results of the 1964–1965 activities?

Yes; in particular, the staff doctors at the Salubridad hospitals received a raise of from 700 pesos to 2,500 pesos per month. ISSSTE physicians' salaries rose approximately 150 per cent, and IMSS doctors who had refused to join the strikers, were rewarded between January and July 1965 by raises amounting to about 200 per cent as well as increased fringe benefits. These raises were made effective in at least some of the government hospitals outside of Mexico City. No reclassification of doctors was ever carried out, however, so it is not known how many physicians, listed on the payrolls in non-professional categories, failed to benefit from the new salary scales.[9]

A comment made by one of Mexico's foremost social scientists seems to accurately summarize the situation:

When mass movements arise . . . (like the railroad strike of 1959, the more recent movements of teachers, doctors, students, et cetera) which by virtue of their own dynamics break out of the narrow framework of [government] control, then the first preoccupation of the corresponding authorities is to break up the movement as such, in the name of the 'principle of authority,' even though later they may in large part grant the demands formulated by the movement. In these cases, the most important thing is that it should not appear that an autonomous mass movement can achieve success outside of the consecrated system. Bargaining may not be open or public.[10]

Another informant, reinterviewed in 1968, took the inquirer on a visit to the handsome new building which had been erected in late 1965 on the grounds of the health department's General Hospital to house residents and interns. Asked whether gains like this had been worth the sacrifices, he shrugged. "Somebody has to pay for progress," he commented. But he was an older physician whose fortunes had been very lightly touched by the events. Whether the men in jail, in exile, or in professional limbo would agree with him as to who should pay, and how much, is doubtful.

If the movement had produced no real heroes, neither had it produced any genuine martyrs. Even those who were jailed were not convicted on charges directly connected with the strikes. There was nothing concrete around which to mobilize antigovernment sentiment. The sour taste of frustration was all that remained; the movement had *malogrado* (miscarried) as had so many before it.

The strike movement was . . . the beginning of a political movement of great proportions, . . . to achieve the overthrow of the government of the Republic and later dictate a new constitution for Mexico. This involves a real conspiracy as part of a general plot to disrupt order and to make feasible the achievement of plans thought out and organized by a foreign country against Mexico and against all the countries of Latin America. . . .[11]

This summation of the prosecution's case, presented by the attorney general of the Republic, has all the classic accusations about subversion. It was released to the mass media at the time of Demetrio Vallejo's arrest in 1959 but was repeated with very little change at the 1970 trial of the student strike leaders.

More than two years after the "night of Tlatelolco," Judge Eduardo Ferrer McGregor sentenced sixty-eight persons found guilty of an assortment of crimes associated with the student movement, on counts such as incitement to riot, sedition, property damage, homicide, looting, illegal possession of arms, and attacks on agents of public authority. The sentences ranged from three to seventeen years in prison, with graduated fines. Included in the group receiving lightest punishment were three foreigners: a Puerto Rican, a North American, and a Chilean.

The prosecution had contended that the student activities were part of an elaborate worldwide conspiracy, conceived at meetings in Prague and Havana and put into operation by a corps of dedicated revolutionaries who had manipulated the unsuspecting Mexican masses to carry out the plan. To support this contention, thousands of documents were introduced in evidence, including reports by secret service agents on protest meetings which took place before and during the strikes, reports on events by eyewitnesses, confessions (that is, depositions dictated to stenographers by investigating officers and signed by imprisoned students), and excerpts from presidential speeches.

After examining the documents, the defense had moved for acquittal, alleging a number of flaws in the government's case. Most important of these flaws was the imputation of guilt by association; individuals had been found guilty of specific crimes (for example, homicide) simply because their presence (among hundreds or even thousands of others) at a particular time and place had been established by the prosecution. Other flaws were also alleged, such as the existence of numerous examples of contradictory accounts of events by different police agents, extraction of confessions by third-degree methods, and inclusion of a vast mass of hearsay and irrelevant testimony. It was alleged that all these flaws, and many others, had been overlooked by an obliging judge who was eager to produce the verdicts sought by the prosecution. (It should be noted that jury trial is not a feature of the Mexican legal system.)

By the summer of 1971, all but nineteen of the sixty-eight persons had been released from prison and placed on parole. Although many students saw the entire movement as having ended in failure, a few of the most optimistic pointed to two developments which they regarded as positive results of their struggle. The first of these was the concession of voting rights to eighteen-year-olds. This enlargement of the franchise did not correspond to any of the demands formulated by the students, nor, in view of the lack of choice offered to the electorate, did it hold out the possibility of any real change in political outcomes.

The repeal of the Law of Social Dissolution (Article 145) was a different matter, as this was one of the demands listed in the students' original six-point petition. The article had been criticized by civil libertarians since its passage in 1941 and since the first case was brought to court under its provisions in 1953.[12] The article under attack read, in its entirety:

> A prison term of from two to twelve years and a fine of from one thousand to ten thousand pesos [one hundred sixty dollars to eight hundred dollars] shall be applied to any foreigner or Mexican national who in speech or in writing, or by any other means, carries on political propaganda among foreigners or Mexican nationals, spreading ideas, programs, or forms of action of any foreign government which disturb the public order or affect the sovereignty of the Mexican State. Public order is disturbed when those acts specified in the previous paragraph tend to produce rebellion, sedition, riot, or mutiny.
>
> National sovereignty is affected when said acts may place in danger the territorial integrity of the republic, obstruct the functioning of its legitimate institutions, or propagate contempt on the part of Mexican nationals toward their civic duties.
>
> The same penalties shall be applied to any foreigner or Mexican national who by any means leads or incites one or more individuals to carry out acts of sabotage, subvert the institutional life of the country, or carry out acts of provocation for the purpose of disturbing the public order or peace as to the one who effects such acts. In the case where the same acts constitute other crimes, the sanctions prescribed for those crimes shall also be applied.
>
> Imprisonment for from ten to twenty years shall be applied to any foreigner or Mexican national who, in any way, carries out or morally prepares for invasion of the national territory or submission of the country to any foreign government.
>
> When the convicted person in the case of the previous paragraphs is a foreigner the penalties previously referred to shall be applied without prejudice to the faculty conceded to the President of the Republic by Article 33 of the Constitution.[13]

In 1969, the president of Mexico directed a legislative commission to hold hearings with respect to the possible elimination of the offending article. The Mexican congress formally repealed the article in July of 1970, but at the same time it amended the Penal Code in such a way as to include in new or already existing articles all of the crimes formerly described and sanctioned by Article 145. Moreover, the penalties for these and other crimes of subversion were increased.

After the first wave of euphoria caused by the repeal of this article, many thoughtful Mexicans realized that the congress's action did not significantly liberalize the existing legislation. The most notable and perhaps the only positive result of the change was the release of the railroad union leaders, Demetrio Vallejo and Valentín Campa, jailed for their participation in the 1958–1959 strikes. Their release was in accordance with Article 57 of the Penal Code which reads:

When the law removes from an act or omission the character of crime which had been given to it by a previous law . . . those prisoners who are serving or who are about to serve their sentence [under previous law] and, as of right, all effects which that law and sentences would have had for the future will also cease.

With respect to the sixty-eight students sentenced to jail in December of 1970, the fact that Article 145 had been repealed had no practical effect. They had not been prosecuted under Article 145; the crimes of which they had been convicted were all present in other parts of the federal criminal code.

"wasting so much energy in pursuing mistaken paths. . . ." This judgment, explicit in the quotation at the head of this chapter, haunted the veterans of all three protest movements studied here. Many of the most dedicated workers continued to ask themselves and each other, "Where did we go wrong? What mistakes did we make, and how could we have avoided them?"

Perhaps these are not the questions most likely to provide an understanding of the complex processes which constitute a political event in Mexico. They assume that there is a correct line of action which, if unfalteringly pursued, will lead triumphantly to achievement of all, or almost all, of a movement's goals. This point of view assumes that similar movements of the past failed only because of some avoidable misstep. In 1968, the organizers of the CNH believed they had discovered why the physicians had lost their struggle:

> The students did not allow themselves to become disconcerted. As of then, their demands began to assume concrete form in petitions [which were] conditioned by the necessity—in order not to be betrayed by ministerial secrets, as the still recent experience of the physicians' movement had demonstrated—that the dialogue should be public.[14]

But, as we have seen, there was no dialogue, either public or private. The students rejected private dialogue, and the regime rejected public discourse. Instead, there was Tlatelolco and, for many of the survivors, prison. If the movement itself dispersed, however, the spirit of the movement persisted on the two main campuses of Mexico City and in some of the provincial universities. In response to evidences of this spirit, violent repressive measures, whose first small-scale manifestations had been noted in August of 1968, became so widespread in 1971 that a national scandal resulted.

It will be recalled that on 29 August 1968 unidentified groups attacked two vocational schools where students had been active in the strike movement, and a few days later a large contingent of similar individuals attacked another school near Tlatelolco injuring fifty people, some of them residents of the housing project, and inflicting some property damage as well. On the night of 20 September 1968, a gang drove past the Colegio de México and fired a machine gun at the impressive glass facade of the main building.

Some time after the strike ended, these attacks resumed, and became more frequent by the summer of 1971. The attackers were young men who let it be known that they were students who opposed the communist activities of the movement sympathizers. These anticommunists operated as masked gangs; they were well armed, traveled by automobile or in their own buses, attacked their victims with vicious efficiency, and seemed to enjoy immunity from police intervention. Some of these groups even adopted distinguishing names; most notorious, and most feared, were the Falcons (or Hawks). The events were reminiscent of Germany in the 1930s.

In spite of this intimidation, student activism at the UNAM and the Poli refused to die. A new outbreak of protest also occurred at the University of Nuevo León in Monterrey, in May of 1971. Students in that demonstration opposed the proposed new law of the University which would strip the institution of its autonomy.[15] Dozens of persons were wounded, and more than 100 arrests were made.

In Mexico City, UNAM and Poli students decided to include discussion of the Monterrey events in the program of a meeting which they were planning for 10 June. On that date, students from both campuses gathered at the Poli and started to march in the general direction of the center of the city. A few blocks from the campus they were intercepted and attacked by a well-armed contingent of the Falcons, who, eyewitnesses allege, arrived in municipal buses. In the resulting struggle, which lasted over two hours without police intervention, twelve students were killed, and dozens of others were wounded.

Too many circumstances surrounding the event suggested, if not government support, at least official tolerance of the Falcons' bloody attack. Charges were made that the rightist paramilitary group actually operated from an unmarked office in one of the Gobernación buildings. While carefully avoiding the appearance of accusing the regime, the rector of the UNAM stated that it had become public knowledge that the attack was carried out by well-trained shock troops "organized by elements who possess ample financial and material resources." [16]

Public trust in and respect for the regime sank to what may have been the lowest point of the post-Revolutionary period. To save appearances, it was necessary to conduct an inquiry and to find one or more scapegoats to relieve the president from the onus of responsibility. In the supercharged atmosphere of alarm, indignation, suspicion, and fear, no one recalled that the Falcons had begun their operation at a time when President Echeverría had been the secretary of Gobernación. It is hard to believe that if the terrorist group had been operating with the support of the government, the head of the secret service would have been ignorant of its existence.

An investigating commission was appointed, and an inquiry was held. After six weeks of labor, an inconclusive and vaguely worded report evaded the question of responsibility and was silent on the matter of the Falcons' relationship to the regime. Meanwhile, the regent of the Federal District (which includes Mexico City), Alfonso Martínez Domínguez, and the police chief resigned and were replaced. In the face of continued criticism, Attorney General Julio Sánchez

Vargas, who had conducted the inquiry, also resigned.

American newspapers occasionally report that the president is seeking "to open a dialogue with Mexico's rebellious students" (for example, *New York Times*, 17 June 1971), but my Mexican informants say, if this is so, the students are not aware of it.

Dialogue or Debacle?

As we have seen, the demise of each of the movements was accompanied by feeble invocations of the governmental authorities to "engage in a dialogue" with the protesters. The government's answer to those aspirations had been to ignore them. In two of the cases, those of the railroad men and the doctors, wholesale accession to the demands would have required reallocation of economic resources as well as reorganization of important segments of the regime's power base. Some of the implications of that statement will be spelled out in another chapter. At present, it is enough to say that in all three cases the decision makers were adamantly opposed to making any accommodation with the protesters which would have required even minimal modification of their preferred policies. Not only that, but they made plain their refusal even to concede that the protesters had any right to present demands and to be given an explanation as to why the demands would not be granted.

In the first two cases we saw an initial appearance of receptiveness on the part of the government as personified by the president, followed by a breaking off of communication between the authorities and the protesters which preceded a period of ominous silence; after that ensued the repression of the protesters, ending with defeat and dispersal of the movements. In the case of the students, the same sequence can be observed, except that the apparent receptiveness was telescoped almost to the point of being obliterated.

The cases are not simply copies of each other, down to minute details. An important difference can be observed in the amount of violence employed in repressing the movements. But the variation seems to correlate quite accurately with the size of the movements. That of the doctors being the smallest and least effective, sanctions were applied selectively and did not involve bodily harm. The student movement, in contrast, involved tens of thousands of militants and hundreds of thousands of participant-spectators. According to the criterion postulated above, maximum violence was employed in its repression.

The data do not reveal a political system oriented toward the formulation and modification of goals through pluralistic participation in the decision-making process. Instead, we see repression of authentic interest groups and encouragement of spurious groups that can be relied on not to speak out of turn. The regime deals with bona fide groups almost as though they were enemy nations. We shall discuss the significance of this behavior somewhat later, but first it may repay us to inspect some of the weapons in the government's arsenal, in addition to those which inflict death or bodily harm.

Deprivation of liberty is a powerful weapon, both in peacetime and wartime. War has its own special methods, but all modern nation-states have adopted elaborate legal provisions for disarming and isolating the "enemy within" during peacetime. Reference has already been made to Mexico's erstwhile antisubversive law and to the sections of the Penal Code which have replaced that law without sacrificing any of its effectiveness. The regime's ability to use these provisions has proved a thorny problem in the case of protest groups like the three studied in this volume, because the actions and rhetoric of these groups has mainly been patriotic and reformist.

The difficult task of equating protest with subversion is made easier by constant appeals to Mexicans' deeply ingrained xenophobia. The fear of foreign intervention, understandable in light of the nation's history, is spelled out not only in the Penal Code but also in Article 33 of the constitution, which reads in part, "the Executive of the Union shall have the exclusive faculty of requiring the immediate departure from the national territory, without the necessity of previous judicial procedure, of any foreigner whose stay he regards as inconvenient. Foreigners may not, under any circumstances, interfere in the country's political matters." Because the ability to expel unwelcome foreigners from national territory or to prevent their entry into the country is the executive's prerogative in any modern nation-state, it would not have been necessary to include this clause in the constitution. Mexicans, however, derive a peculiar satisfaction in seeing it there. The prohibition against foreigners interfering in the country's political matters can be interpreted to include casual expressions of opinion or even scholarly research. Actually, it is gratuitous because the more general statement which precedes it embraces particular examples like this one.

Article 33 has no practical use in dealing with Mexican nationals of course, but if it can be shown that a domestic protest group has links with foreign meddlers, the task of bringing its leaders within the purview of the antisubversive laws is facilitated. In both the railroad strikes and the doctors' strikes, the executive's prerogative to expel foreigners was used, with the attendant publicity aimed at creating the impression that disloyal Mexicans were working with the clandestine support of representatives of unfriendly nations to overthrow the constitution. An attempt to use this rather crude technique against the student movement was abandoned after it became apparent that it would be easier to use the fact that many students had attended or were alleged to have attended conferences in Cuba and Czechoslovakia as an indication of an international plot. This became the main thrust of the prosecution's argument in the trial of the students. The obliging judge overlooked the prosecutor's failure to establish a causal relationship between such foreign travel and the subsequent events in Mexico.

When legal methods are too cumbersome or time-consuming, extralegal deprivation of liberty is sometimes used against problem individuals who are believed to be obstructing the government's handling of a conflict. Kidnapping is an example of this. In such cases, persons who may or may not identify themselves as secret service agents call upon the obstreperous individual in his home or waylay him en route to his home. They take him to a distant place and hold him there until the conflict is resolved. In two such cases related to the author, the individuals reported that they had been treated courteously and had not suffered discomfort.

A variant of this technique is a modification of the police roundup. An informant who had been involved in an earlier conflict and who had served time in jail reported that he had a more reliable indicator than the mass media when trouble was brewing. "Whenever that happens," he related, "two plainclothes men drop by and invite me to stay with them at 'headquarters' until things calm down. That way the government apparently feels that it has one less enemy to deal with."

The Russian custom of exile is also practiced in Mexico. A troublemaker may be ordered, under pain of imprisonment or bodily harm, to leave the area where he has been exercising his allegedly noxious influence and to reside at a distant place until further notice. When it seems desirable that an individual leave the country and reside abroad, government funds may be furnished to cover his expenses. When the individual is a person of great prestige, he may be prevailed upon to accept an appointment as ambassador to a distant country.

It often proves practicable to blacklist individuals so that they can no longer obtain employment. They are kept so busy trying to eke out an existence that they have no time to engage in protest activities, whether the latter are subversive or innocuous.

Each of these methods was used in one or more of the conflicts studied in this volume, as emergency supplements to the routine methods of control and co-optation described in earlier chapters.

Cost Calculations

8

The Establishment of Economic Priorities

In our discussions of the conflict between the decision makers and the protest groups, we have referred repeatedly to divergent preferences of policy choices by each of the parties, without always being as specific as we might have been. It is time to clarify this ambiguity.

As we have seen, the problem posed for the government by the demands of the protest groups involved a reallocation of resources. This in turn implied the possibility of a shift in emphasis from one aspect to another of the nation's program for achieving economic goals, which brought to the foreground the distinction between economic growth and economic development.

In its simplest form, the notion of economic growth implies a net increase in the national product, without regard for the way this product is distributed among the total population. Economic development, on the other hand, is a more elusive concept. There are almost as many definitions as there are writers on the subject. For our purposes, use of the term requires a stipulation that growth be accompanied by a persistent tendency toward equalization of income (as goods and services) among the population. In this view, development is progress toward the broadest possible participation in the nation's wealth which is compatible with the continued growth of the economy. The interpretation of this proviso about the compatibility of development and growth has lain at the center of Mexico's post-Revolutionary inability to reconcile the several wings of concerned public opinion.

For the *científicos* of Profirio Díaz's day, the problem was extremely simple: growth, taking priority over development, was to be emphasized at all times. These influential advisers to Mexico's longest-entrenched dictator (1876–1910) were, as their popular sobriquet suggests, convinced practitioners of Comtian positivism. José Yves Limantour, secretary of the treasury from 1892 until the fall of the Díaz regime, was their most articulate spokesman. Convinced that development would occur automatically when growth had reached the desired level, Limantour espoused policies which favored industrial and commercial expansion by encouraging massive foreign private investment. Limantour's achievements are a record of the triumph of the *científicos'* philosophy: monetary stability, enviable foreign credit conditions, a balanced budget, and a steady rise in the GNP.

Limantour and his associates were confident that some of the benefits of this fiscal progress would eventually begin to trickle down from the thin layer of Mexico's economic elite into the vast stratum of the nation's appallingly poor people. At the end of the Porfirian regime, this takeoff from growth into development was not yet visible. Whether or not it would have occurred is a question which was left unanswered by the outbreak of the Mexican Revolution in 1910, a revolution whose success was guaranteed by the participation of a sector of the population largely ignored in most of the *científicos'* calculations: the peasants. The nation's decision makers ignored the breadth and depth of impatience with the failure of development to take place.

Although frequent and intense signals were fed into the information system by the numerous peasant uprisings during the Porfirian era, these signals were suppressed by the officially approved violence of President Díaz's federal troops. In the pursuit of the political stability which was regarded as a necessary precondition for economic growth, decision makers turned a deaf ear to vital information concerning the failure of the government's policies in the provinces.

It is doubtful, however, that the *científicos* would have evaluated the signals correctly even if they had cared to listen. Prisoners of the myths they themselves had created, they tended to disregard any contradictory evidence. In the words of one scholar, these "men of the city, friends of the big landowners . . . were ignorant of the inconformity which very rightfully agitated thousands of peasants [working for] wages which were insufficient for their most elementary necessities. They confined themselves to denying the existence of the problem. . . . Experience has demonstrated that these talented Porfirists were completely mistaken." [1]

It took nearly a quarter of a century for the dust of the Revolution to settle and for a leader to emerge who was aware of the need to convert some of the symbolic output of revolutionary rhetoric about development into concrete efforts to effect a reallocation of resources. President Lázaro Cárdenas (1934–1940) translated Articles 27 and 123 of the 1917 constitution (the first concerning agrarian reform and the second concerning the rights of labor) into programs of land distribution to peasants, encouragement of labor unions, support of demands for higher wages, and nationalization of the petroleum industry and the railway network. To accomplish these goals, he tightened the party organization. It is difficult to assert what effect these policies would have had on the nation's economic growth if they had been vigorously promoted by later presidents. The outbreak of World War II and subsequent shifts of emphasis in Mexico's economic policies preclude a definite answer to this question.

From 1946 through 1970, national economic policies were oriented toward growth. Government actions in stimulating and regulating public and private investment, channeled principally toward encouragement of the industrial sector, were chiefly responsible for the average annual growth rate of 6.5 percent.[2] During the same period, efforts were also made to honor the concept of development, but these were concentrated almost entirely in the large industrialized urban centers.[3] Low-cost housing, subsidized staple foods, expansion of the educational system, and the establishment and expansion of a social security system that offered a wide range of benefits were widely publicized aspects of successive administrations. They were available only to a small proportion of the country's total population, the salaried workers in private industrial and commercial enterprises, civil service workers, and regularly employed wage earners in selected geographic areas. The bulk of Mexico's population—the peasants, the urban unemployed, the intermittently employed, and the underemployed—did not have access to these benefits.[4]

In an analysis of the regressive trend of Mexican economic policy, an observer from the United States has destroyed, once and for all, the rose-colored picture of Mexican development which has been painted by official literature. Conceding that real progress had been made under Cárdenas, the writer says, "After 1940 the trends reversed. A development strategy emerged which tightly controlled labor union activity, slowed the pace of agrarian reform, and reduced the relative share of the total income of the bottom sixty per cent of the Mexican population." [5]

Putting all of the nation's economic eggs into one basket may produce more of the desired growth more quickly, but the decision makers must ignore appeals or demands from other groups in the society for a larger share of the available goods. For the economic planners in totalitarian political systems, the necessity of including such demands in their calculations is not an important consideration; manifestation of discontent can be reduced or eliminated by appropriate escalations of violence. In systems whose elites are not so fully convinced of the rightness of their choices, total commitment of the resources for violence is not likely to occur. Under these circumstances, planning and steady progress toward a predetermined goal may still be achieved, although probably at a slower rate, by employing a program of incentives and disincentives to promote the dominance of one sector of the economy, such as mining, industry, agriculture, or services. Incentives for the dominant sector usually include such devices as protection from foreign competition by import substitution, fringe benefits for favored groups, subsidies, direct governmental investment, or nationalization. Disincentives may include neglect, price or wage controls, discriminatory tax rates, and other de jure and de facto methods of restricting access to available resources.[6] The application of such policies is likely to be followed by clashes between the favored and nonfavored sectors of the economy, as the latter try to compete with the former for better treatment and these, in turn, try to prevent erosion of their privileges. In addition, groups within the less favored sectors are likely to compete with each other for a greater share of the diminishing available goods. In a partially open political system, when economic controls are consistently enforced by an elite, much of the competitive activity of the less favored groups will take the form of protest movements.

These observations by foreign writers were nothing new to Mexican intellectuals who had been exposing the regressive tendencies for some time. Two main currents could be discerned in their discussions. The first of these, typified by Narcisco Bassols's defense of the peasants during the Alemán administration, centers on the argument that economic growth will eventually grind to a halt unless the internal market is stimulated by a transfusion of acquisitive power to the less favored groups.[7] This objection gradually lost cogency as it became apparent that the upper-middle group, which has benefited from economic growth, has been buying increasing quantities of durable consumer goods. They have become the customers that have absorbed some of the slack in products which could not compete for foreign markets. In this sense, they have underwritten the Mexican industrialization.

Another argument, much more forcefully advanced and more appealing to a broad spectrum within the concerned public, is that economic growth is meaningless unless it is simultaneously accompanied, or at least rapidly followed, by economic development. In the case of Mexico, it is argued, the lag in development is intolerable. This point of view crops up again and again and is expressed with the greatest clarity in the writings of Horacio Labastida.[8]

That essential development is not and has not been taking place is the opinion, amply documented, of the intellectuals' most articulate spokesmen. Using such criteria as the kinds and amounts of food, shelter, clothing, and public services available to the population, some of these authors insist that the relative economic position of the least favored groups of the less favored sectors has actually been declining since World War II. The statistical evidence available for 1940–1960 has prompted several investigators to affirm that the social change which took place during that period shows a relative deterioration. "The situation of social inequality," states one, "is becoming more acute, being expressed in the deterioration of the participation by the workers in the social wealth [that has been] generated."[9]

In even more forceful terms, another writer has pointed out

that the average salary in Mexico was 6 percent less in 1960 than in 1940, and the minimum agricultural salary had decreased 45 percent during the same period. The steady decline of the economic participation of these groups in the steadily rising national income makes it appropriate to speak of "decisions for growth, but not for development." [10]

Curiously enough, the appeal of the *científicos'* arguments for economic growth has enjoyed a popular revival, at least as reflected in the recent publication and sale of books about the economic policies of the Porfirian epoch.[11] For the first time since the Revolution, the mass media have found it safe during the decade just past to favorably reappraise the work of Porfirio Díaz's economic advisers. Even so respected a *doyen* of the social sciences as Jesús Silva Herzog, after criticizing the political shortsightedness of the *científicos*, grudgingly concludes that "judging with serenity, we should say of the fiscal work of José Yves Limantour that the balance is predominantly favorable." [12] And an examination of the backgrounds of the twenty-two cabinet members appointed by President Díaz Ordaz when he assumed office in 1964 prompted another writer to describe this group as "Mexico's new *científicos*." [13]

Thus the contemporaneity of opposing economic views has lent vitality to the protest movements described in this book. Although alleged heretics may sometimes be burned, it is only in the Mexican sense of being *quemado* (described earlier); Mexican elites have been unable to establish orthodoxy.

Growth, Development, and the Good Life

Underlying most discussions of growth and development in Mexico are a number of explicit and tacit models for achieving the "good life." One model which currently crops up probably with least frequency but which still figures in the speculations of intellectuals influenced by social scientists like the anthropologist Claude Levi-Strauss[14] is that of an agrarian society which experiences no economic growth and in consequence, no economic development. The kind of behavior which would preclude both growth and development might be—to use a Mertonian term—a latent function of a tradition-bound society, or it might be the conscious choice of nostalgically oriented refugees from the pressures of modern industrial societies.

Each of these aspects of the question can be found in Latin-America's Indian problem.[15] From almost the inception of the colonial epoch, Ibero-American literature has been enriched by prose and poetry conceived in a spirit of admiration for the real and imagined virtues of the noble savage.[16] One of the earliest defenses of Indian social and economic organization was the seventeenth-century *Comentarios reales* of Garcilaso de la Vega. Garcilaso's maternal ancestry was linked with the Inca royal house, and his paternal lineage derived from the Spanish *conquistadores*. He pictured a utopian tribal life stabilized at zero economic growth. The strength of this idyllic legend is demonstrated by the fact that more than three hundred years after the Inca's death, essentially the same arguments were updated and fictionalized, earning their author first prize in the Latin-American novel competition of 1941.[17] In spite of these romantic visions, many Latin-American leaders—and especially Mexican politicians and economists—have a decided preference for various mixes of growth and development, all of which presage the eventual extinction of the Indian as a cultural identity.

A number of pragmatically oriented thinkers advocate the fastest possible growth for achieving, at the earliest possible moment, the stage of postindustrial economic organization. Only such a society, it is argued, can support the generalized high level of goods and services which has been described as a welfare state, and only such a state can provide the good life for all its citizens. This is the *desideratum* on which growth policies are presumably focused, although the assumption is not always clearly articulated.[18]

As often happens, a small group of individuals clustered about the universities and other centers of intellectual activity oppose both these points of view. To the advocates of the inviolate agrarian Eden, they point out that the metastasis of modernization has already affected almost all of the traditional societies of the world, in greater or lesser degree, and nothing short of radical social surgery could remove the malignancy from their midst. Even so, they add, the operation might kill the patients. On the other hand, the intellectuals see no reason why the poor nations of the world should pursue economic growth with such haste as to blind themselves to the present material needs of the majority of their citizens. They argue that at least partial satisfaction of these needs justifies a deceleration of the timetable for maximum growth. Thus, as usual, the intellectuals comprise the nucleus—and often the totality—of the opposition to both of the emotionally more appealing extremes, the diehard traditionalists, and the all-out modernists.

The Dilemma Posed by the Protesters

If the foregoing remarks have left the reader with the impression that the controversy over economic policies has been confined to academic circles, reference to the three case studies reported in this book will quickly disperse that notion. These conflicts were, in fact, the transposition into the material world of the intellectual disagreement which already existed.

In the context of the national economy, the organization and distribution of health care and other social security benefits has concentrated the largest share of those goods and services on that sector of the population—the more highly paid regularly employed workers—which is in the most favorable circumstances. From a mass of available data, a picture emerges of discrimination favoring the small group of workers most closely associated with the process of national economic growth. It is also apparent that the more highly paid workers in manufacturing activities are the most favored of all. This has been a constant feature of government policy for nearly thirty years.[19]

The picture was obscured, however, by the extraordinary variety and complexity of health care plans available to different sectors of Mexican society. The individual citizen, only vaguely aware that some groups had access to more and better services, was in a poor position to demand concrete changes that might have increased his share of available resources. The reorganization and consolidation proposed by the striking doctors not only would have resulted in significant economies but also would have effected redistribution that would benefit the disadvantaged sector of society at the expense of the favored industrial workers.

The consolidation and reorganization of the nation's rail system that the STFRM demanded would have gone a long way toward redressing the imbalance between the railroad workers' contribution to Mexico's economic growth and their share of benefits, but it would also have shifted some of the economic burden to the industries which were benefiting from low freight rates. Through their strikes, the railroad men and doctors tried to achieve a reallocation of economic resources in which they envisioned themselves as being the primary beneficiaries, with other sectors of society receiving "fallout" benefits. We are referring here to the objectives of the strikes as seen by the rank-and-file strikers; some leaders undoubtedly operated from an ideological basis that postulated wider and deeper changes in the economic system.

More basic than medical services or wages and freight rates was the problem confronting the regime of a successful challenge to its control of the labor sector. Through co-opted union officials and a manipulated membership, tame labor was important to economic growth by reducing, or keeping to a minimum, the share of goods received by some sectors. It was also essential to the strategy of political control by the PRI because the big labor unions provided the electoral fodder important for guaranteeing continued massive endorsement of the regime. Many rank-and-file workers were aware of this function but remained cynically passive. In 1968, when a truckload of these men was on its way to a counter-demonstration against the students, some of the group began to chant, "We're just little lambs. We're not going, we're being taken." An independent labor sector might throw the outcome of political action in doubt and would introduce an element of uncertainty into economic and political planning. Because the labor sector of the PRI is composed of unions rather than individuals, it is extremely vulnerable to the possibility of change in union leadership. Individual membership in a union is not translated into individual militancy in the party. As long as a union is tightly controlled by its leader, and as long as the leader plays ball with, or forms part of, the regime, labor can be manipulated.

Although the challenge posed by Demetrio Vallejo was crushed in 1959, the dream of an autonomous workers' movement was cherished throughout most of the following decade, and became an article of faith for some student leaders, especially in 1968. The theorists among them—those with an "objective appreciation of reality"—were convinced that by themselves the students were not numerous enough to force the government to change its policies. They believed an alliance with labor was necessary, and they were encouraged when they saw a contingent of electricians and railroad men, the latter easily identified by their distinctive caps, kerchiefs, and coveralls, at the Tlatelolco meeting.

Our account shows that the alliance was never achieved, but for more than ten years it was a recurrent nightmare to the regime, and even the remote possibility of its realization goes a long way toward explaining the vehemence with which the efforts were repressed.

Some of the leaders of the doctors' strikes had also dreamed of an alliance with labor for the purpose of challenging the PRI's control. Even if the workers had shaken off their puppet officials, however, it is unlikely that they would have brought about a radical change in the political system. Quite possibly, they might have manifested an anti-intellectual hard-hat attitude, becoming militantly conservative and engaging in civil war with student protest groups. From the regime's point of view, this would have been less frightening but would still constitute a problem, because much effort would have to be expended in devising and carrying out new methods of indirect control and manipulation.

Considering the great imbalance in the distribution of

benefits to various sectors of society, it is not surprising that protest movements troubled Mexico during the decade just past. If a greater proportion of Mexican citizens had been aware of the possibility of widespread participation, and if they had desired to make the possibility a reality, the regime would have been forced to make important changes in its program. The possibility, however, was not realized. Even during the largest protest movement—that of the students—and at the height of public demonstration of sympathy for the protesters, a probable maximum of 300,000 people participated in public acts. Most of Mexico's population, which had reached nearly 48 million in 1968, did not so much stand firm in loyal support of the regime as remain marginal to these events. They were a "politically nonexistent" collectivity constituting 50 to 70 percent of the population.[20] This lack of revolutionary violence was the basis for what some writers have called political stability based on oligarchical patterns of control and co-optation.[21]

Our three case studies have revealed the efforts of highly politicized, very articulate, activist groups to win support from a significant portion of the population, and we have seen those efforts fail. Two elements were largely responsible for the failure of the protesters: endemic obstacles to expanding pluralism, and the regime's methods of discouraging participation in the political process.

In earlier chapters we have surveyed some of the factors contributing to the "unpolitization" (rather than "depolitization") of the Mexican masses, but it may be useful to recapitulate some of them in this context.

Members of Indian communities have not participated in national political affairs which are controlled by mestizos, partly because such participation is alien to Indian culture, but also because the regime has largely abandoned the effort to "Mexicanize" this sector of the population. In spite of official rhetoric, government policy has, for some years, been evolving toward a custodial type of program. After voicing sharp criticism of U.S. government policies toward its Indian population, the Mexican government has silently adopted many of its methods.

Reticence, that is, the reluctance to press one's demands, is a characteristic of both the Indian and mestizo populations. We have seen protest groups present petitions which were essentially lists of demands, but this behavior was not a common pattern in the society. Most Mexicans have little or no opportunity to learn the skills of pluralistic participation through school or community organizations. This is not the kind of activity fostered by the government, nor are there any autonomous secondary groups with both the inclination and the means to carry out large-scale training programs of this nature. Passivity is linked to reticence in the sense that reticent people are often forced by default to accept the policies and programs advocated by more articulate and aggressive persons or groups. A tendency to obey an authoritarian figure or ruling elite is another characteristic of the passive individual.[22] Illiteracy further limits the participatory horizon of reticent and passive groups.

Drawing on a number of attitude studies, some of which we have already cited, Hansen sums up the sources of widespread diffuse support for the political system, even while noting that most people are receiving very little from the system. He states his proposition in these words:

> The record of stability in Mexico since 1929 clearly indicates that the present political system has succeeded in one or more of the following ways: (1) limiting the number of demands upon it; (2) increasing its capacity to meet growing

demands; (3) stimulating diffuse support for the political system; and (4) retaining the specific support of the *politically relevant* members of Mexican society, e.g., those members who control enough of the society's resources to threaten the system's stability if they choose to do so.[23]

In extending these observations, Hansen offers the opinion that diffuse support and passivity are the chief elements that maintain the system. While I agree that they are important factors, I conclude from my case studies that the regime's success in limiting, discouraging, and manipulating demand input is the system's most distinguishing characteristic.

These characteristics narrow the scope of political action of most Mexicans in such a way as to leave few channels through which to express nonconformity with existing policies or to exert pressures toward adopting alternative policies. Almost the only road open is to associate with other discontented individuals under the leadership of an authoritarian *caudillo* who will insist on complete obedience, choose the group's goals, and direct its activities. Aware of this possibility, the regime has prevented the emergence of potential *caudillos* through a maximum use of violence when necessary (as in the assassination of Jaramillo) and has provided "safe" authoritarian leaders for existing groups like labor unions, deposing "unsafe" leaders when necessary (as in the case of Vallejo). Our studies do not reveal the emergence of authoritarian figures in either the doctors' or the students' movements; in fact, there was a conscious rejection of this kind of leadership. This rejection reflected the fact that the doctors and students differed significantly from most of their fellow Mexicans: they were literate, articulate, and activist. These differences created problems for the regime in handling the protest movements, but the lack of effective leadership proved an even more serious drawback for the protesters.

If effective protest is to take place, that is, activity which actually persuades or forces the governing elite to modify its timetable of economic growth—that kind of protest is likely to come, not from the ranks of the relatively privileged part of the population, but from the marginal people. After surveying the attitudes of groups of different socioeconomic status, a recent writer concludes that the marginals are the base for possibly violent protest movements that combine "values of equalitarian solidarity among the poor, charismatic leadership of a powerful *patrón*, and magical redress of unjust exploitation." [24] To accept the possibility of mobilization, however, we would have to predicate effective politicization of this group.

While the initial spark may come from ideologically oriented individuals in a relatively high socioeconomic stratum, the resulting conflict will most likely be powered by the same kind of men and women who followed Hidalgo and Zapata. This time, however, the mass of militants will probably not be peasants, at least at the outset. Although the new protesters may hold similar values as those of the Zapatistas, a much larger proportion of them will be city dwellers, because of the torrential trend toward urbanization which took place during the decade from 1950 to 1960, and which has continued at a high rate since then. While in 1969 Cornelius could state that "the assumption of uniformly high urban politicization levels and of increased political cognition as a result of migration to the big city appear largely untenable . . . in the Mexican case," it should be noted that the sources cited as a basis for this assertion were the results of studies conducted before the doctors' and students' strikes.[25] It is at least plausible that the crowds that watched the doctors' marches in Mexico City and those that attended the students' rallies and mass meetings in the capital and in other large cities were more intensively exposed to the politicization process than their country cousins or, indeed, previous city dwellers.

Some student leaders were aware that, if their movement were to have massive impact on future policy formulation, they would have to find broad support for their demands from other strata of the population. They sought such support from industrial workers in the Federal District, but, as we have seen, found them unresponsive. Their failure confirmed Kahl's findings which characterized the more successful manual workers as more individualistic, more confident of their ability to improve their own life chances, and more politically conservative.[26]

Even if the doctors and students were aware of the greater revolutionary potentiality of the marginal people—the landless peasants and the unemployed or underemployed working class—they had no means of establishing an effective alliance with them. Like Francisco Madero, they could only translate the masses' grievances into intellectual terms which were all but incomprehensible to the masses themselves. In spite of this lack of intellectual rapport, the two movements of the 1960s, unlike the earlier railroad strike, had an unmistakably widespread emotional impact on the marginals.

For those who place their faith in an expanding elite or a circulating elite as an effective hedge against conflict, the record provides little cause for optimism. If by expansion is meant the transfusion through co-optation of young blood, it should be remembered that the only blood that is accepted is that which is compatible to the organism. Just because young people enter the PRI and rise through the ranks does not mean that they bring a new pressure for substantive change in political or economic goals. The fallacy of the assumption is illustrated from the record of American party politics: "young Republicans" usually prove to have "old Republican" attitudes.

Thus, while new recruits are welcomed, new goals are rejected. A Mexican intellectual offers this explanation: "Orthodoxy, docility, caution, and even inhibition, coupled with the periodic renewal of hope for upward mobility or for circulation in the different scales of the hierarchy, contribute powerfully to the adherence and subordination of political personnel." [27]

Fear of being *"quemado"* is very realistic. The reference in Chapter 3 to the temporary ascendancy of new young technocrats in the PRI at the beginning of President Díaz Ordaz's term of office reflected an interesting but inconclusive development. During their brief incumbency, their actions indicated only the intention of introducing efficient methods for achieving previously enunciated objectives. Of course, to substitute rationality for rhetoric can in itself result in radical change, and perhaps this is what they, or Madrazo, the new party chief, intended to accomplish. But pursuit of such a policy depended on their operating with the consent and protection of the chief, "*el mero jefe*," and as we have seen, Madrazo was ousted from party leadership after a short struggle. The technocrats made their exit soon thereafter.

The determination to limit participation in decision making seems to be a product of the regime's conviction that to do otherwise would endanger its economic program by putting too great a burden on the available resources. Limited plurality is seen as a necessary condition for political stability, which in itself is regarded as a prerequisite of economic growth.

Each of the three protest movements thus required a

comparative calculation of costs, that is, the cost in terms of momentum lost in the achievement of economic policy preferences versus the cost of applying violence to repress autonomous participation in the political process. Apparently, the decision makers concluded that repression was the most economical course. Because the challenge posed by the students was the most serious one of the decade—and indeed, of the whole post-Revolutionary period—it elicited the most strenuous of all repressive efforts. The blood shed was in direct proportion to the magnitude of the threat.

In its present incarnation, the Mexican political system has endured more than forty years. This longevity is not the result of chance but of several factors, among which are (1) spectacular satisfaction of aspirations for economic growth followed by some, if insufficient, economic development; (2) evolution of structures for efficient control and manipulation of popular participation in the decision-making process; and (3) culture traits that raise the level of tolerance to frustration. Realizing this, many Mexican intellectuals are pessimistic about the possibility of peaceful change in the near future. While reiterating the desirability of a more equitable distribution of psychic and economic dividends, they shrink at the cost of achieving them. Some believe that Mexico's system of domination and subjection through the apparatus of the party has been necessary to provide a stable basis for economic growth. They say it is not easy to democratize the process of protest and response without dismantling the entire political and economic framework.[28]

Choices for the 1970s

9

In discussing "communication, Mexican style," we described a number of behavioral traits which seem to distinguish the Mexican system of processing political information. We found many techniques that helped to avoid direct confrontation between the makers of national policies and those who expressed a preference for different policies. These techniques seemed to drain the force out of protest and response alike, leaving the regime free to implement its decisions with only minor concessions to the protesters. Although some policy makers were always inclined to view dissent as threats to the stability of the political system, they had not been free to indiscriminately employ their legitimized violence to eliminate the supposed threat.

During the decade 1958–1968, events reflected a gradual abandonment of the indirect style by protesters and decision makers alike, with the former becoming less dependent on intermediaries, more impatient with delay, and more insistent in their demands for change. The regime seemed to become less receptive to new information, more reliant on stereotypes, more rigid in its suspicion of dissenters, and less reluctant to resort to violence in silencing them. We might gain further understanding of past, and possible future, events by placing what we know in the framework of information and decision making.

Changing Patterns of Communication

Although the Mexican system of information and decision making is by no means an hermetically closed one, it manifests a progressive tendency toward closure, seen in such aspects as manipulation of the mass media and of the sector divisions of the dominant party. Inevitably, such manipulation has impoverished the content of messages transmitted over the system.

Lower echelon decision makers define each new situation to conform with the stereotyped images which have shaped their political world. In effect, they have decided a priori to confine their responses to an extremely narrow range of actions, which present protest groups with a reduced range of choices as to their subsequent behavior. Decision makers at higher levels lack, or are deprived of, information which might enable them to reevaluate the situation and search for alternative methods of dealing with it. Actions at all levels often seem to push the problem all the way to the top of the ladder, where it can be deposited in the hands of the chief executive, whom the lower level officials see as the *only* executive. Like other powerful rulers in many historical periods and many parts of the world, modern Mexican presidents must fight vigorously to avoid becoming prisoners of their own advisers. If not, by the time the problem reaches the top, it has been shaped into a standardized product divested of any distinguishing characteristics which might cause the Ultimate Decision Maker to hesitate in his applying the tried-and-true formula, and perhaps even to search for alternatives.

The positive feedback thus engendered moves the whole system farther and farther away from reality. Upper-echelon decision makers, seeing their symbols treated by the lower echelons as reality, and having few independent sources of information against which to check and compare, increasingly orient their plans and actions toward the symbols rather than toward the real world. Unless the tendency is reversed, or at least checked, the system will become totally autistic, with messages from the real world being treated as irrelevant or dangerous.

If the information and decision-making systems of some other Latin-American nations reveal similar tendencies, we may gain some insight into an apparent inconsistency which has baffled many observers. The paradox is concerned with the almost complete divergence of the informal political life in those countries from the formal-legal prescriptions embodied in their constitutions. Foreign observers find it impossible to reconcile the actions of Latin-American decision makers with what appears to be the clear language of the constitutions. But those decision makers, their attention fixed on the symbols which have replaced reality, are convinced that their actions are consistent. Only in this way can we understand how in present-day Mexico reformers are branded as counterrevolutionaries, protesters are convicted as subversives, and supporters of established policies call themselves true revolutionaries.

In this setting, even the most determined efforts to establish contact with reality often meet with frustration. In the absence of reliable statistics, economic planning can degenerate into a profession of faith in received dogma. Suppressing certain sectors of the economy to stimulate others is viewed as the only road to salvation rather than being seen as an expedient to be pragmatically adjusted as new information about its effects becomes available.

At the periphery of the decision-making apparatus—indeed, in many ways independent of that apparatus—exist groups that are aware of a significant change in their own social or economic status. Other peripheral groups are attentive to the gradual shift in value preferences reflected in government policies. Intellectuals perceive the first indications, but inevitably as the gap between revolutionary rhetoric and actual practice widens, other sectors share the disillusionment. They experience this in ways which cannot be denied or glossed over by reference to the symbol system. These groups are often peripheral only with respect to that facet of reality with which they have immediate and personal contact; in all other respects, they are consumers of the generalized symbolic input supplied by the upper-level decision makers. For example, railroad men are indistinguishable from other components of public opinion when they state that doctors "went too far" in their strikes, and doctors join the great mass of symbol consumers when they emit similar opinions about railroad men. Imprisoned in the same frame of reference, economic planners may view the behavior of both of the above groups as inimical to the public interest without realizing that, however defined, this interest itself must be constantly reexamined. This empirical examination can only be conducted if the planners have access to the raw data, that is, data which have not been screened through the prevailing myths and then processed into symbols.

Decision makers in the grip of the very symbols which they have helped produce constantly reassure themselves, and each other, that they are not unalterably opposed to any modification of their programs; it is simply that the proponents of the current attempt at change have "gone too far."

In the context of Mexican politics during the decade examined, this phrase became a magic formula, substituting, on one hand, for a careful examination of the failure of protest groups to achieve their objectives and, on the other hand, justifying the government's use of severe sanctions against those groups. In the interviews for the present study, for example, informants who had been involved in or affected by the railroad strikes or the doctors' strikes were asked to evaluate the strikes' significance. A frequent answer, repeated with only slight variation, was, "I was in sympathy with them at first [or "I was active in the initial stages"] because I felt they were justified in protesting, but I lost sympathy [or "I became inactive"] because I thought *they had gone too far*."

A review of the case studies involving a comparison between the stories disseminated by the mass media and the accounts given by participants or eyewitnesses reveals important discrepancies between the two types of information. Dependence on the mass media alone would certainly give the impression of intolerable excesses perpetrated by the protesters. One author, citing only newspaper accounts as sources, explained the failure of the railroad strikes in terms of Vallejo's "senseless . . . demands, which he knew would be rejected." These demands, states the author, "could and did lead only to political conflict and his [Vallejo's] own destruction." [1]

Step-by-step comparison of the mass media coverage of the three protest movements reveals a remarkable similarity in the timing and sequence of the use of symbols and the content of messages leading to identical conclusions in all cases. Moreover, a cursory survey of mass media coverage of other protest movements during the past decade suggests that a detailed study of each might reveal similar regularities. The record is available for the interested student with a penchant for pursuing such matters.

Another theme which occurs with insistent regularity is that of subversion. The term appears first in the allegations published in the form of advertisements over the names of apocryphal groups, and, shortly thereafter, on the editorial pages, from whence it passes into the news stories, having apparently progressed from the status of opinion to that of datum. Finally, the accusation is voiced by the attorney general's office in the prosecution of certain key personalities. In this final stage, the subversive tendencies first alluded to in the advertisements have expanded to a plot.

Two principal types of evidence are adduced as conclusive proof of a plot; the first of these is the discovery and confiscation of items described as "subversive literature and propaganda." [2] The second type of evidence gains particular force from its appeal to the xenophobia which is an important element in Mexican culture, and which is enshrined in Article 33 of Mexico's constitution in these words: "Foreigners may not, in any way, meddle in the political affairs of the country." The president, and through him the attorney general's office, has unrestricted power to interpret the word meddle. In the railroad strikes, two members of the Soviet Embassy were singled out as foreign meddlers. In the doctors' strikes, such evidence was harder to produce, but one enterprising newspaper writer finally discovered that one of the accused plotters had been born in Spain and brought to Mexico by his parents when he was five years old. In addition, one of the doctors implicated in the plot, although born in Mexico, had two German surnames.

During a crucial final stage of a protest movement, communication among the members is disrupted, and individuals, cut off from the real world, are forced to fall back on symbols provided by the mass media. Each individual, convinced that while he and others within his limited range of empirical experience have labored for their cause from the purest of motives, another group outside of his range of immediate perception has betrayed the movement through treason, poor judgment, or intemperance. Thus the stage is set for action by a new group which believes itself to have a legitimate motive for calling the attention of the decision makers to its particular grievance through the use of protest techniques. The leaders of the new group are convinced that they will succeed where others failed because *they* will take every precaution not to "go too far." This concern with moderation is often reflected in compulsive emphasis on formal safeguards, for example, incorporation and registration of the group, presentation of petitions to the appropriate bureaucrats, and consultation with legal advisers as to the propriety of each action.

Limitation and distortion of information input affects formative groups in another way. Since the mass media often omit reference to the number of casualties suffered by protest groups, attention is concentrated on a few scapegoats who are brought to trial on charges of plotting to overthrow the government. Although rumors of deaths or imprisonments fly thick and fast for a short time, the symbol consumers are eventually convinced that most of this information is false and that as long as they are innocent of any subversive intent, they will be relatively safe if they join a protest movement. At the same time, however, communication between groups is inhibited by the fears entertained by the leaders of each group that to join forces with another would, by associating with people who "go too far" doom their own group to reprisals and eventual failure.

The reactions described above give some indication of the importance which decision makers attach to public opinion, which during the past twenty years has become progressively less public, with the isolation of individuals and subgroups from access to a free flow of information and from communication with each other. As long as this isolation continues, as long as the bulk of an individual's information intake is symbolic, private opinion is unlikely to pose serious obstacles to the continuation of present policies.

Changing Attitudes toward Violence

Small-scale violence as a repressive tool is still fairly common in the provinces, especially in the rural areas.[3] Even at the level of state governments it is by no means rare, but until recently it had appeared that there had been a diminution in the more public kinds of large-scale violence.

It has often been possible for the regime to avoid large-scale violence because the government also has recourse to a wide range of coercive measures which avoid bloodshed. These measures include both legal and extralegal acts; for reasons explained elsewhere, the regime has shown a preference for the use of extralegal measures.[4]

Probably the most widely used of these latter measures is the manipulation of organized groups to replace leaders who are outspokenly critical of government policy preferences with progovernment leaders. This has been particularly successful in the labor sector, with increasingly sophisticated techniques being developed during the past thirty-five years. Co-optation, subsidization, and selective enforcement of legal measures (for example, exclusion clause, arbitration machinery, writ of *amparo*) are only a few of the devices available. As we saw in the railroad strikes, however, these techniques have not always ensured the unquestioning support of labor leaders, and the government has resorted to other measures.

The repertoire of these measures includes a number of techniques which can be subsumed under the category of covert violence, such as kidnapping of selected leaders at critical junctures of protest movements. The leaders may be well treated, and may be held only long enough to insure a resolution of the conflict compatible with the government's policy preferences. The period of sequestration is usually brief: from one or two days to one or two weeks.

When removal of troublesome individuals is required for longer periods of time, temporary exile may be resorted to. Less fortunate individuals may be given a few hours notice, be provided with passport and plane fare to a nearby Latin-American nation, and warned not to return to Mexico for a specified period of time. In some cases, exile is self-imposed, as in the case of some of the leaders of the doctors' movement, individuals were blacklisted and unable to find employment in Mexico. Others may be given scholarships or travel grants involving several months' absence from the country, and really prominent persons may be prevailed upon to accept a diplomatic post in a distant nation.

Overt violence includes all public forms of physical attack on the participants in protest movements. The range extends from the organized and directed heckling of protest marchers (recorded during the doctors' strikes), to the use of government troops to dislodge protesters from strategic locations (railroad men's, doctors', and students' strikes), and even beyond that to firing upon protest groups, wounding or killing participants. The most recent addition to the repertoire of techniques has been the sponsorship of terrorist street gangs to attack protesters.

As recently as 1968, it was still possible to state that the limits of acceptable use of overt violence had been undergoing steady attrition since the 1920s. Since the use of violent measures to repress the student disorders of the latter part of 1968 (and especially with reference to the tragic event at the Plaza of the Three Cultures), the trend appears to have reversed.

The contrast between the railroad workers' protest and the physicians' protest may be instructive. If violence or the threat of violence can be regarded as information, it would appear that Mexican decision makers exercised discrimination in responding to messages in the same idiom. In the case of the physicians, probably the most that could be hoped for was that procrastination would eventually so discourage the strikers that they would drop their demands. There is much to be said for delay, when a system undergoing rapid development is subjected to massive demands which strain its capacity to respond adequately. At the end of six months, however, it was clear that this tactic would not succeed.

Next in order of desirability was the introduction of so much new information into the communication network (for example, activities of company unions, slanderous accusations by anonymous groups, ambiguous decrees promulgated by the president) that first the concerned public, and eventually many of the strikers, would begin to doubt the legitimacy of the doctors' claims. That this result was at least partially achieved was evident in the comments of several informants, some of whom had supported the strikers unreservedly until August 1965, but who felt that the last strike was unnecessary and unwise.

The refusal of the regime to consolidate the railroad lines and the failure of the STFRM to organize on an industry-wide basis helped immeasurably in diluting the impact of the railroad strikes. In 1958–1959 the government met force with force to break the railroad strike and to oust Vallejo from his leadership. Vallejo's supporters were not soft-handed theoreticians; they fought roughly and were treated roughly in return. Or perhaps the sequence was inverted: they were treated roughly and fought back. There is no way of ascertaining the real order of events, as all available accounts are partisan. Thousands were seized and jailed for a short time; hundreds were fired and never rehired; less than a dozen were tried and imprisoned for many years. Even the most pro-Vallejo accounts claim less than half a dozen deaths directly attributable to repressive measures by the regime.

In the case of the doctors' strikes, each health and welfare official retained a relatively wide scope of freedom in dealing with the strikers in his own institution. This slowed down the unification of the striking doctors by confronting them with apparently quixotic and disparate official actions. Thus, ground seemingly gained in one health agency had to be fought for anew in every other agency. Whenever this kind of inefficient behavior could be called into play, there was a corresponding reduction in the need to employ violent repressive measures. As a result, the doctors suffered less physical harm. None were killed; only a few were even roughly treated; two were jailed for a short time, and less than half a dozen eventually received long-term prison sentences. The most serious large-scale reprisal measure used was the firing and blacklisting of hundreds of physicians. While many were eventually able to reinstate themselves in the good graces of the regime, others remained permanently beyond the pale, with no prospect of being able to work at their profession. While an unemployed railroad worker might possibly find employment in some other kind of work, the possibilities open to an unemployed doctor are very slim in a system characterized by massive governmental participation in health care services.

Although all of the above responses were brought into play against the students in 1968, the most impressive difference was in the abrupt escalation of violence. The tendency was manifested during the first week of student activity; it continued intermittently during the ensuing two months, and peaked with the horrifying bloodshed at the Plaza de Tres Culturas on 2 October. It did not cease then: violent repression has occurred on several subsequent occasions, most notable of which was the killing of several students in June of 1971.

A charitable attitude toward the regime might prompt an observer to concede that the events of 2 October 1968 were deliberately triggered by revolutionary agents provocateurs in the expectation that public indignation at the killing of students would push the nation into revolt. By June 1971 however, it was impossible to sustain such a point of view. At that time the police made no attempt to prevent well-organized gangs of toughs from attacking the student marchers. Accusations that these gangs were supported by and operated under orders from the government were never satisfactorily dealt with.

Viewed in the context of responses to protest movements during the previous thirty years, the regime's behavior toward the students is startling and irrational. It seems to be the product of a different mentality, one that stresses winning the point even though it means losing the game, one that is not too fastidious about covering up evidence of foul play, and one that cannot tolerate an occasional boo from the bleachers. These metaphors should not mislead us into thinking simply that the present regime is headed by a group of bad sports. They are not engaged in a genteel game; as Mr. Dooley put it, "politics ain't beanbags." People have been hurt; they have been killed, too often in recent times and in numbers too large to be dismissed as the result of accident or aberration. The irrationality has not consisted in the use of violence, but in its use in disproportionate response to the behavior which evoked it.

The behavior patterns exhibited by the regime in response to the different protest movements reported here seem to indicate that all levels of decision makers have been afflicted with hardening of the arteries. During the decade examined, a formula for dealing with such movements was taking shape, and now it appears that rigidity is setting in with respect to the application of that formula. A salient characteristic is denial of the legitimacy of any kind of protest against officially approved policy choices, and the most discouraging sign is the recent escalation of violence.

A precedent for this kind of behavior was the "Porfiriato" when, from 1876 to 1910, the regime of Porfirio Díaz used violent repressive measures to ensure a clear field for the implementation of his policies for economic growth. The "Pax Porfiriana" was followed by the Revolution and eighteen years of another kind of violence: chaotic struggles between groups and individuals contending for the privilege of imposing their value choices on the nation.

For some years after the outbreak of the 1910 Revolution, political behavior was a matter of loser-lose-all. Local *caciques* and guerrilla chieftains sometimes banded together temporarily to pursue an immediate objective, but inevitably quarreled, separated, and tried to kill each other. Capture of the seat of national government at Mexico City was seen as the prize of victory, the symbol of domination by one chieftain over all his rivals. Men accepted the leadership of one or another chieftain out of personal loyalty rather than from adherence to particular political views, and followers were aware that they must share the eventual fate of their leaders, whether that be a share of the spoils of victory or a violent death. That these attitudes and this behavioral style were regarded as the essence of *machismo* is indicated by the folk songs and stories that are preserved in the present-day culture.

Why has Mexican political behavior reverted not to the immediately post-Revolutionary era but to that which preceded the great Revolution?

The government could quash *any* group by using brutal and unrestrained force. It has a monopoly on organized violence; it also has as much control as it wants over mass communication, as well as an efficient intelligence structure for collecting information. In other words, the elites now have at their command the *technological* capabilities for establishing and maintaining total or virtually total control over the activities of all actual or potential groups. The elites could impose their value choices nearly all the time. They can now do much more efficiently what the Porfirian regime did in the rough-and-ready turn-of-the-century fashion.

Unless a regime is willing to make full use of new modes of repression, it must operate within certain boundaries. Decision makers must make *some* concessions to protesters, even though most of these concessions may be symbolic satisfactions rather than real policy changes. To understand the trend away from concession and possible future changes toward increasingly violent repression of dissent, it may be helpful to express these changes in the idiom of information theory.

History as Information

Old information (that is, information about past events), about what finally happened to the Porfirian regime in spite of—or perhaps because of—the uses of violence is stored in the memory bank of the political system and deters total use of coercive capabilities. But old information is a curious thing. There are degrees of oldness. The older a datum is, the further back it is stored in the memory bank and the less accessible it is to immediate recall for calculating the possible outcomes of current policy choices. Old information is most accessible when it is still in oral form. When it can be recalled and recounted by persons within whose lifetime the event actually occurred, this kind of information is likely to figure almost as prominently in calculations as current information. When these bearers of oral information have top decision-making roles, policy choices will be influenced by this circumstance.

One result of this is the so-called generation gap, where there is a sharp discontinuity between the calculations influencing policy preferences of the older generation and those of the younger generation, the latter of whom are insulated from direct contact with data about certain events in the not-so-distant past. They can read about them in history books, but they rarely do, and when they do, the data have lost their impact.

Curiously, the generation gap doesn't occur, or occurs only in a very attenuated form, in preliterate societies, where all members of the community are constantly exposed to oral history. Anthropologists have often been baffled by the failure of bearers of oral history to distinguish between events of the present, the recent past, and the remote past. The field workers feel frustrated in their attempts to compile written histories of such communities and to assign neat dates to each important event. But the members of the communities are not uncomfortable at all in such a situation; on the contrary, they make their calculations within a frame of reference which shifts so slowly as to appear, to the impatient visitor from a literate society, to be completely immobile. Sharp breaks with the past do not occur because in a very real sense the past is present. Advocates of rapid change show their appreciation of this fact when they stress the importance of literacy; the sooner old information can be removed from the oral domain and consigned to history books, the easier it will be to disregard the past in making current policy choices. McLuhan to the contrary notwithstanding, the "global village"—at least in this sense of oral history—simply has not come into being.

Until about 1940, Mexico's top decision makers had all lived through the Revolution; many of them had taken part in it. They knew the uses of violence, but were also familiar with its limitations, and this knowledge figured importantly in the calculations which resulted in the founding of the PRI, which made possible the manipulation of large groups of people with a modicum of violence. This element of caution in the use of violence is a salient characteristic of the period 1930–1950 which has been noted by almost every non-Mexican student of that country's political life.

Since 1940, the ranks of the old revolutionaries have been undergoing the inevitable process of attrition. General Cárdenas, revered as the most revolutionary of all the Mexican presidents, died in 1970 at seventy-five. By 1950, the influence of such personages over policy choices was rapidly declining, and by 1960, the period of revolutionary upheaval was relegated to a series of commemorative volumes bearing the imprimatur of a government-approved publisher.

If our speculations about the relative ease of retrievability of oral versus written history are valid, it can be expected that information about the uses and limitations of violence will have figured less prominently in the calculations of elites and protest groups during the decade 1950–1960 and may have declined precipitately in the following ten years.

Only a very small percentage of Mexico's present population is old enough to have experienced the violence and bloodshed of the post-Revolutionary period. A mere handful can recall the repression of the Porfirian era. Must the new generations again lay the ghost of Mexico's violent past? As Huntington has suggested, history is full of examples that belie the optimists' certainty of unbroken progress toward political perfection.[5]

Changing Styles of Communication

Our examination has revealed some major shifts in the patterns of information transmittal and reception as well as in the decision-making process. I would like to suggest that there may also have been a comparable shift in the *style* of political communication.

In an earlier essay I advanced the notion that the comparative peacefulness of the post-Revolutionary period was due, at least in part, to a feminization of political behavior.[6] Although the "cult of virility" is little more than a myth, it is a myth whose power must still be respected by politicians.[7]

If it is true, as a number of writers have suggested, that revolution is most likely to occur when dissatisfied groups perceive the government as weak, it may have been necessary for Mexican leaders to create an appearance of strength in order to maintain public confidence in their ability to enforce their decisions.[8] This appearance corresponded to deep feelings about the appropriate style for conducting political activities. Mexicans still believe that politics is men's business and ideally, male and female styles are polarized, becoming mutually exclusive.

While the most visible characteristic of the cult of virility is a preoccupation with sexual prowess, a survey of scholarly and popular literature reveals that other traits are considered more important components of the *macho* behavioral constellation. Included in these are strength, courage, invulnerability, dominance, and violence in relationships with members of both sexes.[9] Most important of all is intransigence, shown in a rigid adherence to a previous course of action in the face of all opposition or attempts at persuasion. The ideal *macho* is as unyielding as a diamond; once he has made a decision, he must stick to it, admitting no modification or compromise. In the *machismo* framework, violence is an acceptable tool for imposing one's decisions on others, and death by violence is the recognized cost of failure to prevail over the opposition.[10]

In contrast, men regard "any kind of gentleness or refinement of attitude, any kind of moderation in action" as feminine traits.[11] It is generally assumed by Mexican men and by foreign observers that Mexican women are passive, submissive, and completely dominated by men.[12] Occasionally, however, an observant researcher finds that under the stereotyped attitudes, women have developed elaborate strategies for imposing their will.[13] Even in intrafamilial relationships they skillfully bargain, maneuver, propagandize, and temporize until they attain their goals. By concentrating on selected objectives and ceding ground on others which they consider less important, they cultivate the illusion that men make all the decisions. Such behavior is typical of the highly skilled political activity which avoids confrontations and implements policy choices without the need of resorting to violence.

Mexican men, always hypersensitive to any suspected imputation of lack of virility, believe it necessary to eschew this modus operandi, at least at the level of public visibility. For this reason, I have argued, the dominant political party was created in 1929 and for three decades utilized as a screen behind which peaceful negotiation could take place while a facade of intrànsigence could be maintained. As a result, policy choices were implemented at a relatively low cost in terms of violence.

During the thirty-year period just described, there was enough flexibility, enough give and take, and enough built-in limitations on unbridled aggressiveness to prevent a relapse into the bloody warfare and chaotic struggles that had characterized the 1910–1928 period. The reduction in violence enabled decision makers to utilize a greater proportion of available resources to implement economic programs. Although important sectors of the population remained marginal with respect to the distribution of political and economic goods, their frequent acceptance of symbolic gratification in lieu of real satisfaction of their needs and demands cannot be simply written off as the result of widespread repressive measures.

The regime's use of violence as a tool to implement policy choices was never entirely abandoned, but it appears that top-level decision makers usually exercised discrimination in selecting appropriate methods for achieving acceptance of their programs. Their restraint was imitated by lower-level officials, and occasional lapses in the provinces were concealed or minimized by the public communications media. The repertoire for decision enforcement included co-optation, manipulation, corruption, procrastination, apparent irrationality, legalized sanctions, covert illegal sanctions (for example, officially ignored kidnappings, occasional assassinations, exile of undesirable individuals), and—rarely, during the period under question—large-scale repressive measures. A review of challenges to official policies suggests that all levels of government (federal, state, local) were usually economical in their use of the resources at their disposal, employing a conscious choice of the least violent method compatible with enforcement of decisions.[14]

Where did the shift take place? This essentially feminine style of protest and response was fairly constant until the late 1950s. Although the railroad strike was not the first sign of an important shift (having been preceded by significant but small-scale disturbances in 1956), the massive retaliatory measures of 1959 employing the full range of legalized sanctions, covert illegal measures, and maximal violence were experienced directly on a scale unknown for at least a generation. In 1964–1965, the style employed by the striking doctors permitted a temporary and partial return to less violent methods of coercion. Unwilling to give in so easily, the students of 1968 made it clear that they would not settle for symbolic satisfactions, nor would they be frightened by masculine posturing.

What will happen if Mexican policy makers entirely abandon the covert use of feminine strategies and resort to unrestrained force? What will happen if they retreat from their rhetoric and negotiate openly with the protest groups that seem to become stronger every day? Either alternative seems to involve enormous danger for Mexico's future. The middle way, the way that characterized the most tranquil thirty years in the nation's history, will require clear vision, hard choices, and an act of political will that can liberate Mexico from repeating historical mistakes.

Notes

Chapter 1

1. David Apter, *Choice and the Politics of Allocation* (New Haven: Yale University Press, 1971).

2. Juan J. Linz, "An Authoritarian Regime: Spain," in *Cleavages, Ideologies and Party Systems, Contributions to Comparative Political Sociology*, ed. Erik Allardt and Yrjö Littunen (Helsinki: Transactions of the Westermarck Society, 1964).

3. Ibid., p. 297.

4. Susan Kaufman Purcell, "Decision Making in an Authoritarian Regime: Mexico," mimeographed (Paper presented at the 1971 Annual Meeting of the American Political Science Association).

5. Stanley Ross, ed., *Is the Mexican Revolution Dead?* (New York: Alfred A. Knopf, 1966).

Chapter 2

1. Gabriel Almond and Sidney Verba, *The Civic Culture* (Boston: Little, Brown and Company, 1965 paperback), p. 311.

2. Kalman Silvert, *Man's Power* (New York, The Viking Press, 1970).

3. Edward Twitchell Hall, *The Silent Language* (Garden City, N.Y.: Doubleday & Co., 1959).

4. Octavio Paz, *El laberinto de la soledad* (México: Fondo de Cultura Económica, 1959), Chapter 3, passim.

5. Salvador Reyes Nevárez, *El amor y la amistad en el Mexicano* (México: Porrúa y Obregón, 1952, Serie "México y lo Mexicano," Vol. 6), pp. 15–16.

6. Ibid., pp. 22–23.

7. For an early description of the interminable formalities of polite conversation in Mexico, see Frances Calderón de la Barca, *Life in Mexico During a Residence of Two Years in that Country* (London: J. M. Dent & Sons, and New York: E. P. Dutton & Co., 1968), pp. 82–83. This chronicle covers the years 1839–1842.

8. Carlos A. Echánove Trujillo, *Sociología mexicana* (México: Editorial Porrúa, S.A., 1963).

9. Compare, for example, Charles Emil Kany, *American–Spanish Euphemisms* (Berkeley: University of California Press, 1960), with

Camilo José Cela, *Diccionario secreto I* (Madrid: Ediciones Alfaguara, S.A., 1969).

10. See the articles by Santiago Ramírez and Felipe Montemayor in A. Jiménez, *Picardía mexicana* (México: Libro Mex, 1960, Twentieth Edition, April, 1965), pp. 219–223 and 229–232. (N.B.: Each new printing is designated in Mexico as a new edition. *Picardía* is a best seller and in 1970 was already in its 28th printing.)

11. Joyce O. Hertzler, *A Sociology of Language* (New York: Random House, 1965), p. 252.

12. The word *quemado* is rich in other connotations as well as the one cited here. I am indebted for the explanation of this nuance to Informant No. 116, interview dated 31 August 1965, who explained that by inquiring about the meaning of the term I had "burned" myself.

13. David Riesman, Nathan Glazer, and Reuel Denney, *The Lonely Crowd,* abridged edition (Garden City, N.Y.: Doubleday and Company, 1953), pp. 210–212.

14. See, for example, American Academy of Political and Social Science, *Annals: Latin America Tomorrow* 360 (July 1965), passim. See also in *El Día*, 15 September 1965, article entitled "Una falla en la economía de América Latina es la falta de estadísticas."

15. Rogelio Díaz-Guerrero, L. Lara-Tapia, H. M. Capella, et al., "Preliminary Study on International Tensions," mimeographed (conducted under the auspices of the Mexican Group for Study of International Tensions, México, February 1963), p. 1.

16. Zygmunt Gostkowski, "Algunas consideraciones en torno a la validez de las técnicas de investigación utilizadas en los países en vías de desarrollo," *Ciencias Políticas y Sociales* 10 (July–September 1964): 441–451.

17. Gabriel Almond and Sidney Verba, *The Civic Culture* (Princeton: Princeton University Press, 1963), presents an impressive amount of interview data from Mexico and other countries included in the study. Pablo González Casanova and Ricardo Pozas Arciniega, "Un estudio sobre estratificación y movilidad social en la ciudad de México," *Ciencias Políticas y Sociales* 11 (January–March 1965): 115–185, are in the vanguard of Latin American social scientists who are optimistic about developing new techniques for eliciting unbiased responses.

18. For descriptions of these aspects of communication, see especially the Epilogue in Rodolfo Usigli, *El gesticulador* (México: Editorial Stylo, 1947), and, by the same author, "Rostros y Máscaras," in *México: realización y esperanza* (México: Editorial Superación, 1952), pp. 47–56.

19. Informant No. 107, interview dated 4 August 1965. See also Luis Castaño, *Temas de sociología política mexicana* (Mexico: Universidad Nacional Autónoma de México, Instituto de Investigaciones Sociales, 1960), pp. 46–48.

20. An exception, notable because of his rarity, is the cartoonist Abel Quezada of *Excelsior*, who slyly needles his readers.

21. *Excelsior*, Friday, 11 March 1966.

22. Dr. Guillermo Montaño, "La otra cara de la luna," *Siempre!* (25 November 1964): 77 and 86.

23. Edward D. Beechert, Jr., "The Gap Between Planning Goals and Achievement in Latin America," *Inter-American Economic Affairs* 19 (Summer 1965): 59.

24. For arguments contrary to the view expressed by this informant as to municipal autonomy, see L. Cárdenas, Jr., "Contemporary Problems of Local Government in Mexico," *Western Political Quarterly* 18 (December 1965): 858–865.

25. Francisco González Pineda, *El mexicano: su dinámica psicosocial* (México: Editorial Pax, 1959), pp. 35–36.

26. Phyllis Ann Weigand Procter, "Mexico's Supermachos: Satire and Social Revolution in Comics by Rius" (Ph.D. diss., University of Texas, Austin, 1972).

27. Renfro Cole Norris, "A History of La Hora Nacional: Government Broadcasting via Privately Owned Radio Stations in Mexico" (Ph.D. diss., University of Michigan, 1963).

28. Eleazar Díaz Rangel, in his *Pueblos sub-informados* (Caracas, Venezuela: Imprenta Universitaria de Caracas, 1967), argues that the massive use of U.S.-produced syndicated features and wire service material constitutes a form of journalistic colonialism.

29. This seems to be a characteristic of many Latin-American newspapers. See, for example, Christian Rudel, "La Presse d'Amérique Latine," *Presse Actualité* (January 1966); 18–19. This author estimates that 75 percent of space is filled with "soft" news.

30. Erling Halvard Erlandson, "The Press of Mexico, with Special Consideration of Economic factors" (Ph.D. diss., Northwestern University, 1963), p. 145.

31. Following Merle Kling's pioneering study, *A Mexican Interest Group in Action* (Englewood Cliffs, N.J.: Prentice-Hall, 1961), almost every writer on Mexico has acknowledged the attempts of business groups to influence government policy making. (See, for example, Brandenburg; Glade and Anderson; Vernon.)

32. Informant No. 108, a multimillionaire industrialist, reported on one such visit in detail in an interview with this author on 18 August 1965.

33. See the remarks on the network of personal relationships in Chapter 3.

34. Informant No. 111, interview dated 25 September 1965.

35. See the following section of this chapter for a description of this powerful government agency.

36. Informant No. 110, interview dated 22 September 1965.

37. Consuelo Medal, *El periodista como orientador social* (México: Universidad Nacional Autónoma de México, Thesis, Escuela Nacional de Ciencias Políticas y Sociales, 1965), p. 93. This was confirmed by several Mexican newspapermen who were interviewed for the present study.

38. Arnaldo Pedroso D'Horta, "Reportaje sobre México: situación de la prensa," *Espejo* 5 (November–December 1964): 28. However, informants canvassed in 1965–1966 stated that the top monthly salary paid by newspapers was around 3,000 pesos (240 dollars). All agreed that the standard of living of many newspapermen was on a much higher level. This was confirmed by personal observation.

39. Fortino Ibarra de Anda, *El periodismo en México*, vol. 1 (México: Imprenta Mundial, 1934).

40. Medal, *El periodista como orientador social*, p. 92.

41. *Excelsior*, 9 December 1965.

42. Erlandson, "The Press of Mexico," pp. 139–140.

43. Informant No. 109, interview dated 3 September 1965.

44. Medal, *El periodista como orientador social*, pp. 96–97. See the

article by Rodolfo Alcaraz "Sesenta años de periodismo mexicano," *Historia y Sociedad* 6 (1966): 107–125.

45. Guillermo Enríquez Simoní, *La libertad de prensa en México, una mentira rosa* (México: B. Costa-Amic, Editor, 1967), pp. 73 and 76.

46. See, for example, the stories in *Excelsior* and *El Día* of that date.

47. *Excelsior*, 5 November 1965.

48. *El Día*, 11 December 1965.

49. Source: Marynka Olizar, ed., *Guía a los mercados de México* (México: 1968), p. 283.

50. *Novedades*, Sunday, 29 August 1965 (emphasis mine).

51. Informant No. 109, interview dated 3 September 1965, was the first of several expert observers to offer this explanation.

52. Erlandson, "The Press of Mexico," p. 184.

53. Communication to author, from an official of the Audit Bureau of Circulations, Chicago, Illinois, dated 18 May 1967.

54. *Editor and Publisher Yearbook*, 1973, pp. 446–450.

55. Enríquez Simoní, *La libertad de prensa en México*, p. 111.

56. Claude Bataillon, "Communications de masse et vie urbaine au Mexique" *Communications* (March 1964): 31. For an earlier view in general agreement, see Marvin Howard Alisky, "Growth of Newspapers in Mexico's Provinces" *Journalism Quarterly* 37 (Winter 1960): 75–82.

57. Interview with Srta. María del Carmen Ruiz Castañeda, in charge of the catalógo analítico, Hemeroteca Nacional, 28 July 1965. See also the pertinent remarks in Moisés Ochoa Campos, *Reseña histórica del periodismo mexicano* (México, Editorial Porrúa, S.A., 1968), p. 153.

58. Estados Unidos Mexicanos, Secretaría de Industria y Comercio, Dirección General de Estadística, *9° Censo General de Población, 1970; resumen de las principales características por entidad federativa* (México: November 1970); *resumen general abreviado* (México: 1972).

59. Centro de Estudios Educativos, *Boletín Mensual Informativo*, vol. 1 (1965), pages not numbered. See also Thomas V. Greer, "An

Analysis of Mexican Literacy," *Journal of Inter-American Studies* 11 (July 1969): 476. See also Rodrigo A. Medellín E. and Carlos Muñoz Izquierdo, "Sistema escolar y sociedad en México," Mimeographed. Paper presented at IV International Congress of Mexican Studies, Santa Monica, California, October 17–21, 1973.

60. Antonio Castro Leal, "El pueblo de México espera: Estudio sobre la radio y la televisión" *Cuadernos Americanos* 150 (January–February 1967): 90. Compare with the UNESCO estimate that as much as 65 percent of the world's population is functionally illiterate. See United Nations, UNESCO *World Illiteracy at Mid-Century* (Westport, Conn.: Greenwood Press, 1970), p. 191.

61. Shirley Brice Heath, *Telling Tongues: Language Policy in Mexico, Colony to Nation* (New York and London: Teachers College Press, Columbia University, 1972), p. 171.

62. See, for example, Wilbur Lang Schramm, *Mass Media and National Development: The Role of Information in the Developing Countries.* (Stanford: Stanford University Press, 1964).

63. Instituto Nacional Indigenista, *Realidades y proyectos, 16 años de trabajo*, vol. 10 (Mexico: Editorial Libros de México, S.A., 1964), p. 44.

64. Source: Organization of American States, *América en Cifras, 1970, Sección Cultural* (Washington, D.C.: Organization of American States, 1971).

65. Ibid.

66. Interview with PAN official, 29 September 1965. This official assured the author that a tape recording of the telephone conversation had been made and was preserved in the party's files in Mexico City, but it was not produced in evidence even after several requests had been made. Similar allegations were made with respect to the temporary suspension of broadcasting by five radio stations in Morelia during the 1966 student disturbances there. Pablo G. Macías, *Octubre sangriento en Morelia* (México: Editorial Acasim, 1968), p. 92.

67. Estados Unidos Mexicanos, Secretaría de Gobernación, *Ley Federal de Radio y Televisión* (Capítulo III, Art. 62; *Diario Oficial*, 19 January 1960).

68. Renfro Cole Norris, "A History of La Hora Nacional," p. 15.

69. *Excelsior*, 3 December 1952.

70. Antonio Castro Leal, "Radio y televisión," in *Los medios de communicación de masas en México*, ed. Enrique González Pedrero (México: Universidad Nacional Autónoma de México, Facultad de Ciencias Políticas y Sociales, Serie Estudios 10, 1969), p. 26.

71. Interview dated 29 September 1965.

72. *El Día*, 7 October 1965.

73. Estados Unidos Mexicanos, "Reglamento de las estaciones radiodifusoras comerciales, culturales, de experimentación científica y aficionados," *Diario Oficial* (Articles 114 and 115, 20 May 1942). (This Regulation was based on the law of General Channels of Communication—Ley de las vías generales de comunicación—of 1940. Although the law was amended in 1960, the earlier Regulation has remained in effect. The new law extends the scope of the regulatory power to television.)

74. Ibid., Articles 28 and 36 (italics mine).

75. Oscar Bravo Santos, *La radiodifusión comercial en la legislación mexicana* (México: Universidad Nacional Autónoma de México, Thesis, Facultad de Derecho, 1956).

76. Castro Leal, "Radio y televisión," p. 43.

77. International Research Associates, S.A. de C.V., *El radiómetro coincidente* and *El Videómetro de México* (México: July 1965), pp. 1 and 18, respectively.

78. Castro Leal, "El pueblo de México," pp. 90–98, passim.

79. Olizar, *Guía a los mercados de México.*

80. *Excelsior*, 2 March 1966.

81. See, for example, Rodolfo Usigli, *Corona de luz: la virgen* (México: Fondo de Cultura Económica, Colección Popular, 1965), p. 71.

82. Horacio Flores de la Peña, ed., *Bases para la planeación económica y social de México* (México: Siglo XXI, 1966), pp. 6 and 93.

Chapter 3

1. Gerardo Medina Valdés, "El problema médico: gran oportunidad para una revisión al fondo," *La Nación* 24 (1 February 1965): 9–15.

2. See Luis Islas García, *Apuntes para el estudio del caciquismo en México* (México: Editorial Jus 1962), and Jacques Lambert, "Structure sociale dualiste et administration publique en Amérique Latine," *Bulletin de l'Institut International de l'Administration Publique* (April–June 1967): 23–35.

3. Bernabé Rodríguez Aranda, *El caciquismo y el comisariado ejidal* (México: Universidad Nacional Autónoma de México, Thesis, Facultad de Derecho, 1960), pp. 41–46.

4. Karl M. Schmitt, *Communism in Mexico* (Austin: University of Texas Press, 1965).

5. Luis González de Alba, *Los días y los años* (México: Ediciones Era, 1971), p. 21.

6. See later in same chapter.

7. Fernando Carmona, "Reflexiones sobre el desarrollo y la formación de las clases sociales en México," *Cuadernos Americanos* 154 (September–October 1967): 116.

8. I am aware that there is a body of literature which denies the validity of the concept of "two cultures" and that there is also a persuasive argument for the concept of a "culture of poverty," but observation of Mexican social organization lends credence to the views expressed by Jacques Lambert in *Amérique Latine, Structures Sociales et Institutions Politiques* (Paris: Presses Universitaires de France, 1963), p. 51.

9. Partido Revolucionario Institucional, *Estatutos* (México: November 1963), Article 18.

10. Carlos A. Madrazo, "Memorandum" to Gonzalo Martínez Corbalá, mimeographed (Mexico: 22 June 1965).

11. Many Mexicans are convinced that Madrazo's death was not accidental. See Kenneth Johnson's discussion of this point in *Mexican Democracy: A Critical View* (Boston: Allyn and Bacon, 1971), p. 82.

12. See, for example, Frank Brandenburg, *The Making of Modern Mexico* (Englewood Cliffs, N.J.: Prentice-Hall, 1964), p. 244.

13. Estados Unidos Mexicanos, *Constitución Política* (México: Editorial Olimpo, 1966), Article 54.

14. Estados Unidos Mexicanos, *Ley electoral federal y prontuario* (México: 1964), Articles 29 and 33, and amendments.

15. The speech was reported in full in *El Día*, 31 December 1965, and occupied half a page.

16. Quoted in Allan Nevins, *Ordeal of the Union*, vol. 1 (New York: Charles Scribner's Sons, 1947), p. 96.

17. Mario Moya Palencia, *La reforma electoral* (México: Ediciones Plataforma, 1964), p. 178.

18. Virginia Pauline Stullken, "Keystone of Mexican Government—The Secretaría de Gobernación" (M.A. Thesis, University of Texas, Austin, 1954), pp. 101–102.

19. Arnaldo Pedroso D'Horta, "Reportaje sobre México: situación de la prensa," *Espejo* 5 (November–December 1964): 27.

20. *Sucesos para Todos*, 27 November 1965, p. 24.

21. At that time, the Mexican press, like that of most Latin-American nations, was devoting much space to the "operation Camelot" affair. It may be assumed that in view of subsequent developments, the author's research task would later have become even more difficult. See, for example, Elinor Langer, "Foreign Research: CIA plus Camelot Equals Troubles for U.S. Scholars," *Science* 156 (23 June 1967): 1583–1584.

22. This emphasis on blood ties has been paralleled in other places and times. "In France, in speaking of kinsfolk, one called them simply 'friends' (*amis*) . . . the general assumption seems to have been that there was no real friendship save between persons united by blood"—Marc Bloch, *Feudal Society* (Chicago: University of Chicago Press, 1961), pp. 123–124.

23. See, for example, Sidney W. Mintz and Eric Wolf, "An Analysis of Ritual Co-Parenthood (Compadrazgo)," *Southwestern Journal of Anthropology* 6 (Spring 1950): 341–369.

24. George M. Foster, "The Dyadic Contract: A Model for the Social Structure of a Mexican Peasant Village," Part I, *American*

Anthropologist 63 (December 1961): 1173–1192; Part II, *American Anthropologist* 65 (December 1963): 1280–1294.

25. Salvador Reyes Nevárez, *El amor y la amistad en el mexicano* (México: Porrúa y Obregón, S.A., 1952, Serie "México y lo mexicano," vol. 6), p. 86.

26. Official biographical details from Plataforma de Profesionales Mexicanos, *Nuestro voto razonado por Luis Echeverría* (México: 22 October 1969, no publisher), pp. 7–9.

27. Eric Wolf, "Aspects of Group Relations in a Complex Society: Mexico," *American Anthropologist* 58 (December 1956): 1075.

28. Linda Sue Mirin, "Public Investment in Aguascalienties: A Study in the Politics of Economic Policy" (Ph.D. diss., Harvard University, 1964), p. 16.

29. Ibid., pp. 56–57.

30. Informant No. 137, interview dated 8 December 1965.

31. Informant No. 172, interview dated 28 July 1965.

32. Edmundo Flores, "On Financing Land Reform: A Mexican Casebook," *Studies in Comparative International Development* 3 (1967–1968): 116–117.

33. See, for example, *Taharumara*, prize-winning Mexican film of 1965.

34. See Oscar Lewis, *Life in a Mexican Village* (Urbana: University of Illinois Press, 1951), p. 45.

35. Hubert Herring, *History of Latin America* (New York: Alfred A. Knopf, 1961), pp. 379–380.

36. This is the contention of Gilberto Balam in *Cuarto menguante, los valores de una sociedad que se eclipsa* (México: B. Costa-Amic, 1967), pp. 137–138.

37. Robert Scott, *Mexican Government in Transition*, rev. ed. (Urbana: University of Illinois Press, 1964), pp. 24 and 131.

38. Talcott Parsons' sets of paired dichotomies of values (for example: ascriptive vs. achievement, particularistic vs. universalistic) was an effort to describe and classify the bases of different social systems. See his *The Social System*, Glencoe, Illinois, The Free Press, 1951, pp. 58–67. Other American social

scientists have used Parsons's taxonomy to predict that "underdeveloped" societies will never "develop" (that is, achieve political stability and economic growth) unless they abandon "their" set of values and adopt "ours." See for example Lucian Pye, *Politics, Personality and Nation Building: Burma's Search for Identity*, New Haven, Yale University Press, 1962. These writers ignore the fact that important sectors of "developed" societies are based on values usually associated with underdevelopment. As an illustration, the ascriptive practice of keeping incompetent brothers-in-law and superannuated uncles on the payroll has not prevented Jewish firms from contributing to the U. S. gross national product.

Chapter 4

1. Rafael de Zayas Enríquez, *Apuntes confidenciales al Presidente Profirio Díaz*, reprinted with a foreword by Leonardo Pasquel (México: Editorial Citlaltépetl, 1967).

2. For a concise but informative description of the development of Mexico's rail system, see Andrés Caso, "Las Comunicaciones," in *México, cincuenta años de Revolución*, abridged version (México: Fondo de Cultura Económica, 1963), p. 238.

3. Raymond Vernon, *The Dilemma of Mexico's Development* (Cambridge: Harvard University Press, 1963), p. 41.

4. Caso, "Las Comunicaciones," p. 239.

5. See John Hamilton McNeely, *The Railways of Mexico: A Study of Nationalization* (El Paso: Texas Western College, Southwestern Studies, Mongraph 5, 1964).

6. Arthur Neef, *Labor in Mexico* (Washington, D.C.: United States Department of Labor, Bureau of Labor Statistics, B.L.S. Report No. 251, 1963), p. 92.

7. William P. Glade, Jr., "Revolution and Economic Development," in *The Political Economy of Mexico*, William P. Glade, Jr., and Charles W. Anderson (Madison: University of Wisconsin Press, 1963), p. 77.

8. For independent confirmation of the steep rise in the cost of living in Mexico during the 1950s, see Neef, *Labor in Mexico*, p. 80. Although the totals tabulated in this report should, like all statistical

material based on Latin-American figures, be used with caution, there can be no doubt as to the nature of the problem.

9. See, for example, Joe C. Ashby, *Organized Labor and the Mexican Revolution Under Lázaro Cárdenas* (Chapel Hill: University of North Carolina Press, 1963), p. 288.

10. Jorge Basurto, "El líder obrero en México," *Mundo Nuevo* (March–April 1971): 71–76. The author states that all organized labor is completely subservient to government policy.

11. See Neef, *Labor in Mexico*, p. 85, for legal basis of this practice.

12. For contrasting and obviously biased accounts see Jesús Topete, *Terror en el riel de "El Charro" a Vallejo; páginas de la lucha sindical* (México: Editorial Cosmonauta, 1961), pp. 199–200, and Ferrocarriles Nacionales, *La verdad sobre el tortuguismo en los Ferrocarriles Nacionales de México* (México: 1956, no publisher).

13. Topete, *Terror en el riel*, p. 214.

14. Karl M. Schmitt, *Communism in Mexico* (Austin: University of Texas Press, 1965), p. 162.

15. For details of the events between 2 July and 27 August 1958, see ibid., pp. 162–163.

16. *Excelsior*, 3 January 1959, p. 4.

17. See, for example, Schmitt, *Communism in Mexico*, p. 163.

18. *Excelsior*, 17 January 1959, pp. 1 and 9.

19. Ibid., pp. 1 and 11.

20. Ibid., p. 10.

21. *Excelsior*, 23 January 1959, pp. 1 and 9.

22. Schmitt, *Communism in Mexico*, p. vi.

23. *Excelsior*, 11 February 1959, pp. 1 and 13.

24. Ibid.

25. *Excelsior*, 12 February 1959, p. 19.

26. *Excelsior*, 13 February 1959, p. 10.

27. *Excelsior*, 21 February 1959, pp. 1 and 9.

28. "The right to assemble or associate peaceably for any lawful purpose cannot be restricted; but only citizens of the Republic may

do so to take part in the political affairs of the country. No armed deliberative meeting is authorized."

"No meeting or assembly shall be deemed unlawful that has for its object the petitioning of any authority or the presentation of a protest against any act; nor may it be dissolved, unless insults are proffered against said authority or violence is resorted to, or threats are used to intimidate or compel such authority to render a favorable decision"—Gerald E. Fitzgerald, ed., *The Constitutions of Latin America* (Chicago: Henry Regnery Company, 1968), p. 146.

29. *Excelsior*, 23 February 1959, p. 9.

30. Union advertisement in *Excelsior*, 7 March 1959, p. 23.

31. *Excelsior*, 24 March 1959, p. 13.

32. Informant No. 329, interview dated 22 July 1968.

33. *Excelsior*, 26 March 1959, p. 1.

34. Guillermo Flores Portuguez, *La inexistencia jurídica de la huelga* (México: Universidad Nacional Autónoma de México, Thesis, Facultad de Derecho, 1965), p. 129.

35. Topete, *Terror en el riel*, p. 269.

36. See, for example, *Excelsior*, 26 March 1959, p. 6.

37. Raúl Beethoven Lomeli, "Reconquista Sindical por los comunistas," *Excelsior*, 27 March 1959, p. 1.

38. *Excelsior*, 30 March 1959, p. 1.

39. Ibid., p. 1.

40. *Excelsior*, 1 April 1959, p. 1.

41. *Excelsior*, 9 April 1959, p. 1, italics mine.

Chapter 5

1. For the significance of different lengths of waiting periods, see Edward Twitchell Hall, *The Silent Language* (Garden City, N.Y.: Doubleday & Co., 1959), Chapters 1 and 9.

2. *Movimiento médico, datos históricos*, typewritten, undated, from the files of the Alianza de Médicos Mexicanos.

3. *El Universal*, 4 December 1964, p. 10.

4. *El Universal*, 6 December 1964, p. 6.

5. Informant No. 202, interview dated 19 November 1965.

6. Informant No. 203, interview dated 16 November 1965.

7. *El Universal*, 10 December 1964, pp. 1, 8, and 13.

8. See especially the issues of the weekly magazine, *Siempre!* for the period 1 September–1 December 1964.

9. See "La polémica sobre el primer año del régimen," *El Día*, 29 August 1965.

10. Frank Brandenburg, "The Relevance of Mexican Experience to Latin American Development," *Orbis* (Spring 1965): 194–195.

11. Informant No. 221, interview dated 10 March 1966.

12. Estados Unidos Mexicanos, Presidencia de la República, *El Gobierno Mexicano* (México: Dirección General de Difusión y Relaciones Públicas, December 1–31, 1964), p. 79.

13. Ibid., pp. 85–90.

14. Ibid., p. 79.

15. Ibid., p. 79.

16. Informant No. 206, interview dated 25 November 1965.

17. Informant No. 205, interview dated 16 February 1966.

18. *Boletín de la Alianza de Médicos Mexicanos*, 15 March 1965, pp. 1–2.

19. Comisión de Conflictos, Alianza de Médicos Mexicanos, "Informe a la Asamblea Nacional," *El Día*, 3 June 1965.

20. Herbert Marcuse, *One-Dimensional Man* (Boston: Beacon Press, 1968), p. 1.

21. Informant No. 206, interview dated 22 November 1965.

22. Informants Nos. 202, 203, 206, interviews on various dates, October–November, 1965.

23. Ibid.

24. An alternative explanation offered by some informants, is that the eighteen delegates had been threatened by agents of the *Secretaría de Gobernación* (Internal Security).

25. "History of Events Occurring Between December 1964, and July 1965, compiled in Compliance with Directive Adopted by Plenary Session of the Alianza . . . ," mimeographed, unsigned, undated.

26. Estados Unidos Mexicanos, Presidencia de la República,

El Gobierno Mexicano (México: Dirección General de Difusión y Relaciones Públicas, 1–28 February 1965), pp. 133–134.

27. *Comunicado de la Secretaría de Salubridad y Asistencia*, 18 February 1965.

28. Estados Unidos Mexicanos, *El Gobierno Mexicano* (1–28 February 1965), Table of Contents.

29. "Información de la A.M.M.R.I.," *Boletín de la Alianza de Médicos Mexicanos*, 15 March 1965, p. 4.

30. Informant No. 202, interview dated 4 March 1966.

31. Ibid.

32. "Notas Informativas de la A.M.M." *Boletín de la Alianza de Médicos Mexicanos*, 15 March 1965, p. 4.

33. Estados Unidos Mexicanos, Presidencia de la República, *El Gobierno Mexicano* (México: Dirección General de Difusión y Relaciones Públicas, 1–31 March 1965), p. 86.

34. Ibid., p. 138.

35. "El triunfo de nuestra dignidad," *26 de Noviembre* (May 1965), pp. 1 and 5.

36. "Médicos del ISSSTE desconocen a su organización sindical," *Memoria de los acontecimientos*, Anexo No. 5.

37. Informant No. 205, interview dated 16 February 1966.

38. Estados Unidos Mexicanos, Poder Ejecutivo Federal, *Diario Oficial* (México: 26 May 1945).

39. Samuel P. Huntington, "Political Development and Political Decay," *World Politics* 17 (1965): 386–430.

40. Informant No. 212 (one of the charter members of the original *Sindicato de Médicos*), interview dated 1 February 1966. With regard to obstacle no. (1), several informants saw the fear of government opposition as well-founded.

41. Robert E. Scott, *Mexican Government in Transition*, rev. ed. (Urbana: University of Illinois Press, 1964), p. 25.

42. Frank Brandenburg, *The Making of Modern Mexico* (Englewood Cliffs, N.J.: Prentice-Hall, 1964), p. 86.

43. Ibid.

44. Alianza de Médicos Mexicanos, *Informe de la comisión de conflictos a la asamblea nacional*, mimeographed (México: 29 May 1965), pp. 2–3.

45. "Los médicos ante la defensa de sus derechos," *26 de Noviembre* (July 1965), p. 8.

46. Informant No. 203, interview dated 16 November 1965.

47. *Excelsior*, 21 April 1965.

48. *Excelsior*, 22 April 1965.

49. *Excelsior*, 20 April 1965.

50. *Excelsior*, 4 May 1965.

51. *Excelsior*, 5 May 1965.

52. *Excelsior*, 29 April 1965.

53. *Excelsior*, 6 May 1965.

54. *Excelsior*, 2 May 1965.

55. *Excelsior*, 14 May 1965.

56. Ibid.

57. *Excelsior*, 20 May 1965.

58. *Excelsior*, 7 May 1965.

59. *Excelsior*, 9 May 1965.

60. *El Universal*, 3 May 1965.

61. *Excelsior*, 14 May 1965.

62. *Excelsior*, 15 May 1965.

63. Luis Milán, "El paro médico: ¿movimiento depurador o confabulación reaccionaria?" *El Día*, 18 May 1965.

64. *Excelsior*, 18 May 1965.

65. *Excelsior*, 19 May 1965.

66. *Excelsior*, 4 May 1965. See also news story, ibid.

67. *Excelsior*, 6 May 1965.

68. *Excelsior*, 12 May 1965.

69. Estados Unidos Mexicanos, *El Gobierno Mexicano* (1–31 May 1965), pp. 25–35.

70. Ibid., p. 33. Of the leaders of the physicians' movement who were interviewed for this study, four reported interruption of telephone service and one reported temporary cessation of electric service. See also *Boletín de la Alianza de Médicos Mexicanos*, 31 August 1965. It was impossible to determine whether these instances were deliberate or accidental.

71. *Excelsior*, 19 May 1965.

72. Ibid.

73. Alianza de Médicos Mexicanos, *Informe de la comisión de conflictos*, p. 5.

74. *El Día*, 26 May 1965.

75. Ibid.

76. *Boletín de la Alianza de Médicos Mexicanos*, 15 June 1965, pp. 6–7.

77. Informant No. 115, interview dated 11 February 1966.

78. Dr. Jorge Vélez Trejo, "El paro se levantó en forma condicional," *26 de Noviembre* (July 1965), p. 1.

79. *El Día*, 30 May 1965.

80. *Excelsior*, 21 June 1965.

81. Vélez Trejo, "El paro se levantó en forma condicional," emphasis in original.

82. Estados Unidos Mexicanos, *El Gobierno Mexicano* (July 1965), p. 12.

83. Informant No. 201, interview dated 8 October 1965.

84. Estados Unidos Mexicanos, *El Gobierno Mexicano* (July 1965), pp. 118–120.

85. Ibid.

86. 1 month-hour = 30 hours per month.

87. *El Día*, 13 July 1965.

88. *Excelsior*, 16 July 1965.

89. *Excelsior*, 17 August 1965 and 20 August 1965.

90. Dr. Treviño Zapata, who led the group pressing for postponement, argued that the doctors should wait until after

President Díaz Ordaz had given his state of the nation address on 1 September.

91. Informant No. 220, interview dated 6 November 1965. For references to the effects of this type of verbal incitement, see Evelyn P. Stevens, "Mexican Machismo: Politics and Value Orientations," *Western Political Quarterly* 18 (December 1965): 848–857.

92. *Excelsior*, 24 August 1965.

93. Informant No. 203, interview dated 18 November 1965.

94. *El Día*, 27 August 1965.

95. *Excelsior*, 28 August 1965.

96. *Boletín de la Alianza de Médicos Mexicanos*, 31 August 1965. (These men were released in November 1965, and on being interviewed by the author, stated that they had been well treated in jail.)

97. *El Día*, 27 August 1965.

98. Emilio Kuri Rame, *Crítica en relación con la distribución de los Médicos* (México: Universidad Nacional Autónoma de México, Thesis, Facultad de Medicina, 1965), p. 48.

99. *Excelsior*, 5 September 1965.

100. Ibid.

101. "The courts are not as yet independent of the central government in their function of administration of justice"—M. H. Fix Zamudio, 10 July 1965 (verbal clarification of paper entitled *Panorama del juicio de amparo*, presented as a part of the Session of Comparative Law conducted under the joint auspices of the Universidad Nacional Autónoma de México and the Faculté International Pour l'Enseignement du Droit Comparé a Strasbourg).

102. *Excelsior*, 13 September 1965.

Chapter 6

1. Details of the narrative in this chapter have been drawn from many different sources, including the author's firsthand observation of some of the events of July and August 1968, the official government version and several versions written by individuals who participated in or were sympathetic with the students' cause, and

other versions by groups claiming to be impartial or objective. See especially: by various authors, *Los procesos de México 68: Acusaciones y defensa* (México: Editorial Estudiantes, 1970); Tarsicio Ocampo, compiler, *México: Conflicto estudiantil, 1968* (Mexico: Centro Intercultural de Documentación, CIDOC Dossier No. 23, 2 vols., 1969); Elena Poniatowska, *La noche de Tlatelolco* (Mexico: Ediciones Era, 1971); Ramón Ramírez, *El movimiento estudiantil de México, julio–diciembre de 1968*, 2 vols. (México: Ediciones Era, 1969); Luis González de Alba, *Los días y los años* (México: Ediciones Era, 1971); and Jorge Carrión et al., *Tres culturas en agonía* (México: Editorial Nuestro Tiempo, 1969).

2. See the comments on Mexico's Communist Party, chapter 3.

3. Newspaper photographs of the day's events show only males, but at least two young women were reported among the injured. Their ages—twenty-two and twenty-four years—suggest that they may have been spectators. See *El Día*, 27 July 1968. By 30 July, a small number of girls were actively engaged in student protests. See photographs in *Ultimas Noticias de Excelsior*, 2nd ed., 30 July 1968.

4. *Excelsior*, 27 July 1968.

5. *El Día*, 27 July 1968.

6. César Sepúlveda, "Student Participation in University Affairs: The Mexican Experience," *The American Journal of Comparative Law* 17 (1969): 384–389.

7. Compare this with the findings of Glaucio Ary Dillon Soares, "Intellectual Identity and Political Ideology Among University Students," in *Elites in Latin America*, Seymour Martin Lipset and Aldo Solari, eds. (New York: Oxford University Press, 1967), pp. 431–456.

8. Pablo G. Macías, *Octubre sangriento en Morelia* (México: Editorial Acasim, 1968), p. 4.

9. Rafael Segovia, "The Strike and its Aftermath, A Narrative and Perspective," in *Political Power in Latin America: Seven Confrontations*, R. R. Fagen and W. A. Cornelius, Jr., eds. (Englewood Cliffs, N.J.: Prentice-Hall, 1970), pp. 316–323.

10. *El Día*, 29 July 1968.

11. Interview by author with eyewitness, 31 July 1968.

12. *El Día*, 30 July 1968.

13. *Ovaciones*, 2nd ed., 30 July 1968.

14. *Ultimas Noticias de Excelsior*, 2nd ed., 30 July 1968.

15. Ibid., 31 July 1968.

16. *Excelsior*, 31 July 1968, pp. 6–7.

17. Ibid.

18. *Los procesos de México 68*, p. 42.

19. Jorge Carrión, "Biografía política del movimiento," in *Tres culturas en agonía*, p. 33.

20. Poniatowska, *La noche de Tlatelolco*, pp. 29–30.

21. Evelyn P. Stevens, "Mexican Machismo: Politics and Value Orientations," *Western Political Quarterly* 18 (December 1965): 848–857.

22. Evelyn P. Stevens, "*Marianismo:* The Other Face of *Machismo* in Latin America," in *Female and Male in Latin America*, Ann Pescatello, ed. (Pittsburgh: University of Pittsburgh Press, 1973).

23. Robert F. Peck and Rogelio Díaz Guerrero, "The Meaning of Love in Mexico and the United States," mimeographed, no date.

24. James N. Goodsell, "Mexico: Why the Students Rioted," *Current History* 56 (January 1969): 31–35, 53.

25. Report by a government agent, in *Los procesos de México 68*, p. 43.

26. Carrión, in *Tres culturas en agonía*, p. 33.

27. *Excelsior*, 2 August 1968, p. 8A.

28. Ibid., p. 14A.

29. Poniatowska, *La noche de Tlatelolco*, p. 97.

30. For a discussion of Article 145, see chapter 8 of this book.

31. *Excelsior*, 23 August 1968, p. 1.

32. Eugenio Mendoza Navarro, "140 años de historia, el informe presidencial," *Mañana* 22 (4 September 1965): 8–17.

33. See Salvador Hernández, *El PRI y el movimiento estudiantil de 1968* (México: Ediciones "El Caballito," 1971), p. 88; and González de Alba, *Los días y los años*, p. 84.

34. Tarsicio Ocampo, compiler, *México, conflicto estudiantil 1968*,

CIDOC Dossier No. 23, Mexico, Centro Intercultural de Documentación, 1969.

35. *Siempre!* 18 September 1968, p. 10.

36. Pablo González Casanova, "El conflicto estudiantil; decisiones y riesgos," *Excelsior*, 13 September 1968, p. 7.

37. *El Día*, 2 September 1968.

38. *Los procesos de México 68*, pp. 31–33.

39. See, for example, the report of a six-hour confrontation at Tlatelolco, published in *Novedades*, 22 September 1968.

40. See *New York Times*, 1 October 1968.

41. *El Día*, 3 October 1968.

42. Goodsell, "Mexico: Why the Students Rioted," pp. 32–33.

43. *Le Monde*, Paris, 5 October 1968.

44. Secret service report in *Los procesos de México 68*, pp. 38–39.

45. *La Prensa*, 3 October 1968.

46. *Le Monde*, Paris, 5 October 1968.

47. *La Prensa*, 3 October 1968.

48. See, for example, *Le Monde*, 5 October 1968; *Figaro*, Paris, 4 October 1968, and *Look* magazine, 12 December 1968 ("The Shooting of Oriana Fallaci").

49. Poniatowska, *La noche de Tlatelolco*, p. 175.

50. *Excelsior*, 3 October 1968.

51. *New York Times*, 9 July 1970.

52. Jorge Ibargüengoitía, "La literatura Tlatelolco," *Libro Abierto* (November 1971): 38–40.

53. *El Día*, 4 October 1968.

54. *El Día*, 5 October 1968.

Chapter 7

1. Armando Hinojosa and Adriana Cosío Pascal, *Análisis psicológico del estudiante universitario* (México: La Prensa Médica Mexicana, 1967), p. 11.

2. Mexican jurisconsults are proud of their constitutional device of

amparo, which they regard as superior to the Anglo-American writ of habeas corpus. See Title Three, Chapter IV, Article 107 of the Mexican Constitution. For a discussion of the history and operation of this writ, see Richard D. Baker, *Judicial Review in Mexico* (Austin: University of Texas Press, 1971).

3. George M. Foster, "Treasure Tales, and the Image of the Static Economy in a Mexican Peasant Community," *Journal of American Folklore* 77 (January–March 1964): 39–44.

4. *Excelsior*, 21 August 1966.

5. Ernesto Julio Teissier, "De domingo a domingo," *Novedades*, 21 August 1966.

6. *Excelsior*, 8 December 1967.

7. The new medical school is located on the UNAM campus in a southern suburb of Mexico City.

8. Informant No. 203, reinterview dated 21 July 1968.

9. Ibid.

10. Rodolfo Stavenhagen, "Un modelo para el estudio de las organizaciones políticas en México," *Revista Mexicana de Sociología* 29 (April–June 1967): 333.

11. *El Popular*, 9 April 1959.

12. See Carlos Sánchez Cárdenas, *Disolución social y seguridad nacional* (México: Ediciones Linterna, 1970), pp. 113–161.

13. For the circumstances surrounding the original passage of this measure during World War II, and its subsequent amendment, see Evelyn P. Stevens, "Legality and Extra-Legality in Mexico," *Journal of Inter-American Studies and World Affairs* 12 (January 1970): 62–75.

14. Jorge Carrión et al, *Tres culturas en agonía* (México: Editorial Nuestro Tiempo, 1969), p. 33.

15. *El Día*, 25 May 1971.

16. *El Día*, 13 June 1971.

Chapter 8

1. Jesús Silva Herzog, *El pensamiento económico, social y político de México, 1810–1964* (México: Instituto Mexicano de Investigaciones Económicas, 1967), p. 321.

2. Raymond Vernon, *The Dilemma of Mexico's Development* (Cambridge: Harvard University Press, 1963); Raymond Vernon, ed., *Public Policy and Private Enterprise in Mexico* (Cambridge: Harvard University Press, 1964); Gustavo Romero Kolbeck, "Economic Development in Mexico," in *Economic Development Issues: Latin America*, Committee for Economic Development (New York, Washington, London: Frederick A. Praeger, 1967), pp. 177–214.

3. Helio Jaguaribe, *Economic and Political Development* (Cambridge: Harvard University Press, 1968), pp. 9–12. Fourteen years earlier, Sanford A. Mosk described the trend toward concentration on industrialization in Mexico. See his *Industrial Revolution in Mexico* (Berkeley: University of California Press, 1954), especially pp. 306–307.

4. See especially Pablo González Casanova, *Democracy in Mexico* (New York: Oxford University Press, 1970), and Calixto Rangel Contla, *El desarrollo diferencial de México, 1940–1960* (México: Universidad Nacional Autónoma de México, Thesis, Escuela Nacional de Ciencias Políticas y Sociales, 1965).

5. Roger D. Hansen, *The Politics of Mexican Development* (Baltimore and London: The Johns Hopkins Press, 1971), p. 95.

6. For a fuller exposition of the problems arising from this approach to economic planning, see Markos J. Mamalakis, "The Theory of Sectoral Clashes," *Latin American Research Review* 4 (Fall 1969): 9–46.

7. Narciso Bassols Batalla, *La revolución mexicana cuesta abajo* (México: Editorial Impresiones Modernas, S.A., 1960), and *Las pisadas de los días* (México: Guión de Acontecimientos Nacionales e Internacionales, Talleres Gráficos de Impresiones Modernas, 1965).

8. See his "Programación social," in *Bases para la planeación económica y social de México* (proceedings of the seminar of the same title held in April 1965, under the auspices of the National School of Economics [México: Universidad Nacional Autónoma de México, Siglo XXI Editores, S.A., 1966]), pp. 177–198.

9. Rangel Contla, *El desarrollo diferencial de México*, pp. 107–108.

10. González Casanova, *Democracy in Mexico*, pp. 139 and 146.

11. A good example is the resurrection of José Yves Limantour's *Apuntes sobre mi vida* (México: Porrúa Hermanos, 1965).

12. Silva Herzog, *El pensamiento económico*, p. 324.

13. James D. Cochrane, "Mexico's 'New Científicos': The Díaz Ordaz Cabinet," *Inter-American Economic Affairs* 21 (Summer 1967): 61–72.

14. Claude Levi-Strauss, *Tristes Tropiques: An Anthropological Study of Primitive Societies in Brazil* (New York: Criterion Books, 1961).

15. Charles Wagley and Marvin Harris have described the controversy over the Indian (to let be or not to let be) in their *Minorities in the New World* (New York: Columbia University Press, 1958).

16. For a concise scholarly overview of this genre, see Concha Mélendez, *La novela indianista en Hispanoamérica*, 2nd ed. (Río Piedras, Ediciones de la Universidad de Puerto Rico, 1961).

17. Ciro Alegría, *El mundo es ancho y ajeno* (Santiago, Chile: Ediciones Ercilla, 1941).

18. See, for example, Benito Rey Romay, "La planeación del desarrollo industrial," *Cuadernos Americanos* 28 (January–February 1969): 119–130.

19. Lucila Leal de Araujo, *Aspectos económicos del Instituto Mexicano del Seguro Social* (México: Cuadernos Americanos, 1966), pp. 84–85.

20. González Casanova, *Democracy in Mexico*, p. 134.

21. Bo Anderson and James D. Cockroft, "Control and Cooptation in Mexican Politics," *International Journal of Comparative Sociology* 7 (March 1966): 2–28.

22. Rogelio Díaz Guerrero, "The Active and the Passive Syndromes," *Revista Interamericana de Psicología* 1 (December 1967): 263–272; Rogelio Díaz Guerrero, "Socio-Cultural and Psychodynamic Processes in Adolescent Transition and Mental Health," mimeographed (presented at the University of Oklahoma Fifth Social Psychology Symposium, May 1964); Rogelio Díaz Guerrero and Robert F. Peck, *Respeto y Posición Social en Dos Culturas*, mimeographed (no dates).

23. Roger D. Hansen, *Mexican Economic Development* (Washington, D.C.: National Planning Association, Studies in Development Progress, No. 2, 1971), p. 93.

24. Joseph Alan Kahl, *The Measurement of Modernism: A Study of Values in Brazil and Mexico* (Austin and London: University of Texas Press, 1968), pp. 118–119.

25. Wayne A. Cornelius, Jr., "Urbanization as an Agent in Latin American Political Instability: The Case of Mexico," *American Political Science Review* 63 (September 1969): 838 and 846.

26. Kahl, *The Measurement of Modernism*, p. 117.

27. Victor Flores Olea, "Política y Desarrollo," in *Los problemas nacionales* (México: Universidad Nacional Autónoma de México, 1971), p. 119.

28. Ibid., pp. 126–127.

Chapter 9

1. Karl M. Schmitt, *Communism in Mexico* (Austin: University of Texas Press, 1965), p. 164.

2. For the railroad case, see *Excelsior*, 30 March 1969, p. 1; and for the doctors' case, see *El Día*, 19 August 1966, p. 1 and "De Domingo a Domingo," in *Novedades*, 21 August 1966.

3. See, for example, Bernabé Rodríguez Aranda, *El caciquismo y el comisariado ejidal* (México: Universidad Nacional Autónoma de México, Thesis, Facultad de Derecho, 1960), passim.

4. Evelyn P. Stevens, "Legality and Extra-Legality in Mexico," *Journal of Inter-American Studies and World Affairs* 12 (January 1970): 62–75.

5. Samuel P. Huntington, "Political Development and Political Decay," *World Politics* 17 (1965): 386–430.

6. Evelyn P. Stevens, "Mexican Machismo: Politics and Value Orientations," *Western Political Quarterly* 18 (December 1965): 848–857.

7. Evelyn P. Stevens, "*Marianismo:* The Other Face of *Machismo* in Latin America," in *Female and Male in Latin America*, Ann Pescatello, ed. (Pittsburgh: University of Pittsburgh Press, 1973), pp. 89–101.

8. See the concept of "power deflation" developed by Chalmers Johnson in his *Revolutionary Change* (Boston: Little, Brown, and Co., 1966), pp. 27–33.

9. Evelyn P. Stevens, "Mexican Machismo."

10. Eric Wolf, *Sons of the Shaking Earth* (Chicago: University of Chicago Press, 1959, Phoenix Books paperback), p. 239.

11. Angelina C. de Moreleón, "Algunas formas del valor y de la cobardía en el mexicano," *Filosofía y Letras* 23 (January–June 1952): 165–174.

12. See, for example, "Importing Hembrismo," *Human Behavior* (September–October 1972): 41.

13. May Nordquist Díaz, *Tonalá: A Mexican Peasant Town in Transition* (Berkeley: University of California Press, 1967), p. 177.

14. Evelyn P. Stevens, "Legality and Extra-Legality in Mexico," p. 73.

Glossary

Alianza
Alianza de Médicos Mexicanos
(Alliance of Mexican Physicians)

AMMRI
Asociación Mexicana de Médicos Residentes e Internos
(Mexican Association of Resident Physicians and Interns)

BUO
Bloque Unido de Obreros
(United Workers' Bloc)

CGT
Confederación General de Trabajadores
(General Confederation of Workers)

CNED
Central Nacional de Estudiantes Democráticos
(National Central [Organization] of Democratic Students)

CNH
Consejo Nacional de Huelga
(National Strike Council)

CNT
Central Nacional de Trabajadores
(National Central [Organization] of Workers)

CROC
Confederación Regional de Obreros y Campesinos
(Regional Confederation of Workers and Peasants)

CROM
Confederación Regional Obrera Mexicana
(Regional Workers' Confederation of Mexico)

CTM
Confederación de Trabajadores Mexicanos
(Confederation of Mexican Workers)

FNET
Federación Nacional de Estudiantes Técnicos
(National Federation of Technical Students)

FSTSE
Federación de Sindicatos de Trabajadores al Servicio del Estado
(Federation of Unions of Civil Service Workers)

FUM
Frente Universitario Mexicano
(Mexican University Front)

IMSS
Instituto Mexicano de Serguro Social
(Mexican Institute of Social Security)

IPN
Instituto Politécnico Nacional
(National Polytechnic Institute)

ISSSTE
Instituto de Seguridad Social al Servicio de los Trabajadores del Estado
(Institute of Social Security at the Service of the Civil Service Workers)

MURO
Movimiento Universitario de Renovadora Orientación
(University Movement of Renovational Orientation)

PAN
Partido de Acción Nacional
(National Action Party)

PARM
Partido Auténtico de la Revolución Mexicana
(Authentic Party of the Mexican Revolution)

PC
Partido Comunista
(Communist Party)

PIPSA
Productora e Importadora de Papel, Sociedad Anónima
(Paper Producer and Importer, Inc.)

PPS
Partido Popular Socialista
(Popular Socialist Party)

PRI
Partido Revolucionario Institucional
(Institutional Revolutionary Party)

SNTIMSS
Sindicato Nacional de Trabajadores del Instituto Mexicano de Seguro Social
(National Union of Workers of the Mexican Institute of Social Security)

STFRM
Sindicato de Trabajadores Ferrocarrileros de la República Mexicana
(Union of Railroad Workers of the Mexican Republic)

STMMSRM
Sindicato de Trabajadores Mineros, Metalúrgicos y Similares de la República Mexicana
(Union of Mining, Metallurgic, and Associated Workers of the Mexican Republic)

UNAM
Universidad Nacional Autónoma de México
(National Autonomous University of Mexico)

Bibliography

"Poor Mexico—so far from Heaven and so near to the United States!"

Surely every foreign researcher who has done field work in Mexico has had this old saw quoted to him at least a dozen times, and each time courtesy constrains him to chuckle as though he had never heard it before. This proximity has resulted in Mexico's being the most frequently studied of all Latin-American nations; in some respects the research waters have been overfished. Because the author assumes that serious students are aware of the immense bibliographic resources available to them in English, in the areas of their own particular interests, no attempt is made here to duplicate listings available elsewhere. Instead, emphasis is placed on materials which are especially pertinent to the topics discussed in this book.

Academia Nacional de Medicina de México. *Problemas del ejercicio profesional del médico en México* (Mesas Redondas de las V jornadas Médicas Nacionales). México: Imprenta Universitaria, 1960.

Alarcón, Donato G. "Planeación de la enseñanza y del ejercicio de la medicina." *Revista de la Facultad de Medicina* 7 (May 1965): 525–535.

———. *Valuación de la necesidad de médicos de la República Mexicana y planeación de la enseñanza médica.* México: Universidad Nacional Autónoma de México (Facultad de Medicina), 1965.

Alba, Victor. *Historia del movimiento obrero en America Latina.* México: Libreros Mexicanos Unidos, 1964.

———. *Las ideas sociales contemporáneas en México.* México: Fondo de Cultura Económica, 1960.

———. *The Mexicans: The Making of a Nation.* New York: Praeger, 1967.

Alcaraz, Rodolfo. "Sesenta Años de periodismo mexicano." *Historia y Sociedad* 6 (1966): 107–125.

Alegría, Ciro. *El mundo es ancho y ajeno.* Santiago (Chile): Ediciones Ercilla, 1941.

Alexander, Robert J. *Organized Labor in Latin America.* New York: The Free Press and London: Collier-Macmillan, 1965.

Alianza de Médicos Mexicanos. *Informe de la comisión de conflictos a la asamblea nacional.* Mimeograph. México: 29 May 1965.

Alisky, Marvin Howard. "Educational Aspects of Broadcasting in Mexico." Ph.D. dissertation, University of Texas, Austin, 1953.

———. "Growth of Newspapers in Mexico's Provinces." *Journalism Quarterly* 37 (Winter 1960): 75–82.

———. "Mexico's National Hour on Radio." *Nieman Reports,* October 1953.

Almond, Gabriel, and Sidney Verba. *The Civic Culture: Political Attitudes and Democracy in Five Nations.* Princeton: Princeton University Press, 1963.

———. *The Civic Culture: Political Attitudes and Democracy in Five Nations.* Boston: Little, Brown and Company, 1965 paperback.

Alvear Acevedo, Carlos. *Historia sumaria del periodismo.* México: Universidad Nacional Autónoma de México (Facultad de Filosofía y Letras), 1963.

American Academy of Political and Social Science. *Annals: Latin America Tomorrow* 360 (July 1965).

Anderson, Bo, and James D. Cockroft. "Control and Cooptation in Mexican Politics." *International Journal of Comparative Sociology* 7 (March 1966): 11–28.

Andreu González, Arquímedes. *La supremacia del poder ejecutivo como institución adversa al principio de división de poderes.* México: Universidad Nacional Autónoma de México (Thesis, Facultad de Derecho), 1958.

Anonymous. "Auge de las vías de comunicación en el progreso de todo el país." *Revista Fiscal y Financiera* 17 (31 October 1957): 124.

Apter, David. *Choice and the Politics of Allocation.* New Haven: Yale University Press, 1971.

Araiza, Luis. *Historia del movimiento obrero mexicano.* México: Editorial Cuautémoc, 1964.

Aramoni, Aniceto. *Psicoanálisis de la dinámica de un pueblo (México, tierra de hombres)*. México: B. Costa-Amic, 1961.

Aron, Raymond. "Student Rebellion: Vision of the Future or Echo of the Past?" *Political Science Quarterly* 84 (June 1969): 289–310.

Arrow, Kenneth J. *Social Choice and Individual Values*. New York: Wiley, 1951.

Ashby, Joe C. *Organized Labor and the Mexican Revolution Under Lázaro Cárdenas*. Chapel Hill: University of North Carolina Press, 1963.

Asociación Mexicana de Servicio Social, A.C. "Directorio." Offset. México: 1964.

Austin, Rubén Vargas. "The Development of Economic Policy in Mexico with Special Reference to Economic Doctrines." Ph.D. dissertation, State University of Iowa, 1958.

Baker, Richard Don. *Judicial Review in Mexico*. Austin: University of Texas Press, 1971.

Balam, Gilberto. *Cuarto menguante, los valores de una sociedad que se eclipsa*. México: B. Costa-Amic, 1967.

———. *Tlatelolco: reflexiones de un testigo*. México: Talleres Lenasas, 1969.

Baruch Velázquez, Dinah Estela. *El problema de los ferrocarriles nacionales de México*. México: Universidad Nacional Autónoma de México (Thesis, Facultad de Economía), 1945.

Bassols Batalla, Narciso. *Las pisadas de los días*. México: Guión de Acontecimientos Nacionales e Internacionales (Talleres Gráficos de Impresiones Modernas), 1965.

———. *La revolución mexicana cuesta abajo*. México: Editorial Impresiones Modernas, S.A., 1960.

Basulto Jaramillo, Enrique. *Libertad de prensa en México*. México: 1954 (no publisher).

Basurto, Jorge. *La Influencia de la economía y del estado en las huelgas; el caso de México*. México: Universidad Nacional Autónoma de México (Escuela Nacional de Ciencias Políticas y Sociales), 1962.

Basurto, Jorge. "El líder obrero en México." *Mundo Nuevo* (March–April 1971): 71–76.

——— "México: el movimiento estudiantil." *Mundo Nuevo* (December 1968): 4–11.

Bataillon, Claude. "Communications de masse et vie urbaine au Mexique." *Communications* (March 1964): 19–35.

Beals, Ralph Leon. *Politics of Social Research: An Inquiry into the Ethics and Responsibilities of Social Scientists.* Chicago: Aldine Publishing Co., 1969.

Beechert, Edward D., Jr. "The Gap Between Planning Goals and Achievements in Latin America." *Inter-American Economic Affairs* 19 (Summer 1965): 59–74.

Béjar Navarro, Raúl. *El mito del mexicano.* México: Universidad Nacional Autónoma de México (Thesis, Escuela Nacional de Ciencias Políticas y Sociales), 1966.

Bermúdez, María Elvira. *La vida familiar del mexicano.* México: Antigua Librería Robredo (series México y lo Mexicano), 1955.

Beteta, Ramón. *Pensamiento y dinámica de la revolución mexicana.* México: Editorial México Nuevo, 1950.

Blanco Moheno, Roberto. *Tlatelolco: historia de una infamia.* México: Editorial Diana, S.A., 1969.

Bloch, Marc. *Feudal Society*, 2 vols. Translated by L. A. Manyon. Chicago: University of Chicago Press, 1961.

Brandenburg, Frank. "A Contribution to the Theory of Entrepreneurship and Economic Development: The Case of Mexico." *Inter-American Economic Affairs* 16 (Winter 1962): 3–23.

———. *The Making of Modern Mexico.* Englewood Cliffs, N.J.: Prentice-Hall, 1964.

———. "Organized Business in Mexico." *Inter-American Economic Affairs* 12 (Winter 1958): 26–50.

———. "The Relevance of Mexican Experience to Latin American Development." *Orbis* (Spring 1965): 190–213.

Bravo Santos, Oscar. *La radiodifusión comercial en la legislación mexicana.* México: Universidad Nacional Autónoma de México (Thesis, Facultad de Derecho), 1956.

Brickman, William W., and Stanley Lehrer. *Conflict and Change on the Campus: The Response to Student Hyperactivism.* New York: School and Society Books, 1970.

Briseño, Romo. *Confiaencialmente: México social y burocrático al descubierto.* México: B. Costa-Amic Editor, 1967.

Brothers, Dwight S., and Leopoldo Solís M. *Mexican Financial Development.* Austin and London: University of Texas Press, 1966.

Cabrera, Amilcar. "The Peasant Struggle in Mexico." *Revolution: Africa, Latin America, Asia* 1 (February 1964): 38–41.

Calderón de la Barca, Frances. *Life in Mexico During a Residence of Two Years in that Country.* London: J. M. Dent & Sons, and New York: E. P. Dutton & Co., 1968.

Calvert, Peter. "The Mexican Political System: A Case Study in Political Development." *Journal of Development Studies* 4 (July 1968): 464–480.

Cañibe Rosas, Juan Manuel. *Estudio exploratorio sobre el prestigio de algunas ocupaciones.* México: Universidad Nacional Autónoma de México (Thesis, Escuela Nacional de Ciencias Políticas y Sociales), 1965.

Cárdenas, L., Jr. "Contemporary Problems of Local Government in Mexico." *Western Political Quarterly* 18 (December 1965): 858–865.

Carmona, Fernando. "Reflexiones sobre el desarrollo y la formación de las clases sociales en México." *Cuadernos Americanos* 154 (September–October 1967): 89–119.

Carrasco Puente, Rafael. *La prensa en México.* México: Universidad Nacional Autónoma de México, 1962.

Carreño, Alberto. "Las clases sociales en México." *Revista Mexicana de Sociología* (September 1950): 333–350.

Carrión, Jorge, Daniel Cazés, Sol Arguedas, and Fernando Carmona. *Tres culturas en agonía.* México: Editorial Nuestro Tiempo, 1969.

Carter, Roy E., Jr. "Some Problems and Distinctions in Cross-Cultured Research." *The American Behavioral Scientist* 9 (March 1966): 23–24.

Castaño, Luis. "El desarrollo de los medios de información en América Latina y crisis de la libertad de expresión." *Ciencias Políticas y Sociales* 8 (April–June 1962): 291–306.

———. *Temas de sociología política mexicana.* México: Universidad Nacional Autónoma de México (Instituto de Investigaciones Sociales), 1960.

Castillejos Escobar, Marcos. *Examen dogmático de disposiciones penales contenidas en la ley federal del trabajo; trabajo elaborado en el Seminario de Derecho Penal.* México: 1965.

Castro Adeath, Evangelina. *Esquema para un estudio del ejecutivo gubernamental.* México: Universidad Nacional Autónoma de México (Thesis, Escuela Nacional de Cienicas Políticas y Sociales), 1963.

Castro Leal, Antonio. "El Pueblo de México espera: Estudios sobre la radio y la televisión." *Cuadernos Americanos* 150 (January–February 1967): 75–102.

Cela, Camilo José. *Diccionario secreto I.* Madrid: Ediciones Alfaguara, S.A., 1969.

Centro de Estudios Educativos. *Boletín Mensual Informativo*, vol. 1, 1965.

Cerqueira, S. "Mouvements agraires, mouvements nationaux et révolution en Amerique Latine." *Revue Française de Science Politique* 19 (October 1969): 1018–1041.

Chávez Orozco, Luis. "Orígenes de la política de Seguridad Social." *Historia Mexicana* 16 (October–December 1966): 155–183.

Chellet Osante, Roberto. *Organización administrativa y política de la República Mexicana.* México: Editorial de la Secretaría de Hacienda y Crédito Público, Academia de Capacitación, 1955.

Cherry, Colin. *On Human Communication: A Review, A Survey, and A Criticism.* 2nd ed. Cambridge: The MIT Press, 1966.

Chevalier, François. " 'Ejido' et Stabilité au Mexique." *Revue Française de Science Politique* 16 (August 1966): 717–752.

Clark, Marjorie Ruth. *Organized Labor in Mexico.* Chapel Hill: University of North Carolina Press, 1934.

Cline, Howard F. *Mexico: From Revolution to Evolution.* New York: Oxford University Press, 1963.

———. *The United States and Mexico.* Cambridge: Harvard University Press, 1963.

Cobo Ortiz, Héctor. *La terminación de la huelga.* Mèxico: Universidad Nacional Autónoma de México (Thesis, Facultad de Derecho), 1965.

Cochrane, James D. "Mexico's 'New Científicos': The Díaz Ordaz Cabinet." *Inter-American Economic Affairs* 21 (Summer 1967): 61–72.

Cole, William E., and Richard D. Sanders. "Income Distribution, Profits, and Savings in the Recent Economic Experience of Mexico." *Inter-American Economic Affairs* 24 (Autumn 1970): 49–63.

Coleman, James S. "Foundations for a Theory of Collective Decisions." *The American Journal of Sociology* 71 (May 1966): 615–627.

Commitee for Economic Development. *Economic Development Issues: Latin America.* New York, Washington, London: Frederick A. Praeger, 1967.

Cornelius, Wayne A., Jr. "Urbanization as an Agent in Latin American Political Instability: The Case of Mexico." *American Political Science Review* 63 (September 1969): 833–857.

Cosío Villegas, Daniel. *American Extremes.* Austin: University of Texas Press, 1964.

———. *El sistema político mexicano: las posibilidades de cambio.* Austin: The University of Texas (Institute of Latin American Studies), 1972.

Covarrubias, José. "Trascendencia política de la reforma agraria." *Problemas agrícolas e industriales de México* 5 (July–September 1953): 129.

Cumberland, Charles Curtis. *Mexico: The Struggle for Modernity.* New York: Oxford University Press, 1968.

Dealy, Glen. "Prolegomena on the Spanish American Political Tradition." *Hispanic American Historical Review* 48 (February 1968): 37–58.

De Castro, Josué, Irving Louis Horowitz, and John Gerassi, eds. *Latin American Radicalism: A Documentary Report on Left and National Movements.* New York: Random House, 1969.

De la Riva, Dr. Xavier, Dr. Miguel A. Cervantes, Dr. Felipe García Sánchez, and Dr. Gustavo Viniegra. *Planeación, administración y evaluación de los programas de salud pública en México.* México: Secretaría de Salubridad y Asistencia, Segundo Congreso Mexicano de Salud Pública, April 1963.

Deutsch, Karl W. *Nationalism and Social Communication.* New York: John Wiley & Sons, 1953.

———, and Leroy N. Rieselbach. "Recent Trends in Political Theory and Political Philosophy." *Annals* 360 (July 1965): 139–162.

Deutschmann, John, T. McNelly, and Huber Ellingsworth. "Mass Media Use by Sub-Elites in 11 Latin American Countries." *Journalism Quarterly* 38 (Autumn 1961): 460–472.

Díaz, May Nordquist. *Tonalá: A Mexican Peasant Town in Transition.* Berkeley: University of California Press, 1967.

Díaz-Guerrero, Rogelio. "The Active and the Passive Syndromes." *Revista Interamericana de Psicología* 1 (December 1967): 263–272.

———. *Estudios de psicología del mexicano.* México: Editorial F. Trillas, S.A., 1968.

———. "Neurosis and the Mexican Family Structure." *American Journal of Psychiatry* 112 (December 1955): 411–417.

———. "Socio-Cultural and Psychodynamic Processes in Adolescent Transition and Mental Health." Mimeograph. Paper presented at the University of Oklahoma Fifth Social Psychology Symposium, May 1964.

———. Rogelio, L. Lara-Tapia, H. M. Capella, et al.

"Preliminary Study on International Tensions." Mimeograph. México: The Mexican Group for Study of International Tensions, February 1963.

———, and Robert F. Peck. *Respeto y Posición Social en Dos Culturas.* Mimeograph. No date.

Díaz Rangel, Eleazar. *Pueblos sub-informados.* Caracas: Imprenta Universitaria de Caracas, 1967.

Easton, David. "Political Anthropology." In *Biennial Review of Anthropology,* edited by Bernard J. Siegel, pp. 210–249. Stanford: Stanford University Press, 1959.

Echánove Trujillo, Carlos A. *Sociología mexicana.* México: Editorial Porrúa, S.A., 1963.

Encinas, Luis. *La alternativa de México.* México: Ediciones Sonot, 1969.

Enríquez Simoní, Guillermo. *La libertad de prensa en México, una mentira rosa.* México: B. Costa-Amic, Editor, 1967.

Erlandson, Erling Halvard. "The Press of Mexico, with Special Consideration of Economic Factors." Ph.D. dissertation, Northwestern University, 1963.

Estados Unidos Mexicanos, Secretaría de Industria y Comercio *Anuario estadístico* 1962–1963, 1963–1964. México: Talleres Gráficos de la Nación, 1965 and 1966.

Estados Unidos Mexicanos, Secretaría de Industria y Comercio, Dirección General de Estadística, *9°Censo General de Población, 1970; resumen de las principales características por entidad federativa.* México: November 1970.

Estados Unidos Mexicanos, *Colección de testimonios, documentos, acuerdos, decretos y leyes importantes para la historia de un régimen.* México: Ediciones del Centro de Estudios Nacionales, 1965, Nos. 3 and 4.

Estados Unidos Mexicanos. *Constitucion política.* México: Editorial Olimpo, 1966.

Estados Unidos Mexicanos, Poder Ejecutivo Federal *Diario Oficial.* México (no publisher, serial publication).

Estados Unidos Mexicanos, Secretaría de Educación Publica, Dirección General de Acción Social. *Doctrina, métodos y realizaciones de trabajo social educativo durante el sexenio 1952–1958.* México: Talleres Gráficos de la Secretaría de Educación Pública, 1958.

Estados Unidos Mexicanos, Presidencia de la República. *El Gobierno Mexicano.* México: Dirección General de Difusión y Relaciones Públicas, 1964–1965 Nos. 1 (1–31 December 1964) through 9 (1–31 August 1965).

Estados Unidos Mexicanos, *Ley electoral federal y prontuario.* México: 1964.

Estados Unidos Mexicanos, *Ley del Instituto de Seguridad y Servicios Sociales de los Trabajadores del Estado.* México: December 28, 1959.

Estados Unidos Mexicanos, *Leyes y códigos de México: código penal para el Distrito y territorios federales, octava edición.* México: Editorial Porrúa, S.A., 1964.

Estados Unidos Mexicanos, *Leyes y códigos de México—nueva ley federal de derechos de autor.* México: Editorial Porrúa, S.A., 1964.

Estados Unidos Mexicanos, Secretaría de Obras Públicas. *Memoria de la construcción del ferrocarril Chihuahua al Pacífico.* México: Editorial Rabasa, 1963.

Estrada Sámano, Miguel I. *Notas sobre la democracia y la representación política.* México: Universidad Nacional Autónoma de México (Thesis, Facultad de Derecho y Ciencias Políticas), 1959.

Ezcurdia, Mario. *Análisis teórico del Partido Revolucionario Institucional.* México: B. Costa-Amic, 1968.

Fagen, Richard R. *Politics and Communication.* Boston: Little, Brown and Co., 1966.

———, and William S. Tuohy. "Aspects of the Mexican Political System." *Studies in Comparative International Development* 7 (Fall 1972): 208–220.

Fajardo Ortiz, Enrique. *Libertad de expresión en la prensa, el cine, la radio y la televisión.* México: Universidad Nacional Autónoma de México (Thesis, Facultad de Derecho y Ciencias Sociales), 1957.

Fals Borda, Orlando. "Marginality and Revolution in Latin America." Sage Publications *Studies in Comparative International Development* 6 (1970–1971) No. 4.

Farace, Vincent, and Lewis Donohew. "Mass Communication in National Social Systems: A Study of 43 Variables in 115 Countries." *Journalism Quarterly* (Spring 1965): 253–261.

Favre, Henri. "La vie Politique Mexicaine." In *Notes et Etudes Documentaires: Problèmes d'Amerique Latine.* Paris: Secrétariat Général du Gouvernement, Direction de la Documentation, No. 3.317, 9 September 1966.

Feder, E. "Sobre la impotencia política de los campesinos." *Revista Mexicana de Sociología* (April–June 1969): 323–386.

Ferrocarriles Nacionales. *La verdad sobre el tortuguismo en los Ferrocarriles Nacionales de México.* México: 1956 (no publisher).

Fitzgerald, Gerald E., ed. *Constitutions of Latin America.* Chicago: Henry Regnery Company, 1968.

Flores, Edmundo. "On Financing Land Reform: A Mexican Casebook." *Studies in Comparative International Development* 3 (1967–1968): 115–121.

Flores Olea, Victor. "Política y Desarrollo." In *Los problemas nacionales.* México: Universidad Nacional Autónoma de México, 1971.

Flores de la Peña, Horacio, ed. *Bases para la planeación económica y social de México.* México: Siglo XXI, 1966.

Flores Portuguez, Guillermo. *La inexistencia jurídica de la huelga.* México: Universidad Nacional Autónoma de México (Thesis, Facultad de Derecho), 1965.

Foster, George M. "The Dyadic Contract: A Model for the Social Structure of a Mexican Peasant Village." Part I, *American Anthropologist* 63 (December 1961): 1173–1192; Part II, *American Anthropologist* 65 (December 1963): 1280–1294.

———. *Empire's Children, The People of Tzintzuntzan.* México: Imprenta Nuevo Mundo, S.A., 1948 (Publication No. 6 of the Institute of Social Anthropology, Smithsonian Institution).

Foster, George M. "Treasure Tales, and the Image of the Static Economy in a Mexican Peasant Community." *Journal of American Folklore* 77 (January–March 1964): 39–44.

Frank, Andrew Gunder. "Mexico: The Janus Faces of 20th Century Bourgeois Revolution." *Monthly Review* 14 (November 1962): 370–388.

Friedrich, Paul W. "A Tarascan Cacicazgo: Structure and Function." In *Systems of Political Control and Bureaucracy in Human Societies.* Proceedings of the 1958 Spring Meeting of the American Ethnological Society, Seattle, 1958, pp. 23–29.

Fuentes Delgado, Rubén. "Presente y futuro de los ferrocarriles en México." *Investigación Económica* 24 (Second Trimester 1964): 293–303.

Fuentes Díaz, Vicente. *El problema ferrocarrilero de México.* México: edición del autor, 1951.

Gándara, Francisco Javier. *Alegato contra la prensa.* México: Universidad Nacional Autónoma de México (Thesis, Escuela Nacional de Ciencias Políticas y Sociales), 1959.

García Sancho, Francisco. *Planeación, planificación y democracia en México.* México: Universidad Nacional Autónoma de México (Thesis, Facultad de Derecho), 1959.

García Treviño, Rodrigo. *Precios, salarios, y mordidas.* México: Editorial América, 1953.

Garizurieta, César. *Isagoge sobre lo mexicano.* México: Porrúa y Obregón, S.A., 1952.

Gasio Campuzano, Alfonso. *La abolición del derecho de huelga en las empresas de servicios públicos.* México: Universidad Nacional Autónoma de México (Thesis, Facultad de Derecho), 1963.

Geertz, Clifford. "The Impact of the Concept of Culture on the Concept of Man." *Bulletin of the Atomic Scientists* (April 1966): 2–8.

Gill, Clark C. *Education in a Changing Mexico.* Washington, D.C.: U.S. Department of Health, Education, and Welfare, Office of Education, 1969.

Gill, Mario. *Los ferrocarrileros.* México: Editorial Extemporáneos, 1971.

Glade, William P., Jr., and Charles W. Anderson. *The Political Economy of Mexico: Two Studies.* Madison: University of Wisconsin Press, 1963.

Glenn, Norval D., and J. L. Simmons. "Are Regional Cultural Differences Diminishing?" *Public Opinion Quarterly* 31 (Summer 1967): 176–193.

Gómez Robleda, José. *Psicología del mexicano.* México: Universidad Nacional Autónoma de México (Biblioteca de Ensayos Sociológicos), 1962.

González de Alba, Luis. *Los días y los años.* México: Ediciones Era, 1971.

González Casanova, Pablo. *Democracy in Mexico.* Translated by Danielle Salti. New York: Oxford University Press, 1970.

———. "L'évolution du système de classes au Mexique." *Cahiers Internationaux de Sociologie* 28 (July–December 1965): 113–136.

———. "México: desarrollo y subdesarrollo." *Desarrollo Económico* 3 (April–September 1963): 285–302.

———. "La opinión pública." In *México: cincuenta años de Revolución.* México: Fondo de Cultura Económica, 1961.

———, and Ricardo Pozas Arciniega. "Un estudio sobre estratificación y movilidad social en la ciudad de México." *Ciencias Políticas y Sociales* 11 (January–March 1965): 115–185.

González Diaz Lombardo, F. "Esquema de la Seguridad Social Mexicana." *Justicia* (May 1965): 45–64.

González Navarro, Moisés. *La Confederación Nacional Campesina: un grupo de presión en la reforma agraria mexicana.* México: B. Costa-Amic Editor, 1968.

González Pedrero, Enrique, ed. *Los medios de comunicación de masas en México.* México: Universidad Nacional Autónoma de México (Facultad de Ciencias Políticas y Sociales, Serie Estudios 10), 1969.

González Pineda, Francisco. *El mexicano: su dinámica psicosocial.* México: Editorial Pax, 1959.

———. *El mexicano, psicología de su destructividad.* México: Editorial Pax-México (Asociación Psicoanalítica Mexicana, A.C.), 1961.

Goodsell, James N. "Mexico: Why the Students Rioted." *Current History* 56 (January 1969): 31–35, 53.

Gostkowski, Zygmunt. "Algunas consideraciones en torno a la validez de las técnicas de investigación utilizadas en los países en vías de desarrollo." *Ciencias Políticas y Sociales* 10 (July–September 1964): 441–451.

Greer, Thomas V. "An Analysis of Mexican Literacy." *Journal of Inter-American Studies* 11 (July 1969): 466–476.

Grimes, C. E., and Charles E. P. Simmons. "Bureaucracy and Political Control in Mexico: Towards an Assessment." *Public Administration Review* 29 (January–February 1969): 72–78.

Guémez Troncoso, Dr. José. *Manual de procedimientos contables para hospitales y catálogo de cuentas.* México: 1966 (no publisher).

Guerrero, Euquerio. *Manual de derecho del trabajo, Tomo II.* México: Talleres Gráficos "Galeza," 1962.

Hall, Edward Twitchell. *The Silent Language.* Garden City, N.Y.: Doubleday & Co., 1959.

Hall, Thomas L. *Health Manpower in Peru, A Case Study in Planning.* Baltimore: The Johns Hopkins Press, 1969.

Handy, Rollo, and Paul Kurtz. "Current Appraisal of the Behavioral Sciences." *The American Behavioral Scientist* 7 (February 1964), Supplement, pp. 97–120.

Hansen, Roger D. *Mexican Economic Development.* Washington, D.C.: National Planning Association (Studies in Development Progress, No. 2), 1971.

———. *The Politics of Mexican Development.* Baltimore and London: The Johns Hopkins Press, 1971.

Hawkins, C. "Reflections on Labor's Relation to Government and

Politics in Latin America." *Western Political Quarterly* (December 1967): 930–940.

Heath, Shirley Brice. *Telling Tongues: Language Policy in Mexico, Colony to Nation.* New York and London: Teachers College Press, Columbia University, 1972.

Hernández, Salvador. *El PRI y el movimiento estudiantil de 1968.* México: Ediciones "El Caballito," 1971.

Herring, Hubert. *History of Latin America.* New York: Alfred A. Knopf, 1961.

Hertzler, Joyce O. *A Sociology of Language.* New York: Random House, 1965.

Hinojosa, Armando, and Adriana Cosío Pascal. *Análisis psicológico del estudiante universitario.* México: La Prensa Médica Mexicana, 1967.

Hoffmann, Stanley, et al. *In Search of France: The Economy, Society and Political System in the Twentieth Century.* New York: Harper–Row, 1963.

Horowitz, Irving Louis, ed. *The Rise and Fall of Project Camelot: Studies in the Relationship Between Social Science and Practical Politics.* Cambridge: MIT Press, 1967.

Huerta Maldonado, Miguel. *Manual de geomédica mexicana.* México: Instituto Mexicano del Seguro Social, 1963.

Hunt, William H., Wilder W. Crane, and John C. Wahlke. "Interviewing Political Elites in Cross-cultural Comparative Research." *The American Journal of Sociology* 70 (July 1964): 59–68.

Huntington, Samuel P. "Political Development and Political Decay." *World Politics* 17 (1965): 386–430.

Hyman, Herbert Hiram. *Interviewing in Social Research.* Chicago: University of Chicago Press, 1954.

Ibargüengoitía, Jorge. "La literatura Tlatelolco." *Libro Abierto* (November 1971): 17, 19.

Ibarra de Anda, Fortino. *El periodismo en Mexico*, vol. 1. México: Imprenta Mundial, 1934.

Instituto Mexicano del Seguro Social. *La seguridad social en México.* México: Editorial Helio–México, 1964.

Instituto Mexicano del Seguro Social. *Ley del seguro social.* México: 1964 (no publisher).

Instituto Nacional Indigenista. *Realidades y proyectos, 16 años de trabajo,* vol. 10. México: Editorial Libros de México, S.A., 1964.

International Press Institute. *Les pressions du Pouvoir sur la Presse.* Zurich (Switzerland): L'Institut International de la Presse, 1955.

International Research Associates, S.A. de C.V. *El radiómetro coincidente* and *El videómetro de México.* México: July 1965.

Islas García, Luis. *Apuntes para el estudio del caciquismo en México.* México: Editorial Jus, 1962.

Iturriaga, José E. *La estructura social y cultural de México.* México: Fondo de Cultura Económica, 1951.

Jaguaribe, Helio. *Economic and Political Development: A Theoretical Approach and a Brazilian Case Study.* Cambridge: Harvard University Press, 1968.

Jiménez, A. *Picardía mexicana.* México: Libro Mex, 1960 (Twentieth Edition, April 1965).

Johnson, Chalmers. *Revolution and the Social System.* Stanford: Stanford University (The Hoover Institution on War, Revolution, and Peace), 1964.

———. *Revolutionary Change.* Boston: Little, Brown, and Co., 1966.

Johnson, Kenneth F. *Mexican Democracy: A Critical View.* Boston: Allyn and Bacon, 1971.

Kafel, Mieczyslaw. "Materia, métodos, tareas y tendencias de la investigación científica de la prensa en el mundo contemporáneo." *Ciencias Políticas y Sociales* 8 (April–June 1962): 307–323.

Kahl, Joseph Alan. *The Measurement of Modernism: A Study of Values in Brazil and Mexico.* Austin and London: University of Texas Press, 1968.

Kany, Charles Emil. *American-Spanish Euphemisms.* Berkeley: University of California Press, 1960.

Klapp, Orrin E. (of San Diego State College). "Mexican Social Types." *The American Journal of Sociology* 69 (January 1964): 404–414.

Kling, Merle. *A Mexican Interest Group in Action.* Englewood Cliffs, N.J.: Prentice-Hall, 1961.

Kuri Rame, Emilio. *Crítica en relación con la distribución de los médicos.* México: Universidad Nacional Autónoma de México (Thesis, Facultad de Medicina), 1965.

Labastida, Horacio. "El desarrollo de Mexico y las ciencias sociales." *América Latina* 7 (January–March 1964): 93–99.

Lambert, Jacques. *Amérique Latine, Structures Sociales et Institutions Politiques.* Paris: Presses Universitaires de France, 1963.

———. "Structure sociale dualiste et administration publique en Amérique Latine." *Bulletin de l'Institut international de l'Administration publique* (April–June 1967): 23–35.

Langer, Elinor. "Foreign Research: CIA plus Camelot Equals Troubles for U.S. Scholars." *Science* 156 (23 June 1967): 1583–1584.

Lazo Cerna, Dr. Humberto. *La medicina social en México.* México: Imprenta Zavala, 1966.

Leal de Araujo, Lucila. *Aspectos económicos del Instituto Mexicano del Seguro Social.* México: Cuadernos Americanos, 1966.

Lerdo de Tejada, Francisco. *Veinte mil horas de antesala.* México: Editorial Letras, S.A., 1968.

Lerner, Daniel. *The Passing of Traditional Society.* Glencoe: The Free Press, 1958.

———, and Wilbur Schramm. *Communication and Change in the Developing Countries.* Honolulu: University Press of Hawaii, 1967.

———. "Communications Systems and Social Systems: A Statistical Exploration in History and Policy." *Behavioral Science* 2 (October 1957): 266–275.

Levi-Strauss, Claude. *Tristes Tropiques: An Anthropological Study of Primitive Societies in Brazil.* New York: Criterion Books, 1961.

Lewis, Oscar. *Five Families: Mexican Case Studies in the Culture of Poverty.* New York: Basic Books, 1959.

———. "Husbands and Wives in a Mexican Village: A Study of Role Conflict." *American Anthropologist* 51 (1949): 602–610.

———. *Life in a Mexican Village.* Urbana: University of Illinois Press, 1951.

———. *Life in a Mexican Village: Tepoztlán Restudied.* Urbana: University of Illinois Press, 1963.

———. *Pedro Martínez: A Mexican Peasant and His Family.* New York: Random House, 1964.

Limantour, José Yves. *Apuntes sobre mi vida.* México: Porrúa Hermanos, 1965.

Linz, Juan J. "An Authoritarian Regime: Spain." In *Cleavages, Ideologies and Party Systems, Contributions to Comparative Political Sociology.* Edited by Erik Allardt and Yrjö Littunen. Helsinki: Transactions of the Westermarck Society, 1964.

Lipset, Seymour M. and Aldo Solari, eds. *Elites in Latin America.* New York: Oxford University Press, 1967.

Long, Norton E. "The Political Act as an Act of Will." *The American Journal of Sociology* 69 (July 1963): 1–6.

López Gallo, Manuel. *Economía y política en la historia de México.* México: Ediciones Solidaridad, 1965.

López Palacios, Manuel. *La autonomía municipal.* México: Universidad Nacional Autónoma de México (Thesis, Facultad de Derecho), 1959.

López Rosado, Diego G. *Ensayos sobre historia económica de México.* México: Universidad Nacional Autónoma de México, Dirección General de Publicaciones, 1965.

Lowry, Dennis T. "Radio, TV, and Literacy in Mexico." *Journal of Broadcasting* 14 (Spring 1970): 239–244.

Maccoby, Michael. "Love and Authority; A Study of Mexican Villagers." *Atlantic* 213 (March 1964): 121–126.

Macías, Pablo G. *Octubre sangriento en Morelia.* México: Editorial Acasim, 1968.

McNeely, John Hamilton. *The Railways of Mexico: A Study of Nationalization.* El Paso: Texas Western College (Southwestern Studies, Mongraph 5), 1964.

Mamalakis, Markos J. "The Theory of Sectoral Clashes." *Latin American Research Review* 4 (Fall 1969): 9–46.

Marcuse, Herbert. *One-Dimensional Man.* Boston: Beacon Press, 1964.

Martínez Corbalá, Gonzalo. *Problemas y soluciones de la vivienda popular en México: Tema No. 13.* México: Editora Agrícola Mexicana, 1965. (Partido Revolucionario Institucional, IV Asamblea Ordinaria, 28, 29 y 30 de abril de 1965.)

Medal, Consuelo. *El periodista como orientador social.* México: Universidad Nacional Autónoma de México (Thesis, Escuela Nacional de Ciencias Políticas y Sociales), 1965.

Medina Valdés, Gerardo. "El problema médico: gran oportunidad para una revisión al fondo." *La Nación* 24 (1 February 1965): 9–15.

Mélendez, Concha. *La novela indianista en Hispanoamérica.* 2nd ed. Río Piedras: Ediciones de la Universidad de Puerto Rico, 1961.

Mendieta y Nuñez, Lucio. "Un balance objetivo de la Revolución Mexicana." *Revista Mexicana de Sociología* 22 (May–August 1960): 529–542.

———. *México: realización y esperanza.* México: Editorial Superación, 1952.

———. "La sociología en México." *Cuadernos Americanos* 23 (1964): 122–137.

———. "Sociología de la burocracia." *Cuadernos de Sociología.* México: Universidad Nacional Autónoma (Instituto de Investigaciones Sociales), 1961.

Mendoza Navarro, Eugenio. "140 años de historia, el informe presidencial." *Mañana* 22 (4 September 1965): 8–17.

Millán, Dr. Alfonso. *El amor en el mexicano.* México: Colección Panorama, 1957.

———. "Los sueños y las pautas socioculturales." *Revista de Psicoanálisis, Psiquiatría, y Psicología* (January–April 1966): 62–70.

Mintz, Sidney W., and Eric Wolf. "An Analysis of Ritual Co-Parenthood (Compadrazgo)." *Southwestern Journal of Anthropology* 6 (Spring 1950): 341–369.

Mirin, Linda Sue. "Public Investment in Aguascalientes: A Study in the Politics of Economic Policy." Ph.D. dissertation, Harvard University, 1964.

Monroy Rivera, Oscar. *El mexicano enano, un mal de nuestro tiempo,* vol. 1. México: B. Costa-Amic, Editor, 1966.

Monsiváis, Carlos. *Días de guardar.* México: Ediciones Era, 1971.

Montaño, Dr. Guillermo. "La otra cara de la luna." *Siempre!* (25 November 1964): 77 and 86.

———. "El problema médico." *Siempre!* (23 December 1964): 6 and 70.

Monteforte Toledo, Mario, and Francisco Villagrán Kramer. *Izquierdas y derechas en Latinoamérica.* Buenos Aires (Argentina): Editorial Pleamar, 1968.

Moore, Wilbert E. *Industrialization and Labor, Social Aspects of Economic Development.* Ithaca and New York: Cornell University Press, 1951. (Published for the Institute of World Affairs, New School for Social Research.)

Moreleón, Angelina C. de "Algunas formas del valor y de la cobardía en el mexicano." *Filosofía y Letras* 23 (January–June 1952): 165–174.

Morones Prieto, Dr. Ignacio, and Sergio Novelo. "Modalidad de formación del médico latinoamericano como promotor del desarrollo económico y social de su país." *Universidades* 7 (July–September 1967): 117–126.

Mosk, Sanford A. *Industrial Revolution in Mexico.* Berkeley: University of California Press, 1954.

Moya Palencia, Mario. *La reforma electoral.* México: Ediciones Plataforma, 1964.

Navarrete, Ifigenia. *La Distribución del Ingreso y el Desarrollo Económico de México.* México: Universidad Nacional Autónoma de México, 1960.

Needler, Martin C. *Politics and Society in Mexico.* Albuquerque: University of New Mexico Press, 1971.

Neef, Arthur. *Labor in Mexico.* Washington, D.C.: United States Department of Labor, Bureau of Labor Statistics (B.L.S. Report No. 251), 1963.

Nevins, Allan. *Ordeal of the Union.* New York: Charles Scribner's Sons, 1947.

Nida, Eugene A. "Principles of Translation as Exemplified by Bible Translating." In *On Translation*, edited by Reuben A. Brower. Cambridge: Harvard University Press, 1959.

Noriega, Raúl. "Los mexicanos, analisis y síntesis." In *México, realización y esperanza*, pp. 39–46. México: Editorial Superación, 1955.

Norris, Renfro Cole. "A History of La Hora Nacional: Government Broadcasting via Privately Owned Radio Stations in Mexico." Ph.D. dissertation, University of Michigan, 1963.

Ocampo, Tarsicio (compiler). *México: conflicto estudiantil 1968.* 2 vols. México: Centro Intercultural de Documentación (CIDOC Dossier No. 23), 1969.

——— (compiler). *México: Huelga de la UNAM, marzo–mayo, 1966.* México: Centro Intercultural de Documentación (CIDOC Dossier No. 4), 1967.

——— (compiler). *México: los médicos y la socialización de la medicina.* México: Centro Intercultural de Documentación (CIDOC Dossier No. 18), 1968.

Ochoa Campos, Moisés. *Reseña histórica del periodismo mexicano.* México: Editorial Porrúa, S.A., 1968.

Oliveira Campos, Roberto. *Reflections on Latin American Development.* Austin: University of Texas Press, 1967.

Olizar, Marynka. *Guía a los mercados de México.* México (no publisher, serial publication, annual).

Organization of American States. *América en Cifras, 1970, Sección Cultural.* Washington, D.C.: Organization of American States, 1971.

Ortiz, Orlando (compiler). *Jueves de Corpus.* México: 1971.

——— (compiler). *La violencia en México.* México: 1971.

Padgett, L. Vincent. *The Mexican Political System.* Boston: Houghton Mifflin Co., 1966.

Parks, Richard W. "The Role of Agriculture in Mexican Economic Development." *Inter-American Economic Affairs* 18 (Summer 1964): 3–28.

Parsons, Talcott. *The Social System.* Glencoe: The Free Press, 1951.

Partido Revolucionario Institucional, Dirección de Relaciones Públicas. *Algunos servicios públicos.* México: 1967 (no publisher).

Partido Revolucionario Institucional. *Empadronamiento y afiliación de la ciudadanía al Partido Revolucionario Institucional.* México: Editora Agrícola Mexicana, 1965.

———. *Estatutos.* México: November 1963.

———. *Integración y funcionamiento de los órganos del partido.* México: Editora Agrícola Mexicana, 1965.

Paz, Octavio. *El laberinto de la soledad.* México: Fondo de Cultura Económica, 1959. (Now available in English as *The Labyrinth of Solitude: Life and Thought in Mexico.* Evergreen: 1961.)

———. *Posdata.* México: Siglo Veintiuno, Editores, 1970.

Peck, Robert F., and Rogelio Díaz Guerrero. "Two Core-Culture Patterns and the Diffusion of Values Across Their Border." Mimeograph. México: Paper presented at VII Congreso Interamericano de Psicología, Sociedad Interamericana de Psicología, 1963.

———. "The Meaning of Love in Mexico and the United States." Mimeograph. No date.

Pedroso D'Horta, Arnaldo. "Reportaje sobre México: situación de la prensa." *Espejo* 5 (November–December 1964): 21–33.

Pérez López, Enrique, et al. *Mexico's Recent Economic Growth.* Translated by Marjory Urquidi. Austin and London: University of Texas Press, 1967.

Plataforma de Profesionales Mexicanos. *Nuestro voto razonado por Luis Echeverría.* México: 22 October 1969, no publisher.

Poder Ejecutivo de la Nación, Secretaría de Estado, Negocios Interiores. *Ley de imprenta expedida por el C. Primer Jefe del Ejército constitucionalista.* México: Imprenta del Gobierno, 1917.

Poniatowska, Elena. *La noche de Tlatelolco.* México: Ediciones Era, 1971.

Price, C. "Death on the Mexican Campus." *New Statesman* 78 (28 November 1969): 762.

Procter, Phyllis Ann Weigand. "Mexico's Supermachos: Satire and Social Revolution in Comics by Rius." Ph.D. dissertation, University of Texas, Austin, 1972.

Pruneda, Salvador. *La caricatura como arma política.* México: Talleres Gráficos de la Nación, 1958.

Purcell, Susan Kaufman. "Decision-Making in an Authoritarian Regime: Mexico." Mimeograph. Paper presented at the 1971 Annual Meeting of the American Political Science Association.

Pye, Lucian W., ed. *Communications and Political Development.* Princeton: Princeton University Press, 1963.

———. *Politics, Personality and Nation Building: Burma's Search for Identity.* New Haven: Yale University Press, 1962.

Ramírez, Ramón. *El movimiento estudiantil de México, julio–diciembre de 1968*, 2 vols. México: Ediciones Era, 1969.

Ramírez, Santiago. *El Mexicano: psicología de sus motivaciones.* México: Editorial Pax, 1959.

Ramos, Dr. Pedro, Dr. Jorge Díaz González, Dr. José Manuel Alvarez Manilla, and Dr. Juan Alvarez Tostado M. *Proyección social del médico.* México: Manuel Casas, Impresor, 1965.

Ramos, Samuel. *El perfil del hombre y la cultura en México.* Buenos Aires: Espasa-Calpe, 1951.

———. "En torno a las ideas sobre el mexicano." *Cuadernos Americanos* 57 (May–June 1951).

Rangel Contla, Calixto. *El desarrollo diferencial de México, 1940–1960.* México: Universidad Nacional Autónoma de México (Thesis, Escuela Nacional de Ciencias Políticas y Sociales), 1965.

Rey Romay, Benito. "La planeación del desarrollo industrial." *Cuadernos Americanos* 162 (January–February 1969): 119–130.

Reyes Nevárez, Salvador. *El amor y la amistad en el mexicano.* México: Porrúa y Obregón, S.A., 1952. (Serie "México y lo mexicano," vol. 6.)

Reyna, José Luis. *Algunos aspectos políticos de México.* México: Universidad Nacional Autónoma de México (Thesis, Escuela Nacional de Ciencias Políticas y Sociales), 1967.

Reynolds, Clark W. *The Mexican Economy: Twentieth-Century Structure and Growth.* New Haven and London: Yale University Press, 1970.

Richmond, Patricia McIntire. "Mexico: A Case Study of One-Party Politics." Ph.D. dissertation, University of California, Berkeley, 1965.

Riesman, David, Nathan Glazer, and Reuel Denney. *The Lonely Crowd: A Study of the Changing American Character.* Abridged edition. Garden City, N.Y.: Doubleday and Company, 1953.

Riggs, Fred W. *Administration in Developing Countries: The Theory of Prismatic Society.* Boston: Houghton, Mifflin Co., 1964.

———. "Agraria and Industria." In *Toward the Comparative Study of Public Administration,* edited by William Siffin. Bloomington: Indiana University Press, 1957.

———. "Prismatic Society and Financial Administration." *Adminstrative Science Quarterly* 5 (June 1960): 1–46.

Río Reynaga, Julio del. *Técnica del reportaje.* México: Universidad Nacional Autónoma de México (Thesis, Escuela Nacional de Ciencias Políticas y Sociales), 1964.

de Rita, Lidia. *I Contadini e la Televisione.* Bologna: Societa Editrice Il Mulino, 1964.

Rodríguez Aranda, Bernabé. *El caciquismo y el comisariado ejidal.* México: Universidad Nacional Autónoma de México (Thesis, Facultad de Derecho), 1960.

Rodríguez Sala de Gomezgil, Ma. Luisa. "Incremento de las communicaciones en México e influencia en algunos aspectos socio-económicos." *Revista Mexicana de Sociología* 25 (January–April 1963): 189–202.

Roemer, Milton I. *La atención médica en América Latina.* Washington, D.C.: Secretaría General de la Organización de Estados Americanos (Estudios y Monografías, 15), 1964.

Romanell, Patrick, ed. *Making of the Mexican Mind: A Study in Recent Mexican Thought.* Freeport, N.Y.: Books for Libraries, 1952.

Ross, Stanley, ed. *Is the Mexican Revolution Dead?* New York: Alfred A. Knopf, 1966.

Rudel, Christian. "La Presse d'Amérique Latine." *Presse Actualité* (January 1966): 12–21.

Ruiz, Antonio. "Mexique: Le Tournant du 2 Octobre." *Les Temps Modernes* (March 1970): 1497–1513.

Saenz, Josué. "Estudio relativo a la planificación de una red hospitalaria del I.M.S.S. y problemas de su organización." Typescript. México: 1958.

Sánchez Cárdenas, Carlos. *Disolución social y seguridad nacional.* México: Ediciones Linterna, 1970.

Sánchez, George Isidore. *The Development of Higher Education in Mexico.* New York: King's Crown Press, 1944.

Sartori, Giovanni. "La Sociologia del Parlamento." *Studi Politici* 8 (April 1961).

Schendel, Gordon et al. *Medicine in Mexico: From Aztec Herbs to Betatrons.* Austin and London: University of Texas Press, 1968.

Schmitt, Karl M. *Communism in Mexico.* Austin: University of Texas Press, 1965.

Schramm, Wilbur Lang. *Mass Media and National Development: The Role of Information in the Developing Countries.* Stanford: Stanford University Press, 1964.

Schubert, Glendon. *The Public Interest.* Glencoe: The Free Press, 1961.

Scott, Robert E. *Mexican Government in Transition.* rev. ed. Urbana: University of Illinois Press, 1964.

Segovia, Rafael. "The Strike and its Aftermath, A Narrative and Perspective. In *Political Power in Latin America: Seven Confrontations,* edited by R. R. Fagen and W. A. Cornelius, Jr., pp. 316–323. Englewood Cliffs, N.J.: Prentice-Hall, 1970.

Selser, Gregorio. *Espionaje en América Latina: El Pentágono y las técnicas sociológicas.*. Buenos Aires: Ediciones Iguazú, 1966.

Sepúlveda, César. "Student Participation in University Affairs: The Mexican Experience." *The American Journal of Comparative Law* 17 (1969): 384–389.

Shafer, Robert J. *Mexico: Mutual Adjustment Planning.* Syracuse, N.Y.: Syracuse University Press, 1966.

Silva García, Jorge. "El temor del hombre a la mujer." *Revista de Psicoanálisis, Psiquiatría y Psicología* No. 2 (January–April 1966): 13–24.

Silva Herzog, Jesús. *Inquietud sin tregua: ensayos y artículos escogidos.* México: Cuadernos Americanos, 1965.

———. *El pensamiento económico, social y político de Mexico, 1810–1964.* México: Instituto Mexicano de Investigaciones Económicas, 1967.

Silvert, Kalman. *Man's Power: A Biased Guide to Political Thought and Action.* New York: The Viking Press, 1970.

Sjoberg, Gideon, ed. *Ethics, Politics, and Social Research.* Cambridge: Schenkman Publishing Co., 1967.

Solís Quiroga, Héctor. *Los partidos políticos en México.* México: Editorial Orión, 1961.

Souchère, E. de la. "Le Mexique Remet en Cause son Systéme Agraire." *Le Monde Diplomatique* (July 1967).

Stavenhagen, Rodolfo. "Un modelo para el estudio de las organizaciones políticas en México." *Revista Mexicana de Sociología* 29 (April–June 1967): 329–336.

Stevens, Evelyn P. "Legality and Extra-Legality in Mexico." *Journal of Inter-American Studies and World Affairs* 12 (January 1970): 62–75.

———. "*Marianismo:* The Other Face of *Machismo* in Latin America." In *Female and Male in Latin America*, edited by Ann Pescatello. Pittsburgh: University of Pittsburgh Press, 1973.

———. "Mexican Machismo: Politics and Value Orientations." *Western Political Quarterly* 18 (December 1965): 848–857.

Stullken, Virginia Pauline. "Keystone of Mexican Government—The Secretaría de Gobernación." M.A. Thesis, University of Texas, Austin, 1954.

Tamayo, Jorge L. *Geografía general de México.* 4 vols. and Atlas. México: Instituto Mexicano de Investigaciones Económicas, 1962.

Tardiff, Guillermo. *La libertad de expresión, ideales y realidades americanas, ensayo sociopolítico.* México: Talleres Gráficos de Manuel Casas, 1958.

Taylor, Charles Lewis, and Michael C. Hudson. *World Handbook of Political and Social Indicators.* New Haven and London: Yale University Press, 1972.

Thomas, Dani B., and Richard B. Craig. "Student Dissent in Latin America: Toward a Comparative Analysis." *Latin American Research Review* 8 (Spring 1973): 71–96.

Topete, Jesús. *Terror en el riel de "El Charro" a Vallejo; páginas de la lucha sindical.* México: Editorial Cosmonauta, 1961.

Torres de la Fuente, Julio. *Beneficios a la economía nacional derivados de la construcción de equipo rodante ferroviario.* México: Universidad Nacional Autónoma de México (Thesis, Facultad de Economía), 1967.

Truman, David B. *The Governmental Process: Political Interests and Public Opinion.* New York: Alfred A. Knopf, 1951.

Tucker, W. P. "Mexican Elites." *Journal of Politics* 21 (August 1969): 804–807.

Turner, Frederick C. *The Dynamic of Mexican Nationalism.* Chapel Hill: University of North Carolina Press, 1970.

United Nations. *Economic Survey of Latin America for 1964.* New York: United Nations, 1966.

———. *Economic Survey of Latin America, 1967.* New York: United Nations, 1969.

———. *Statistical Yearbook*, 1966.

———, UNESCO. *World Communications.* 4th ed. Paris: United Nations, 1964.

———, UNESCO. *World Illiteracy at Mid-Century.* Westport, Connecticut: Greenwood Press, 1970.

United States Department of Health, Education and Welfare. *Social Security Programs Throughout the World,* 1967.

Urquidi, Victor L., and Adrián Lajous Vargas. *Educación Superior, ciencia y tecnología en el desarrollo económico de México.* México: Universidad Nacional Autónoma de México (Centro de Estudios Económicos y Demográficos), 1967.

Usigli, Rudolfo. *Corona de luz: la virgen.* México: Fondo de Cultura Económica, 1965.

———. *El gesticulador.* México: Editorial Stylo, 1947.

———. "Rostros y máscaras." In *México: realización y esperanza,* pp. 47–56. México: Editorial Superación, 1952.

Valdés, José C. *El Presidente de México en 1970.* México: Editores Mexicanos Unidos, 1969.

Valencia, Alfonso. *Legislación periodística.* México: Departamento de Prensa e Información, Procuraduría General de Justicia de la República, 1962.

Various authors. *Bases para la planeación económica y social de México.* México: Universidad Nacional Autónoma de México, Siglo 21 Editores, S.A., 1966.

Various Authors. *Las clases sociales de México*. México: Sociedad Mexicana de Difusión Cultural, 1960.

———. "La marginalidad en América Latina." *Revista Latinoamericana de Sociología* (July 1969) Symposium—Special Issue): 174–221.

———. *Mexico: cincuenta años de Revolución*. Abridged version. México: Fondo de Cultura Económica, 1963.

———. *Los problemas nacionales*. México: Universidad Nacional Autónoma de México, 1971.

———. *Los procesos de México 68: Acusaciones y defensa*. México: Editorial Estudiantes, 1970.

Vernon, Raymond. *The Dilemma of Mexico's Development: The Roles of the Private and Public Sectors*. Cambridge: Harvard University Press, 1963.

———, ed. *Public Policy and Private Enterprise in Mexico*. Cambridge: Harvard University Press, 1964.

Wagley, Charles, and Marvin Harris. *Minorities in the New World: Six Case Studies*. New York: Columbia University Press, 1958.

Waisanen, F. B., and Jerome T. Durlak. "Mass Media Use, Information Source Evaluation, and Perceptions of Self and Nation." *Public Opinion Quarterly* 31 (Fall 1967): 399–406.

Ward, Robert E., ed. *Studying Politics Abroad: Field Research in the Developing Areas*. Boston: Little, Brown and Co., 1964.

Wences Reza, Rosalío. *El movimiento estudiantil y los problemas nacionales*. México: Editorial Nuestro Tiempo, 1971.

Weyl, Nathaniel, and Sylvia Weyl. *The Reconquest of Mexico*. New York: Oxford University Press, 1939.

Wildavsky, Aaron. "The Analysis of Issue-contexts in the Study of Decision-Making." *The Journal of Politics* 24 (1962): 717–732.

Wilkie, James W. *The Mexican Revolution: Federal Expenditure and Social Change Since 1910*. Berkeley and Los Angeles: University of California Press, 1967.

Wohlstetter, Roberta. *Pearl Harbor: Warning and Decision.* Stanford: Stanford University Press, 1962.

Wolf, Eric. "Aspects of Group Relations in a Complex Society: Mexico." *American Anthropologist* 58 (December 1956): 1065–1078.

———. "La formación de la nación: un ensayo de formulación." *Notas e Informaciones, Ciencias Sociales* 4 (April 1953): 50–62; 4 (June 1953): 98–111; 4 (July 1953): 146–171.

———. *Sons of the Shaking Earth.* Chicago: University of Chicago Press, 1959. (Phoenix Books paperback.)

Womack, J. Jr. "The Spoils of the Mexican Revolution." *Foreign Affairs* 48 (July 1970): 677–687.

Zabludovsky, Jacobo. *La libertad y la responsabilidad en la radio y televisión.* México: Porrúa, 1967.

Zayas Enríquez, Rafael de. *Apuntes confidenciales al Presidente Porfirio Díaz.* México: Editorial Citlaltépetl, 1967.

Periodicals

Boletín de la Alianza de Médicos Mexicanos

El Día

Excelsior

Gazette

Liberación

La Nación

New York Times

Novedades

Política

Siempre!

Sucesos para Todos

El Universal

26 de Noviembre

INDEX